Jock's Jocks

VOICES OF SCOTTISH SOLDIERS
FROM THE FIRST WORLD WAR

Jock Duncan

Edited by Gary West

in association with
THE EUROPEAN ETHNOLOGICAL RESEARCH CENTRE
AND NMS ENTERPRISES LIMITED – PUBLISHING
NATIONAL MUSEUMS SCOTLAND

Published in Great Britain in 2019 by
European Ethnological Research Centre
Celtic & Scottish Studies
University Of Edinburgh
50 George Square
Edinburgh EH8 9LH

and

NMS Enterprises Limited – Publishing
NMS Enterprises Limited
National Museums Scotland
Chambers Street
Edinburgh EH1 1JF

Text © European Ethnological
Research Centre 2019

Images © as credited

ISBN 978-1-910682-33-3

The rights of Jock Duncan and all
named contributors to be identified as
the authors of this book have been
asserted by them in accordance with the
Copyright, Designs and Patents Act
1988.

**British Library Cataloguing in
Publication Data**

A catalogue record of this book is
available from the British Library.

Cover photographs: Front, upper:
   Gordon Highlanders parade at
   Culter Village, Aberdeen, 1914
   © Aberdeen City Council, Arts &
   Recreation Department, Library
   & Information Services. Licensor
   www.scran.ac.uk. Front, lower:
   Brownhill, Aberdeenshire. Courtesy
   of Alexander Fenton Photographic
   Collection. Back: Jock Duncan.
   Courtesy of Marc Marnie.

Internal text design by
   NMS Enterprises Ltd – Publishing.
Printed and bound in Great Britain by
   Bell & Bain Ltd, Glasgow.

For a full listing of related NMS titles
please visit:
www.nms.ac.uk/books

CONTENTS

ACKNOWLEDGEMENTS

Many people have put a great deal of time, effort and expertise into the preparation and production of this book. Staff and volunteers of The Gordon Highlanders Museum, Aberdeen, went well beyond the call of duty in helping to check facts, trace individuals, source photographs and generally provide support which has been gratefully received.

We'd also like to thank staff in the National Library of Scotland, National Museums Scotland, and the Imperial War Museum for help in sourcing and providing photographs in particular, and for granting permission for their use. Thanks also go to D. J. Johnston Smith for providing a family photograph, and to Calum Beaton, my colleague in the Glasgow Police Pipe Band, for the photographs of his grandfather, Alec Barlow. A chance conversation about Alec having been shot through the cheek led us to realise that he was one of the men who had been interviewed by Jock Duncan and who features in this book. The North-East magazine, *The Leopard*, featured a small selection of extracts from the interviews in the 1980s, when several of those featured were still living. These articles included photographs of a few of the men themselves, which we have gratefully reproduced here. Pete Shepherd, of Spingthyme Records, has been most helpful in providing images, and his liner notes to Jock's album, *Ye Shine Whar Ye Stan*, are highly informative. A trip to the battlefields of the Western Front with my colleagues in the Atholl Highlanders in June 2018 helped to bring some geographical perspective to the stories, and thanks to Regimental Sergeant Major Graham Jack for allowing us to reproduce some of his photographs.

The School of Literatures, Languages and Cultures, University of Edinburgh, provided funding to support the re-typing of the original manuscript into electronic form, and we are hugely indebted to Sheila Findlay who took that task on and completed it in minimal time and with maximum efficiency and accuracy. My colleagues in the European Ethnological Research Centre (EERC) at the University of Edinburgh helped in many ways: thanks in particular go to Colin Gately for help with photographic reproduction, and to Kenneth Veitch and Caroline Milligan whose thoughts and suggestions on a number of issues were invaluable. Most of all amongst my immediate colleagues, Mark Mulhern deserves enormous thanks and credit: he has been the driving force behind much of the production process, and it is fair to say without his invaluable expertise and experience, this book would not have got off the ground! Lynne Reilly, at NMS Enterprises Ltd – Publishing, also deserves our gratitude for her editorial expertise in knocking the text into shape, and for her wise and insightful suggestions for its improvement. Dr Keith Williamson gave generously of his time and deep linguistic knowledge in helping us to steer a course through the complexities of the Scots language, providing a succinct commentary on its use and representation in the text, and compiling the glossary.

In 2016, I wrote a short play based on this collection, also named *Jock's Jocks*, which has been performed several times now, including once in the presence of Jock Duncan himself! I would like to thank my fellow performers, Scott Gardiner, Chris Wright and Charlie West, whose skill in bringing the words on the page to life has been invaluable in helping to appreciate some of the finer points and deeper nuances of these unique testimonies.

Family and friends of Jock Duncan have been immensely supportive from the start of this project. Jock's late wife, Frances, and their daughters Moira and Frances Jnr have provided encouragement in various ways, and their late son, my school pal, Gordon Duncan, first hinted to me many years ago that his father was up to something that involved a typewriter! Jock's daughter-in-law, Chris Ross, and family friend, Gus Clarke, have offered and given of their time generously, while Jock's elder son, Pipe Major Ian Duncan, has been another key driving force behind this project, inviting us to take it on in the first place, and reacting to a steady stream of questions on all manner of detailed points and issues.

Our greatest debt of gratitude, however, is reserved for Jock Duncan himself, and for the 59 men who shared their stories with him. In tracing them, recording them, and transcribing their narratives in their own native tongue, he has spent many thousands of hours over the greater part of his lifetime working to ensure that their voices are heard, and that they can bear witness to one of the most momentous wars in our entire history. For that, Jock, we salute you.

Gary West
European Ethnological Research Centre

LIST OF ILLUSTRATIONS

NOTES ON LANGUAGE

When Jock Duncan put into writing the remembered experiences of the men of North East Scotland who fought in the Great War, he sought to record not just the substance but something of the voices in which they were recounted to him. His texts echo in visible form the tongues of the witnesses. In so doing, he transmits some of the immediacy of their accounts as told to him, and he gives us, as readers, the opportunity to pick up some resonances of the speech that bore the testimonies. Of course, if we have had experience of hearing speakers from the North East, we can cast them into an aural form in our heads and the effect is all the stronger.

To render distinctive features of speech through writing is not easy. The aural has to be encoded as visual for the reader. Speech can never be rendered exactly in writing, even with specialised alphabets. Standard English spelling is to a considerable degree distant from the realities of current speech varieties. It is a system full of orthographic fossils not to mention inconsistencies and inefficiencies, e.g. several spellings for one sound, one spelling for more than one sound. However, for a language such as present-day English, with a vast number of speakers worldwide and considerable variations in the ways of pronouncing it, this abstract character of the spelling is a great advantage – verging on the logographic. This distancing from the spoken word renders communication in writing much more serviceable between speakers of different varieties of English.

Of course, it has always been desirable for some purposes actually to encode specific features of national or more local speech, and writers of Scots (to bring the matter home) have sought to adapt Standard English spelling to this end, since it became fixed and formed the base of general literacy. Writers have sought to reflect the pronunciation of their varieties of Scots. Allan Ramsay, the poet and anthologist, was one of the pioneers of this practice at the end of the seventeenth century. Fergusson, Burns, Scott, Stevenson, MacDiarmid and many others followed his example. In the present day it is still a common practice. The writer takes as a frame the familiarity of the standard spelling system and replaces parts of it to capture salient features of local speech. Jock Duncan has drawn on this tradition, but – as many a writer in Scots must also do – he has also resorted to his own ingenuity. He was clearly a careful listener not only to the words he heard, but also with respect to the patterns of sounds. The North-East varieties of Scots, which the bulk of his witnesses used, contain many distinctive features, not only in vocabulary, but also in forms of articles, pronouns, verbs and prepositions and their combinations. Not all Jock Duncan's witnesses hailed from the same parts, nor did they all speak with the same density of characteristics, as is evident from how he recorded their voices. The testimonies of a few – notably those who had moved furth of Scotland – contain few or no signs of their linguistic origin. Their stories are given in Standard English orthography, implying that they spoke in a pretty standard style with respect to grammar and vocabulary and with an accent that did not admit much of local distinctiveness. Dialect speakers who move beyond their place of upbringing tend to fade their original speech to something that might yet be identifiably regional while lacking strong colouring. Moving to another English-speaking country will tend to push them to adapt their speech far towards that of their new linguistic milieu.

To read these testimonies of extraordinary times may require effort for some readers more than others, but with perseverance the reading becomes easier and more fluent. Of course, writing cannot capture such matters as the rhythm, intonation or voice quality of the original speaker. From the cues given in the spelling a reader has to create a voice. Obviously, this is easier if the reader has heard the speech of the North East – what they may think of as 'Aberdeen(shire)' or 'The Doric'. For other readers, they might want to consider looking for online recordings of North-East speakers.

Allowing that readers will come from different linguistic backgrounds, it has seemed best to provide a straightforward glossary where a look-up of what is found in the text will provide a meaning or explanation of a form that is puzzling.

Dr Keith Williamson
University of Edinburgh

GLOSSARY

The Glossary provides a basic set of definitions of the words and phrases in the text that are (a) Scots vocabulary items, (b) Scots equivalents of historically related Standard English words, though sometimes with different sense, and (c) some military terms. The varieties of Scots represented are to be understood as of North East Scotland. The order of words glossed is strictly alphabetical and looking up the specific spelling in the text should lead to an entry. Grammatical labels are used for disambiguation or clarification. Their main use is in distinguishing verb forms with endings in *-ed, -in, -en, -ing.*

Abbreviatiations used in the Glossary and Notes

~	corresponds to	*lit*	literally
∅	zero, i.e. represents historical loss of a segment	*mil*	military
		n	noun
adj	adjective	*part*	participle
adv	adverb	*pl*	plural
col	colloquial	*pers*	personal
cp	compare	*pres*	present
dem	demonstrative determiner or pronoun	*pron*	pronoun
		St Eng	Standard English
dim	diminutive	*vb*	verb
esp	especially	*vbl n*	verbal noun
Fr	French	*75s*	French Army artillery pieces of 75 mm calibre capable of rapid firing, Fr Soixante
Ger	German		
inf	infinitive		

aa	all/one
aa ae	all of
allist	oldest
aa richt	alright
aa'l, all	I'll
aabody	everybody, *lit* all body
aacre	acre(s)
aat	that
aathegither	altogether, completely
aathing	everything, *lit* all thing
aawy	everywhere
abeen	above *preposition*
aboot	about
acquaint	familiar with (a place)
adee	ado
ae *adj*	one
ae body	anybody
afa	awful
aff o maself	mad with myself
aff	off/go away
afore	before
aften	often
ahin/ahins	behind/behind us
ain	own
airch	arch
airm	arm
alang	along
ald	old
aleen, alene	alone
allist	oldest
alow	below
amon	among
an	and
an(-)idder	another
ana	and all, i.e. and everything, as well
anents	anent us, alongside us
aneth/aneths	beneath, below/beneath us
asides	beside us
ass	so
at *dem pron*	that
ata	at all
atein *vb pres part*	eating
aten *vb past part*	eaten
ats, at's	at us
atween	between
auld	old

ava	at all
awa	away
away	everywhere, *lit* all way(s)
awite	truly, indeed, in truth *lit* I know
aye	always/yes
baalin *vb pres part*	bawling
back an fore	back and forward
bade	lived, dwelt; stayed
baillie	person with the charge of cattle
baith	both
Bantams *mil*	regiment recruited from men not tall enough to enlist under normal Army regulations
baps	bread rolls
barbet weer	barbed wire
bare maited	poorly fed
bare nyaakit	completely naked
barfit	barefoot
barra	barrow
batherin	bothering
becis	because
been	bone
beeried *vb past*/beery	buried/ bury
beets	boots
ben	inside
berbed weer	barbed wire
bet	but
bi wy	as it were
biddin *vb past part*	stayed, bided
biddin *vbl n*	asking
bidin *vbl n*	staying
biffed aff	took a shot
bigake	disappointment, let down
bigg *vb infl*/biggit *vb past*	build/built
biggin *vbl n*	building
biler	boiler
bilin	boiling
billie	lad, fellow
bit	but
bivvies *mil col*	bivouacs, temporary shelters
blaaded	bled, damaged, injured
blaan	blown
blain *vb pres part*	blowing (off) i.e. boasting
blakit *in* it blakit aa	it beat everything
bleed	blood
blin	blind
blin ee	blind eye

bloddy	bloody
bocht	bought
boddom	bottom
bogie roll	a kind of tobacco made up in thin long twists; named from the River Bogie
boord	board
boord ploo	board plough
bowf	thump
bowie	barrel, cask
brae	hillside
brak/brake *vb past*	broke
bree	juice
breed	bread
breenge *n*	jump, plunge, dash, leap away
breenged *vb past*	jumped, thrashed
breet	creature, *lit* brute
breether, bridder, brither	brother
bricks	breeks, i.e. trousers
brig	bridge
brocht	brought
broon	brown
bruiser	machine for crushing grain
brunt	burnt
Bull Ring *mil*	military training ground (at Calais)
bun *vb past part*	bound, bundled
bun up	bandaged
caa *infl* caaed *vb past part*	drive/ driven
caa-d, caaed *vb past*	drove, transported
caad *vb past*	called
caaed aboot	searched around
caaled	called
caalest	coldest
caased (wi) *vb past part*	caused (by)
caff	chaff
caffie	calf
cairried *vb past*	carried
cairry on	carry on, business
cairt	cart
cam *vb infl* cam *vb past*	come/came
cankered	cross, annoyed, angry
canna, cannae	can't
cannle	candle
cant, can't	canned, drunk
cassie stones	cobble stones
cattler	cattleman
cauld/cauldrift	cold/chilly

chaa	chew
chaain *vb pres part*	chewing
chammer	chamber, *esp* a bedroom
chappit *vb past*	knocked
cheenged *vb past*	changed
cheil, chiel	fellow
chick	cheek
chippet *vb past part*	chapped, cracked open
ciest	cast
cis	because
claes	clothes
clim	climb
clip	colt, after having been weaned until put to work
cloort	mess
clort	mud
clort	muddy, mucky
conkit oot	passed out
coored *vb past*	crouche
coored doon	crouched down
coorse	course/coarse, rough; unpleasant
coortin *vb pres part, vbl n*	courting
cottar hoose	house given to a (usually married) ploughman or farm servant as part of his feeing contract
counter louper	shop assistant, often in a draper shop, *lit* 'counter jumper'
coupin *vb pres part*	overturning; knocking down
coured	recovered from
coured up	got cured
cout	colt
covie	cove, i.e. dim chap
craal	crawl
crabbit	in a bad temper, annoyed
craft, craftie	croft
craft eer	croft year
cralled *vb past*	crawled
cratur	creature; *of humans* fellow
criv	enclosure
crood	crowd
croon	crown
crowdie	crowd, company
cwite	coat
daared *vb past*	dared; afraid
dachled *vb past*	hesitated, lingered
dad	bit
dale *in* nae great dale	of poor quality, poor stuff

dale	deal
darging *vb pres part*	working away at, digging
de-et	died
dee	do
deed *adj, n*	dead
deein *vb pres part/pres part*	doing/dying
deeir	doer
deem	woman
deen *vb past part/pres part*	done/doing
deent	done it
deet	do it
delved out *vb past part*	given out, distributed
denner	dinner
depenned *vb past*	depended
deval	stopping, ceasing
dicht	wipe
didna	didn't
dingie	*apparently* dengue (fever) *misapplied* malaria
dirled *vb past*	thrilled or tingled with pain
dis *vb pres*	does
divot	piece of turf
docken in didna care a docken	didn't care a whit
dole up	distribute, dish up
domino!	the end of it!
don	down
doo *n*	do, i.e. military action, party, fuss
dook/dookit	dive, dodge/dived
dookin	bathing
doon	down
dother	daughter
dowie	sad, dispirited
draan	drawn
dram, drammie	dram, i.e. drink or measure of whisky, *cp* nip, nippy
drap	quantity of liquor
drapped, drappit *vb past*	dropped
draps	drops of medication
drave	drove
dreel	drill, i.e. sow seeds in furrows
dreelin	drilling
dreeve *vb past*	drove
drew its neck	wrung its neck
drooking *vb pres part*	drenching, soaking
drooned *vb past part*	drowned
dub/dubs	puddle, pool of (usually) muddy water
dubby	full of pools

dyke	wall
ean *pron*	one
eased	used
eased wi	used to, accustomed to
edder	either
ee/een *n pl*	eye/eyes
ee *pers pron*	you
een *pron*	one
eence	once
eenced, eensed	used
eer	year(s)
eese *n*/eesed *vb past part*	use/used
Eest	East
efter	after
eicht/eichteen/eichty	eight/eighteen/eighty
em	them
eneuch	enough
er	there, in that place
erse	arse, bum
Etabs/Etaps/Etapes	French town of Étaples in Picardy
fa	who
fa ciest	who cast or cut
faain	falling
faar, far, farr	where
fadder	father
fae	from
faes/faet	from us/from it
fain *vb past part*	fallen
fair *adv*	very well
fairly aat	of course, surely
farrer	further
fe-et	engaged as a farm servant/employment
fe-et	feed
feart	afraid
fecht *n*/fechtin *vbl n*	fight/fighting
feein	feeing
feenished	finished
feoy	few
fermer	farmer
file/files/filie	while/sometimes/short while
fin	when
fir	for
firestep *mil*	step or ledge in a trench on which soldiers stand to shoot
fissin *vb pres part*	hissing
fit	what

fit *n*	foot
fit wy	why, *lit* what way
fitba	football
fite	white
fite shooer	shower of snow, lit white shower
fited *vb past*	whittled
5.9s *mil*	artillery shells of 5.9 inch (15 cm) calibre
fizzle	make a wheezing or whistling sound
flappet *vb past*	dropped, laid or lying (down flat)
fleein *vb pres part*	flying
fleer	floor
flees	flies
fleg	fright
flocks	tufts
foon	base, foundation of a haystack
foonered/founered *vb past*	foundered, gave way
foreby	as well
forneen	forenoon, morning
forrat, forrit	forward
fors/ fort	for us/for it
fortnicht	fortnight
fower	four
fu	how
fu	full
fullin *vb pres part*	loading
fun	found
funker *mil col*	funk-hole, foxhole
fur	furrow
fus	how is
fustle	whistle, whistling sound
fut	what
fye (water)	whey
gad/gaed	went/went,gave
gallus	bold, daring
gamie	gamekeeper
gan *vb pres part*	going
gang *vb inf*	go
gee *vb infl* geein *vb pres part*	give/giving
geen *vb past part/past part*	given/gone
geens/geese	given us/give us
geese huds ot	let me have it
geet	get, i.e. child, brat
gettined, gettent	getting it
gid	went
gid *in* gid worth	gave way
gidder *vb infl* giddered *vb past*	gather/gathered

gie *adj*	great, considerable; fine, splendid
gie *adv*	very, extremely
gie *vb inf*	give
gig	gig-horse, for drawing a small carriage
ging *vb inf*	go
girdle	a metal plate set over a fire on which to cook
girse	grass
git	went
githered	gathered
glass men	in stalking people who seek out deer, making use of binoculars or a telescope
glaur	mud
gled	glad
go *in* on the go	out and about
goorhole	mudhole, muck-pit
gotten *vb past part*	got
grabbet *vb past*	grabbed
graip	fork
gran	grand, fine
greet *vb*	cry
grieve	overseer on a farm
grippy	mean, stingy
grun	ground
grutten *vb past part*	cried, wept
guid, gweed	good
gweed kens far fae	goodness knows where from
gweed loon	good lad
gyad sake!	for God's sake!
haaned *vb past*	handed
hade	waited, held back, held on
hae *vb inf*	have
haen, haein, hain *vb pres part*	having
haimes	curved wooden beams fixed to horse harness
hairsin *vb pres part*/ hairst	harvesting/harvest
hale	whole
hame	home
han	hand
hanked	fastened, drew together
hannle	handle
hapnie	halfpenny
happer	hopper
happit	covered up
harly	hardly
hat/het	waerm, hot
hat *in* got into hat	got a severe reprimand
hatchin	swarming

hauddin *vb pres part*	putting
heavies *mil*	heavy artillery
heed/heeded *vb past*	head, top/headed
heedmaister	headmaster
heelan	highland
heelstergowdie	head over heels
heesin *vb pres part*	swarming, heaving
hennie	hen
her	here
het up	heat up, got hot
hich raas o b arbet weer	high rows of barbed wire
hich-ups	high-ups
hichest	highest
hid/ hidna	had/hadn't
hie	hay
hindmist, hinemist	last
hine awa	a distance away
hinging *vb pres part*	hanging
hinner *in* in the hinner end	finally
hinnerine	back end, conclusion
hiv	have
hiz *emphatic*	us
hoose	house
horse draan	horse drawn
horsewark	horsework
hottern *vb pres part*	boiling
howe	hollow
hud	hold
huddin(g) *vb pres part*	holding
hult	Shetland pony
humphin *vb pres part*	carrying (laboriously)
hun dog	hound dog, hunting dog
hunner	hundred
hurl	lift
hurled	given a lift
idder/ ither	other
ile	oil
ilkey	every
ill nettered	ill-natured
in tull	into
inaa	as well, *lit* and all
ine	end
inti	into
iss	this, these
it *rel pron*	that
iver/ivery	ever/every

jag	injection
jaloosed, jaloused	guessed, suspected, worked out
jelly piece	a piece of bread with jam
jine/jined *vb past*	join; transitive enlist/joined
jiner	joiner
jist	just
juket	dodged
kebbick	[a cake of] cheese
keepering *vbl n*	gamekeeping
ken/kent *vb past*	know/knew
kenneling	kindling
kensa muckle	know so much
kent *vb past part*	known
kent grun	known ground
kepperd *vb past part*	kippered
kine *n*	kind, sort
kine	kind (of), you know
kittle	hard/unreliable, excitable
kweets	ankles
laaed *vb past*	landed, ended
laan *vb inf*	land, come down
laand up *vb past*	landed up, ended up
laand, laaned *vb past*	landed
lach *n*/lach *vb inf*	laugh
lachin *vbl n*	laughing
laft	loft
lair	sink, become mired
laired	sunken, mired
landry	laundry
lang	long
laripint	larrupin it, i.e. slapping it, sloshing it
larries, larry	lorries, lorry
lat	let, allow
lat the pinchin ging oot a han	let the pinching get out of hand
lats	let us
lave	rest, remainder, others
lead	carry harvested grain from field to stackyard
learned *vb past*	taught (but also in the *St Eng* sense, to acquire knowledge)
learnt *vb past part*	taught
ledder	ladder
lee *n*	lie, fib
lest/lest *vb*	last
licht	light in varied senses
listin *vbl n*	enlisting
loon	boy, lad

loose box	stable where horses are kept untethered or restrained
loosey	lousy
loup	jump
loupin *vb pres part*	leaping
louse	loose
louse, lowse aff	unhitch, unyoke, untie
luch mait	lush food
luch *vb past*	laughed
lug	ear
lyth	shelter
ma	me, my
Maconnachies	meat stewed with vegetables, tinned as a supply for British soldiers (named after the manufacturer, Maconochie Brothers)
mair	more
mairched *vb past*	marched
mairchin *vb pres part*	marching
mairried *vb past part*	married
mait	meat, food in general
makkin *vb pres part*	making
mammy dooy	namby-pamby
mangin *vb pres part*	desperate, yearning
mannie	man with -ie dim ending
mart	livestock market
masel	myself
meal girnil	place or box for storing grain
mealie Jimmies	white pudding
meenit	minute
meenlichty	moonlit
meer	mare
meeve *vb inf*	move
meeved *vb past, past part*	moved
meevin *vb pres part, vbl n*	moving
Merk	mark, German unit of currency
midden	dung heap
midder	mother
middlin	not good if not bad, so-so
Mills bomb *mil*	type of hand grenade
mind verb	remember
mine (on)	recall
minewerefers	*Ger* Minenwerfer, a trench mortar or its shell
mintin *vb pres part*	attempting, trying
mishunter	mishap, accident
mith	might *vb*
mith hae been	might have been

mony	many
moo	mouth
moose	mouse
mossin *vbl n*	peat cutting
mous ti	complain about
mu	my
muckle	much
mull	mill
mush	must
na fegs!	no, indeed!
nae	not/no
nae neen	not any
naething, neathing, neething	nothing
naewy	nowhere
nea	not
nee	at all, not in any way
neeb *vb*	feed cattle (with turnips)
needin to *vb pres part*	wanting to go to
neen *adv*	in any way
neen *pron*	none
neent	needn't
neep *n*	turnip
neeper	neighbour
neer	nearly
neist	next
nerra	narrow
nesty	nasty
neuk	corner
news, newsie *n*	chat, gossip
newsin *vb pres part*	news *as verb* + ing, i.e. chatting, gossiping
nich, nicht	night
nip, nippy	small measure of (usually) spirits, especially whisky
no(o) in an	now and then
noo	now
nought	needed
nowt	cattle
o	of
on the pannie	preparing the food
ont	on it
ony	only
onybody	anybody
onywy	anyway
oofs *for Fr* oeufs	eggs
oor	hour/our
oors/oorsels	ours/ourselves

oot	out
orra beast	animal used for odd jobs
orra loon	odd job boy
os ot	of us/of it
ower	over; too
ower sair	too sore
owers	over us
oxters	armpits
pairt	part
peel	pail
peer	poor
peyed	paid
peying *vb pres part*	paying
peys *vb pres*	pays
pick	pitch
picket *vb past*	picked, chose
piece	sandwich
pig	pitcher
piket drum	drum with small picks on it for roughening a millstone
ping through	completely through
pint	point
pirk	pot-shot, shot
pirr	state of excitment, fit of anger or panic
pit *vb inf, past*	put
pitify	pitifully
pittin *vb pres part*	puting
plapperin *vb pres part*/plouterin	splashing
plite	mess
plitered *vb past*	splashed, spattered
ploo *n*/plooed *vb past*	plough/ploughed
plooin *vb pres part*	ploughing
plouterin *vb pres part*	splashing
plukket *vb past*	plucked
plunket *vb past part*t	dropped, dumped
pooch	pocket
pooed	pulled
poored	poured (with rain)
poorin *vb pres part*	pouring
poosaned *vb past part*	poisened
pooshon	poison
poukit *vb past*	pierced
poun, pown	pound(s) of money
pu *vb inf*	pull
puckle	amount; few
puckles	lots of, many

puddock	frog
puttees *mil*	protective strips of cloth or leather wound in a spiral around the leg from ankle to knee
putten, puttin *vb past part*	put
quait	quiet
quite	coat
raa	raw/row
rale *adv*	really
rase *vb past*	rose
raxed *vb past, past part*	reached; stretched
rebatted *vb past*	rebelled
red up	clear up
redd	rid
reddin *vbl n*	clearing
reed	red
reef	roof
reek	smoke
reem fu o	overflowing with
reemin fu *vb pres part*	overflowing
remindeds *vb past*	reminded us
richt	right
rin	run
rines	reins
rinnin *vb pres part*	running
risten, ristin *vb pres part*	resting
roaded *vb past part*	directed
roch/rochest	rough/roughest
roon	round
roon *n*	bullet
roons	around us
roost *in* without a roost	without a penny
rotten	rat
roupit *vb past part*	auctioned
rouse! *for Ger* (he)raus!	get out!
row *vb infl* rowin *vbl n*	roll/rolling
ruck	rick (of corn), stack
ruggin *vb pres part*/ ruggit *vb past*	pulling/pulled
rummle	thump, thud
rummel	crash
ruption	commotion
ryput *vb past*	searched, rummaged through
saa *vb past*	saw
sae	so
saft	soft
sair	sore
saired	served

Sally Annes	Salvation Army people
sam *adj*	same kind of, similar
sap *vb, mil*	dig
sark	shirt
sax/saxteen	six/sixteen
saxpence	sixpence, i.e. 6d
schweel/schweeled	school/schooled, i.e. educated
schweelie	dim
schweeling *vb pres part*	squeeling
scised *vb past*	moved away quickly and quietly
sclyte	lump
scoob	splint
scoobed	fixed with a splint
scrapet, scrapit *vb past*	scraped
scrat/scrattit	scratch/scratched
scrattin *vb pres part*	scratching
screed	stretch
scunnered (o)	got sick or fed up (with)
seemit	vest, undershirt
seen	soon
seen *vb past*	saw
seens	(as) soon as
selt	sold
sen	send
shafies	sheaves
shalt	Shetland pony
sharn	cattle dung, manure
shaves	sheaves
sheddie	small shed or hut
sheelocks	particles of chaff or dust
sheet *vb infl*/sheetin *vbl n*	shoot/shooting
sheetin *vb pres part*	sitting
shew *vb past*	hewed, cut
shewed	sewed
shid	shuld
shift	area of land for a crop
shoo(e)r	shower
shooder	shoulder
shooted weet	suited for it
shot	excrement
shotties	short spells
shottin *vb pres part*	shooting
sic	so, like this
sickin *vb pres part*	seeking
siller	money, lit silver
simmer	summer

siven, sivin/siventy	seven/seventy
sklyte	large and clumsy
sma	small
smert	smart, quick
smertin *vb inf*	smarten
smiddereens	smithereens
sna, snaa, snaw	snow
socht	sought, i.e. invited
sock	ploughshare
sodjers/soger	soldiers/soldier
somewy	somewhere
sooghin *vb pres part*	constant or steady rushing
sookin *vb pres part*	sucking
soon/sooned *vb past*	noise, sound/sounded
sooter	shoemaker, cobbler
sooth	south(ern)
sos	so as, i.e. so that
soss	slop, morass
sotter	mess
spad	spade
spak	spoke
spear *vb infl*speired *vb past*	ask/asked
spik ava	speak at all
spickin *vb pres part*	speaking
spikkers	speakers
sprachlin *vb pres part*	scrambling, clambering
spunk box	matchbox
sqeel	school
staas	stalls
stabbit *vb past*	stabbed
staig	stallion
staiger	handler of stallions
stammack, stammock	stomach
stan	stand, tolerate
stannin *vb pres part*	standing
stappit *vb past*	stuffed, shoved
steed *vb past*	stood
steen	stone (also in weight)
steen deaf	stone deaf
steen deed	stone dead
steerin aboot	bustling about
stem mull	steam mill, i.e. threshing mill driven by a steam engine
stookies	(plaster) statues, dummies
stookit *vb past*	made into stooks
stoot	well-built

strachen/stracht	straighten/straight
strack/strack *vb past part*	struck
strae	straw
straich *vb inf*	strafe
strapper	groom
strick	strike
stunnin *vb pres part*	standing
sue (aff) *vb past*	sawed (off)
suitie	suit (of clothes)
swalled *vb past part*	swollen
sweeled *vb past*	swilled
sweem *vb inf*	swim
sweer	swear
swickit *vb past*	cheated, swindled
swingletree	cross bar to which the horse traces are fastened
tac on	commotion, ado
tac *vb inf*	take
tag	tawse, i.e. a leather strap formerly used by schoolteachers in Scotland to punish pupils by striking them with it on the hand.
takkin *vb pres part*	taking
tap	top
tattie chapper grenades *mil col*	'potato-masher' grenades, so called because of their appearance
tatties	potatoes
tee	too
teem *adj, vb*/teemed *vb past*	empty/emptied
teen *vb past part*	taken
telt	told
teuch	tough
The Broch	Fraserburgh
thegidde/thegither	together
this with *pl n*	these
thocht	thought
tholed *vb past*	endured
thon	that/those
thoomb	thumb
thoosan	thousand
thrash	thresh
thrashin *vb pres part*	threshing
thrashin mull	threshing mill
thrawn	grumpy, stubborn
thripence	three pennies, i.e. 3d
throue/throut, throwt	through/through it
throwe	through, during
thunner and lichtnin	thunder and lightning

ti *inf marker*/ti *prep*	to
timmer	wooden
tippence	two pennies, i.e. 2d
to croon aa	to crown it all
toon	town/farm
toonkeeper	person left to mind a farm when the rest of the household are away
toppers	splendid things
tow	cord
traaler	trawler
track	state, condition
traiveled *vb past*	travelled; led or drove around
trauchlin *vb pres part*	trudging, walking wearily
trooties	trouts
tull	till to, until
tull ma	for me/to me
tulla	till the, i.e. to the
tulls	till us, i.e. for us; to us
tult	till it, i.e. to it; to (get to) it
tummeled *vb past*	tumbled
turket	angry, fierce
twa/twal/twinty	two/twelve/twenty
tyav *n*	hard struggle
tyaved *vb past*	struggled
tyavin *vb pres part*	struggling, wrestling
umman	woman
vrocht	worked
wa	wall
waak/waakit	walk/walked
waaled *vb past part*	chosen
waaled *vb past part*	welded
waals	wells (of water)
waar	war/were/worse
waatch	watch (timepiece)
wall	well (of water)
wannerin *vb pres part*	wandering
war	were
wark *n*	work
warna	weren't
warst	worst
watter	water
waur	worse
wee	little
weel *adj*	well
weel-a-wite	I must say
weelin	willing

weemin	women
weer *n*	wire
weer *vb*	wear
wees	with us
weet	with it
weet, weetie	wet
weicht	weight
werna	weren't
wheeshed *vb past*	wheezed
whizzbangs *mil col*	small-calibre shells which travelled faster than the speed of sound so that the noise of their flight through the air was heard before the sound of their firing from the gun which launched them
wi	with
wick, wik	week
wid *n*	wood
wid *vb*	would
widder, wider	weather
widin *vb pres part*	wading
widna	wouldn't
wike/ass wikes	weak/so weak or as weak as
wiled (oot) *vb past*	picked (out)
wilie	wily, cunning
winister	winnower, a person or device that separates chaff from grain
winner	wonder
winnin sough	strong breeze
wint	want, lack
winted for *vb past*	lacked
winted, wintet *vb past*/wintit	wanted
wir/wirsells, wirsels	our/ourselves
wird	word
wis	our/was/with us
wis en	wasn't
wisna	wasn't/weren't
wite	wait
withoot	without
witin *vb pres part*	awaiting/waiting for
worth *in* gid worth	gave way
worth	useless
wrang deeirs	wrongdoers
wun	win
wunnerfu	wonderful
wuppit *vb past*	wound, wrapped
wy	way

yaird	yard
ye/yer	you/your
yoket	yoked, tied
yokit *vb past part*	of horses, harnessed
yonner	yonder, over there

Jock Duncan.
Photo by Louis de Carlo

1. Jock Duncan.

Photo by Davey Stewart, courtesy of Pete Shepheard

INTRODUCTION

Jock Duncan is an extraordinary ordinary man. I knew this long before I found out about his lifetime's hobby of seeking out men who had fought in the Great War, recording their stories and transcribing them word for word in beautifully rich Scots on his small manual typewriter on two thousand Sunday mornings. I have known him all my days, having grown up in Pitlochry in Perthshire just two years apart at school from his younger son, Gordon, and I was taught the bagpipes from the age of nine by his elder son, Ian. Jock and my dad would take turns driving Gordon and me to piping competitions, Jock sometimes opting for his old Volkswagen camper van that always smelled of calor gas and broth. Jock's wife, Frances, was a familiar voice for me too from a young age, and in later life I got to know their daughters, Moira and Frances Jnr.

Jock fascinated me from the off: his deep-rooted Doric tongue seemed impenetrable at first, but soon grew familiar enough for me to at least catch the gist most of the time. To this day I love listening to him talk – and sing – and I rather fancy his rich Buchan dialect has not been diluted in the slightest since the day he left his native North East seven decades ago. And yet my fascination ran much deeper than just the way he spoke. I suppose even as a boy I recognised a gentle wisdom in him, although a wisdom always worn lightly. Our shared world was the world of piping: he had learned for a while himself as a boy, although it was song that became his own main mode of performance in adult life. But in Ian and Gordon he had two boys who were destined to become famous names in piping, Ian as a prolific teacher and one of the most respected pipe band leaders of his generation, and Gordon as an innovating genius whose compositions and unique virtuosic style of playing opened up entire new directions for the art. All three – Jock, Ian and Gordon – have been admitted to the Scottish Traditional Music Hall of Fame, the only family to date with three members thus honoured.[1] Tragically, Gordon's honour was awarded posthumously, having died in 2005 at the age of just 41.

What struck me back then as a young boy was Jock's incredible depth of knowledge of the traditions of piping, of the repertoire and of its history, and he was generous to a fault with his advice. 'Tak it slowly – there's nae guid in rushin it'. By the time Gordon and I joined the local Vale of Atholl Pipe Band in the mid-1970s, which Ian led, Jock seemed to be ever present for the first few years, serving as parking attendant at the weekly 'Highland Nights' held through the summer in Pitlochry, and supporting us at competitions far and wide. He was particularly in his element when we visited his native North East, on trips to Turriff (Turra), Old Meldrum, Keith and Aberdeen, where he and Frances would help keep our bellies full in the camper van, serving up infinite bowls of broth and imploring us to 'tak some loaf'. Our nights were spent in sleeping bags on the hard wooden floor of the Millbrex village hall, kept by Jock's pal Harry Panton, a man who knew how to pour a generous dram. It was on these trips north and east that I began to understand a little of the world Jock had come from, the world he shared with most of the men whose stories he has gifted us in this book.

Born on the small farm of Gelliebrae near New Deer, Aberdeenshire in 1925, there was music all around Jock from the start. His mother was a gifted pianist and was the accompanist of choice for the many fiddlers of the district, and then for those some miles to the South West around Fyvie after the family's move to the farm of South Faddenhill in 1928. Jock's brother, Jimmy, was himself a fiddler, taught by that great 'master of the slow strathspey', J. F. Dickie (1886–1983), and he brought players and singers from all around to regular soirees in the house, young Jock soaking up every nuance and syllable of the songs, ballads and cornkisters, and every phrase and inflection of the pipe and fiddle tunes. Faddenhill became what much further west would have been called the *taigh ceilidh*, the ceilidh house, a key social and cultural hub of the local community, a gathering place for a grand *splore*. Jock's sister, Marion, was a fine singer, and regular visitors included their father's cousin, Charlie Duncan, a master of the bothy ballads, and whose repertoire and style were a significant influence on the youthful Jock. John Strachan, too, was no stranger to Faddenhill. This well-to-do farmer from Crichie near Fyvie was already becoming recognised as one of the great tradition bearers of Scottish folk song: the American collector, James Madison Carpenter, arriving at Crichie from Harvard with his wax cylinder recorder to capture something of John's verbal art in 1930. Carpenter was the first of a steady trail of academics and collectors to beat a path to John Strachan's door, including Hamish Henderson and Alan Lomax in 1951, who invited him to perform in the first Edinburgh People's Festival Ceilidh in August that same year, the event which is often credited as sparking the entire folk revival in Scotland. (Many years later, Jock himself would perform at the 60th anniversary celebration of that seminal evening, held in the same venue, Oddfellows Hall, in 2011.) There was no shortage of quality, then, in the regular *splores* ben the hoose at South Faddenhill. And crucially, perhaps, from childhood, Jock himself had been made aware of the concept of 'collecting'.

Music was deeply embedded in local life, but it didn't put the dinner on the table. It was working the soil that did that. The farm had been in the possession of Jock's grandfather, and so when Jock's father took it on in 1928 it was very much a family concern. Like most children in his situation, Jock was keen to learn the ways of the farm, taking on the role of *orra loon* or apprentice, and he was comfortable driving a pair of horse behind a plough by the age of ten. On leaving school at 14, he began to work full time on South Faddenhill, no doubt mixing with the older men all around the district at sales and marts, and on the many occasions when neighbours helped each other with the tasks that needed more hands than most smallholdings could supply themselves, such as when the travelling steam threshing mills came round. Many of these neighbours, of course, had fought in the Great War, and not a few still bore the scars to prove it.

The year Jock left school, it started all over again. For many, there must have been a dreadful sense of déjà vu, in watching their sons lay down their ploughs as they themselves had once done, swapping the parks of Buchan for these same fields of France. And for women of Jock's mother's generation, whose lives were punctuated by at least three major conflicts beginning with the Boer War, the sentiments later to be penned by songwriter Judy Small would have rung true indeed:

The first time it was fathers, the last time it was sons,
And in between, your husbands marched away with drums and guns.
Yet you never thought to question, you just went on with your lives,
For all they taught you who to be, was mothers, daughters, wives.[2]

At 18, Jock himself followed on, joining the Royal Air Force in 1943 and soon finding himself in France for the final two years of this latest world conflict. Although he talks little of it, no doubt the experience gave him some insight into the psyche of war: of killing and loss, of military rules and traditions, and of the humour and camaraderie that is so crucial for survival. It was an experience he put to good use in his knowledgeable and empathetic style of interviewing that has fuelled the collection of stories he presents here.

After the War, Jock returned to farm work in the North East, where he met and married Frances, and where Ian, Moira, young Frances and Gordon arrived in turn. Yet farming was changing: tractors were replacing horses, and mechanisation in general was reducing the need for human labour, and Jock was one of thousands of his generation who turned to new ways. One of these new ways was the quest to produce enough electricity to power the recovery from war. Since 1943, hydro schemes had started to be built across the nation, a massive project led by the Secretary of State for Scotland and first chair of the North of Scotland Hydro Electric Board, Tom Johnston. Jock and Frances took the decision to embrace this new life, following the work offered within The Hydro Board. Leaving farming and their native county, they moved the family first to Caithness, then later to Pitlochry where they settled for the rest of their days. Frances passed away there in 2017, and Jock, now 93, lives there still.

While Jock has sung the songs he grew up with all his life, it wasn't until the

1970s that his reputation as a public performer began to be built beyond his own close circle. One key part of the folk revival was the introduction of folk festivals, some of them embracing the emerging singer-songwriter community of younger performers, and others focusing more on 'traditional' unaccompanied singing. One of the latter was held annually at Kinross, well within striking distance of Pitlochry, and it was there in 1975 that Jock entered – and won – his first bothy ballad singing contest. The depth and understanding of his repertoire, with a strong and melodic voice to carry it, were a revelation to many, and it was immediately clear that here was a classy and authentic exponent of the real thing. Jock went on to perform widely around the country, recording two full albums late in his career, *Ye Shine Whar ye Stan* in 1996 and *Tae the Green Woods Gaen* in 2001. He is now widely recognised as one of the finest exponents of Scottish traditional singing we have, from any part of Scotland.

The Collector

Well known as he is, and despite being such a natural, outgoing performer on stage, Jock is also a modest man, and one given to playing down his own achievements. Indeed, I rather fear that if there is one thing he will not like about how we have chosen to put together this book, it will be the fact that we have seen fit to write about *him* at all. It is telling, I think, that very few people knew that he was even collecting these stories. I remember Gordon once remarking to me that he thought his father was learning to type because he could hear him tapping away, up in his bedroom, and Frances Jnr can testify to the fact that it was with one finger at a time! Later, Gordon then mentioned to me that he thought it was maybe a book of some kind that his father was working on, but knew no details. And Ian tells me that he knew almost nothing about this until Jock presented him with the full set of typed transcripts in 2015.

When I asked him what motivated him to begin collecting these men's stories, Jock immediately played it down: 'Ach weel, I wis just newsin wi the neebors, ken.' That, indeed, seems to be how it started out. In his chosen title, Jock indicates that he began his collecting in the 1930s, and given that he was born in 1925, he must have been in his early- to mid-teens at most. It began with casual chats with neighbouring men: we can perhaps imagine this inquisitive young lad dropping the odd question into the conversation as they forked oats together into the threshing mill or lifted tatties one October. Perhaps as the country headed for war once again, and Jock realised it might be his own turn soon, a concerned curiosity led him to seek out some sense of 'what it was like'. Or maybe the neighbouring men themselves began to drop the odd aside into their 'newsin' as renewed talk of war made it all come flooding back. But whatever the immediate motivation, Jock got them talking. In the early years he would return home and write their stories down from memory, often in standard school-learned English, and a few men later wrote their memories down for him themselves. But the bulk of the collecting was carried out much later, in the 1970s, the conversations being recorded onto cassette tape.

Two versions of Jock's typescript exist: the original is set out with full transcriptions of each interview in the order in which they were undertaken. However, he clearly felt that this was not the best way to present the material in its entirety, and so he produced a photostat copy of the entire manuscript, then proceeded to literally cut and paste sections of the interviews into a new order, organised by theme. This is the version we have used here, and we have remained true to Jock's own editing decisions and transcription style throughout.

Life on the Land

In the opening chapter, Jock uses the men's words to paint a verbal picture of life in the countryside of North East Scotland in the lead up to the outbreak of war in 1914. While there are certainly other representations of that place and time – we think, perhaps, of Lewis Grassic Gibbon's novel, *Sunset Song*, or Ian Carter's social history, *Farm Life in North East Scotland* – Jock's veterans were the real life equivalents of Long Rob of the Mill, Chae Strachan and Ewan Tavendale. There are, however, few insights here into the thoughts or experiences of the real life equivalents of Grassic Gibbon's imagined heroine, Chris Guthrie. This collection is very much about the local *men* who went off to fight: it is therefore unashamedly masculine in its focus. Yes, mothers, daughters and wives are in their minds at times when recounting their stories, and there is certainly a marked recognition of the anguish of their waiting and the pain of their loss:

> I had a cousin in the Gordon Highlanders blown to pieces. When I was home on leave I went up to see his mother in New Deer and to offer my condolences. She showed me a photograph of his grave. I didn't say anything. This is what makes me sad for the mothers. None of the dead were buried in a real grave but just on the battlefield.
> **Sergeant Alec Robertson, Buchan, 5th Gordon Highlanders**

Yet overwhelmingly, this is the story of life in the fields of rural Scotland, the trenches of Belgium and France, and the shores of Gallipoli as experienced and recalled by the menfolk.

That short extract, in fact, brings out a number of issues. The passage of time allowed Sergeant Alec Robertson to be very candid as he recounted the circumstances of his cousin's death to Jock a half century or so after the event. He would not have described his fate to his aunt in such highly graphic terms at the time – or ever, I suspect. That he could not even bring himself to tell her that her son was buried in an unmarked grave on the battlefield is surely proof of that. His motivation was to protect her, even if it meant hiding the truth by staying silent. Jock's interview gave him the platform to release that truth many years later, which he was clearly prepared to do. That does provide some ethical challenges for us as we now make this public in this book, and it is an issue which has given us much pause for thought. We – and now you – know a truth which his aunt in all likelihood went to her grave *not* knowing. That is the essence of oral history, however: it throws up moral dilemmas which we must deal with as we see fit. On reflection, to report the words exactly as they were given to Jock does seem the right thing to do.

Sergeant Alec Robertson shared a similar early life to most of Jock's interviewees, leaving school at 14 to take up agricultural labour full time, working the 'parks' of Buchan. The employment system involved being 'fe-et' to a particular farm for a period of six months for single men, or for a year for those who were married. To take a 'fee' was to make a verbal bargain with an employer for a set payment, and the deals were done at the twice-yearly feeing or recruiting fairs held at the 'term days' in May and November. The short term of the contract allowed an early chance for employers to rid themselves of poor workers, and good workers to escape tyrannical bosses: or put simply to Jock by William Shearer of Banff, 'ach we aye likit a change'. It also provided the means for good workers to negotiate a wage rise in order to stay on, or enabled them to seek promotion to a higher position on another farm. The workforce structure was rigidly hierarchical, larger units being led by a grieve or gaffer, with a first, second, third and fourth ploughman, depending on the size of the farm. 'To get on for first' was to be appointed to a prized position, first ploughman, with a corresponding higher fee. This hierarchy tended to be clearly marked within the culture and behaviour of the labourers: a second ploughman would never dream of leaving the stable, or finishing up at 'lousin' time, before the first ploughman had done so. It was a tradition which was deeply entrenched, and so when these young lads suddenly found themselves in an Army uniform, adhering to the military chain of command and following orders may have been almost second nature to most of them.

In Perthshire and Angus, the farm servants would live together in bothies, communal outhouses which had been introduced in the late eighteenth century as a cheap mode of accommodating increasingly large workforces, but bothies never really took off in Aberdeenshire, which continued with the older 'chaulmer' system. A chaulmer (from the French, chambre) was usually a loft space above the stable or other outbuilding of the farm steading, and unlike the bothies which were self-catered, those who were 'chaulmered' tended to take their meals in the farmhouse kitchen. The work was hard and conditions were spartan to say the least, as Harry Nicholl from Lumphanan recalled:

My first fee wis £5 the sax month an I hid ti work like a slave fae five in the mornin ti sax at nicht. I got nae holidays or onything and I hid tae bide in a cauldrift chammer up a laft stair abeen the horses in the stable. There wisna a fireplace, an it wis an afa job keepin yersel het – ye jist hid to craal in aboot the blankets. Weel there mith hae been a bit o heat risin aff the horse, bit yi wid niver hae kent it. The place wis Tillyduke.

caudrift chilly; *het* hot, *mith hae* might have

For most, to become a farm servant in lowland Scotland in the early twentieth century was to become a ploughman, and to become a ploughman was to become a horseman. Learning the ways of the horses and how to handle them was a key skill in this trade, and the learning process was institutionalised through the secret society, The Horseman's Word. An invitation to join was a rite of passage which marked a young lad's coming of age, and if he made it unscathed through the initiation ceremony taking the oath of secrecy, he emerged out of the stable door in the dark of night as a horseman. The skills and tips of horsemanship were thus passed from generation to generation in ritualised fashion, although the men featured in this book belonged to one of the final cohorts, as tractors began to replace Clydesdales during their working lifetimes. And it was both men and horses that in 1914 found themselves on the battlefields of Europe and beyond.

That intimate connection between a cavalryman and his horse which is so movingly captured in Michael Morpurgo's *Warhorse*, replicates the sentiments expressed by many of the men interviewed by Jock too. Several recall the occasion when five healthy 'shalts' or ponies were 'recruited' at the church in Fyvie in 1914:

> The Army cam roon the ferms and commandeered ony horses that they fancied. I aye mind fin they cam to Fyvie Kirk on Sunday service and took aa the good shalts that wis there aat day. Of coorse there wis plenty o shalts and gigs, that's aa there wis at that time ye ken.
>
> **Private Dod Carroll, Fyvie, Machine Gun Corps**

And for John Rennie of the 5th Gordon Highlanders, who saw so many of his friends lose their lives during the conflict, it is the memory of two of his working horses that brought him closest to tears:

> I got a letter fae hame sayin that ma gweed pair o horses I vrocht afore I gid awa, hid been commandeered by the Army. I jist could near hae grutten fin I read that. In the letter, my mother speired if I wid look oot for them – but there wis nae much chance o that!
>
> *gweed* good, *vrocht* worked, *grutten* wept, *speired* asked

Recruitment

Recruiting horses was one thing, but recruiting men was quite another. Only a few of those interviewed by Jock were already full-time regular soldiers by the time war broke out in August 1914, serving in regiments which constituted part of the British Expeditionary Force (BEF) which had been set up as a result of the Haldane reforms of the Army in the first decade of the twentieth century. The aim was to establish a well-trained force of full-time soldiers capable of contributing to any potential major war within Europe, and by 1914 it constituted around a quarter of a million men, commanded by Sir John French, and including some 20,000 or so members of 22 Scottish regiments.[3] At the outbreak of war only three of these were stationed at home in Scotland: the 1st Cameron Highlanders, Cameronians (Scottish Rifles) and 2nd Argyll and Sutherland Highlanders, while eight more were in England or Ireland. The rest were overseas, principally in India. It was the UK-based regiments of the BEF, therefore, who first arrived in France in August 1914, but by the end of the year most, including the Scottish contingent, had travelled back to take their place on the Western Front.

While a few of the men Jock interviewed were regular professional soldiers, or had recently served as such and remained as Reservists, there were many others who had already joined 'the Terriers' by the time war was declared – the Territorial Force which had been set up in 1908 as an extra line of home defence. As Albert Connon of Turriff recalled:

> I jined the Terriers at Turra wi a lad caaed Jimmy Finnie. He wis 16, I wis 17. That wis in February 1914. We war fee-d at Haremoss at the time. Fin we cam oot o the drill hall after jinin, Jimmy says to me, 'Fit will we dee if there's a war?' I just looked at him and we baith luch.
> *luch* laughed

It was a prophetic question of course: within six months Albert and Jimmy were on their way to the Western Front. For the Terriers of the rural North East, the call to arms was highly memorable as it came during one of the key festivals and social highlights of the farming year:

> At aat time aabody got off for the Turra Show. I wis in the Terriers, and wis telt to report to the drill hall by oor sergeant. He wis gan roon the show tellin aa the lads that War hid been declared; so I gid hame for my kit and that wis me for the duration.
> **John Rennie, Turriff, 5th Gordon Highlanders**

While John Rennie and his Terrier colleagues were obliged to report for duty under the terms of their service, for most of Jock's men their first encounter with military culture and authority would come when they responded to Kitchener's pointing finger and headed voluntarily to the recruiting offices across the North East. The BEF was well trained and highly professional but far too small for the scale of the War that was emerging, and so the challenge was on to recruit, train and deploy a much larger fighting force in a matter of weeks. Lord Kitchener, the first serving soldier to be appointed to cabinet since the seventeenth century, distrusted the Territorial Force, and opted instead to create a network of special service battalions attached to the regular full time regiments of the Army right across the nation. Setting out to recruit 100,000 volunteers, his 'Your Country Needs You' poster campaign must surely be one of the most successful marketing projects in history as young men from shipyards, factories, transport depots, professional football teams and virtually every walk of life responded enthusiastically and volunteered to fight in the New Army. The farming folk of the North East were no different:

> I jined up wi ma pal Fred Duncan efter the leaflets cam oot fae Kitchener needin a hunner thoosan men. We biket wi a lot mair fae Millbrex ti Peterheed ti jine up in the 5th Gordon Highlanders. We wis teen richt awa ti dee wir trainin an gid oot ti France fae Bedford in the Spring o 1915. Fred wis teen wi a lot o idder volunteers to the newly formed Machine Gun Corps that eer, bit he wis killed on the Somme.
> **Sandy Simpson, Woodhead, 5th Gordon Highlanders**

Others testify to the fact that there were around 30 farm servants who cycled the 25 or so miles together from Millbrex to Peterhead that day – it must have been quite a sight, this peloton of ploughmen! Some local farmers tried to confiscate the posters and hand bills, understandably worried that they would lose their workforce, but it was an ineffective ploy. There was to be no holding them back.

The numerous stories of recruitment and volunteering collected by Jock and presented in Chapter Three generally follow the same grand narrative which applies throughout the nation. What comes through powerfully is the eagerness of these volunteers to sign up, to go, to get involved, to do their bit. There is an edge of excitement there, almost a levity, as these men, reflecting back much later in life, recall their youthful enthusiasm at the start of the great adventure. Several lads admitted to Jock they had lied about their age. Robert More, of the 4th Seaforth Highlanders was just one of an estimated 250,000 boys in the British Army[4] who fought in the Great War while underage:

> I wis in the Terriers at Perth. With their Black Watch Battalion. I was mustered when War started, I went to my officer and told him I wanted back to my own lot in the Black Isle. I was granted my wish and sent back up north to join the 4th Seaforth Highlanders at that time still at Nigg. I was only 14 years old.
>
> We went from there to Inverness and stayed there a while, then later entrained for Bedford Camp. We were sent to France in October 1914 and joined the 1st Corps, 1st Division, 3rd Brigade. … As I had went off in 1914 when I was 14 years old my folk tried to get me home a few times.[5] I always refused when I was called in front of the CO. I suppose I liked it though it was rough at times.

Whatever their age, when the volunteers arrived onto the fields of Belgium and France, the realities of war kicked in very quickly. The bulk of this book comprises detailed and often graphic accounts of the experiences of these men in virtually all of the main theatres of war on the Western Front and in Gallipoli. In almost every case their stories are told in a rather matter-of-fact manner, with little attempt to add further to the drama, and often with a humour that on first reading may seem surprising. Violent death was a daily occurrence, and many of the men represented here were wounded, some several times over. And yet there is very little evidence of bitterness, and almost no politically infused questioning of the reasons why they were there in the first place. In fact, one of the few hints of protest contained in these narratives comes from Alec Robertson of the 5th Gordon Highlanders when recalling the words of his new Commanding Officer who had replaced the highly popular Lt Colonel Grant who had lost an arm to a shell explosion:

> Colonel MacTaggart came after Grant. He was a wee man who came from the Lancers. When we came out of the Somme, he addressed us and said that it was an honour to die for our country, but I don't think we appreciated that.

For sure, Alec would have agreed with Wilfred Owen's rejection of that 'old lie', *Dulce et decorum est pro patria mori.*[6]

The Regiments

Jock Duncan interviewed 59 men representing 26 battalions from 14 regiments. As is to be expected given his North-East upbringing, the Gordon Highlanders is the regiment which has the largest representation, with 33 men. Several men transferred between battalions or even between regiments and so their testimonies reflect a variety of experiences. During the War, a number of battalions came together to form a brigade, with several brigades forming a division. The majority of the men represented here fought within the 51st (Highland) Division, although the 7th, 8th and 15th (Scottish) Divisions are well represented too. The battalions raised for Kitchener's 'New Army' tended to be attached to the 1st battalions of a regular full-time regiment, and so became numbered as 1/4th, 1/5th, etc. However, common usage was to simply refer to them as 4th, 5th, etc. and that is the terminology used by all of the men and by Jock himself, and so we have adhered to that convention throughout the text.

The following regiments and battalions are represented in the interviews:

18th Australian and New Zealand Army Corps (ANZACS)
Army Service Corps
1st Black Watch
1/4th Black Watch
1/5th Black Watch
1/6th Black Watch
1/7th Black Watch
2nd Cameron Highlanders
1/7th Cameron Highlanders
1st Gordon Highlanders
2nd Gordon Highlanders
1/4th Gordon Highlanders
1/5th Gordon Highlanders
1/6th Gordon Highlanders
1/7th Gordon Highlanders
1/8th Gordon Highlanders
1/9th Gordon Highlanders
12th Highland Light Infantry
1st King's Own Scottish Borderers
The Lovat Scouts
Machine Gun Corps
Royal Engineers
Royal Field Artillery
Royal Horse Artillery
1st Scottish Horse
4th Seaforth Highlanders

Timeline of Key Events

1914

June 28th: **Assassination of Archduke Franz Ferdinand.**

July 28th: **Austria declares war on Serbia.**

August 1st: **Germany declares war on Russia.**

August 3rd: **Germany declares war on France and invades Belgium.**

August 4th: **Britain declares war on Germany.**

August 9th: **British Expeditionary Force (BEF) embarks for France.**

August 21st–24th: **Battle of Mons.** The first main action of the War for the BEF took place at Mons near the French/German border, as Allied forces attempted to halt the German invasion and block the intended advance to Paris. Amongst the Scottish contingent who fought there were the 1st Black Watch and the 1st Gordon Highlanders, both battalions having landed in France on 14th August. The BEF attempted to hold the line of the Mons-Condé canal, but the combination of the strength of numbers of the German 1st Army and the decision of the French 5th Army to retreat, forced the BEF to follow suit.

September 6th–12th: **First Battle of the Marne.** The German advance had been slowed when the British troops fought a rear guard action at the Battle of Le Cateau on August 25th and 26th, the 1st Gordon Highlanders in particular suffering heavy casualties. The German progress continued, however, until the Allied forces dug in and faced their foes on September 6th. The battle lasted a full week and resulted in the first key allied victory of the War, forcing the Germans to retreat to the North East where they dug in at the river Aisne. French and German losses at the Marne were huge – around 250,000 each – while British losses were confined to 'only' around 12,700.

September 12th–28th: **First Battle of the Aisne.** The BEF and the French 5th Army pursued the retreating Germans who had secured a strong defensive position on the river Aisne. On September 12th, the Allies began a combined assault, managing to cross the river, but following four days of fierce fighting it became clear that the battle had reached an impasse, with neither side able to secure a victory, yet both refusing to retreat. The result was the beginning of trench warfare and a stalemate which lasted for four years. Both sides began to attempt to search for a route around the enemy, resulting in the 'Race to the Sea' as they followed the Aisne northwards in search of a chance to break through. This simply resulted in many more miles of trenches being dug, setting the scene for a new approach to war, as the opposing sides faced each other across the neutral territory in between the trenches – No Man's Land.

October 19th–November 22nd: **First Battle of Ypres**. At the beginning of October, the BEF began to move quietly from the Aisne to the plains of Flanders in order to regroup and meet up with reinforcements, primarily those regular Army regiments which had been making their way back from service overseas. The ancient Belgian city of Ypres was of great strategic significance at it helped to guard the coastal ports, and it was to become the scene of some of the most prolonged and fiercest fighting throughout the War. The Germans began their Flanders offensive to try to take the city from the Allied forces on October 19th, with fighting lasting over a month before the winter weather and mutual exhaustion brought it to a halt. The bulge of Allied territory stretching a mile or two east from Ypres between the two main lines, from Ypres itself to the town of Menin a few miles to the east, became known as the Ypres Salient, which remained one of the key theatres of the conflict throughout the War.

October 29th: **Turkey enters the War in support of Germany**.

November 2nd: **Russia declares war on Turkey**.

November 5th: **Britain and France declare war on Turkey**.

December 25th: **The Christmas Truce**. At various points along the Western Front, hostilities temporarily ceased on Christmas Day as the opposing sides met in No Man's Land, swapping gifts of food and cigarettes, and in one or two sites, playing football. It lasted up to a week in some places, although in others it was confined to Christmas Day itself. The British high command, especially Sir John French, took a dim view of such fraternisation and gave orders that this should not happen again. Several of the men interviewed by Jock Duncan took part in the truce.

1915

March 10th–13th: **Battle of Neuve Chapelle**. During the winter, the BEF had been joined by reinforcements as Kitchener's New Army began to arrive in Belgium and France, along with significant numbers of Indian troops. The Allies decided to take the initiative and to mount offensives against the German lines, beginning at Neuve Chapelle in the Artois region of France in an attempt to recapture a salient which the Germans had secured some months previously.

The initial surprise attack which began on March 10th met with some success, but ultimately the Allies were unable to follow through to press home this advantage. British casualties were 11,652 killed, wounded or taken prisoner, and two Gordon Highlander battalions lost their commanding officers, Lieutenant Colonel Henry Uniacke of the 2nd, and Lieutenant Colonel Colin McLean of the 1/6th, both being killed in action.

April 17th–7th May: **Battle of Hill 60, Ypres**. The German 30th Division had captured this spoil heap in November 1914, and the British were very keen to recapture it as it provided a key observation point and was therefore of great strategic importance. Northumbrian and Welsh miners were brought in to tunnel into the surrounding area, and many thousands of pounds of explosives were laid. These were detonated at the start of the attack on the 17th of April, which allowed the British troops to take the hill with relative ease and almost no casualties. However, the Germans counter-attacked using gas in early May and succeeded in recapturing the hill which they retained until 1917.

April 22nd–May 25th: **Second Battle of Ypres**. The struggle for control of the town of Ypres was renewed. This involved the first use of chemical weapons in the War, as the Germans released chlorine gas aimed at French troops, who sustained around 6,000 casualties.

April 25th–January 9th: **1916 Gallipoli Campaign**. The Gallipoli Peninsula within the Ottoman Empire guarded the north shore of the Dardanelles, an important communications and supply route to the Russian Empire, and one Britain was keen to secure. Winston Churchill, 1st Lord of the Admiralty, had advocated opening an Ottoman Front in November 1914, suggesting that as the Turks were thought to be weak, Germany would be forced to send significant numbers of troops to defend the peninsula, thus weakening their hand on the Western Front. In mid-January 1915, the British War Council agreed, although there was confusion as to whether they were simply instructing Churchill to begin preparations, or whether he had the authority to go ahead and mount the full attack. Admiral Carden, in charge of the British naval fleet which was anchored off the Dardanelles, was cautious and argued that a gradual approach was necessary, but Churchill preferred to strike with full power immediately. In mid-February, Carden began a naval bombardment, while British and Anzac troops which were currently stationed in Egypt were put on alert. The naval action went well initially, but it was soon realised that the Turkish defences were much stronger than expected, and that they had mined the straits, with British minesweepers proving ineffective. It was decided that a significant body of troops would have to be deployed to reinforce those already stationed in Egypt, and General Sir Ian Hamilton was appointed as the commander of the

Mediterranean Expeditionary Force. This comprised around 70,000 British, French, Australian and New Zealand troops and included 17 Scottish battalions. On March 18th, a Turkish attack took out two-thirds of the British naval vessels, and so it was decided that a land attack was now necessary. The first troops landed on April 25th, and what followed was an unmitigated disaster. Planning and communication between the commanders was poor, and the Turks proved a defiant foe. While initial British landings at Cape Helles were unopposed, those at Sedd-el-Bahr and later at Suvla Bay were fiercely resisted, while those at what came to be called Anzac Cove proved equally problematic. By December, it was decided that the Allies should cut their losses and evacuate. This was one of the few aspects of the entire campaign that was achieved with great success, and was fondly and indeed proudly recalled by some of Jock's interviewees. They were less impressed, however, by the memory that their horses had to be shot as they left.

May 9th: **Battle of Aubers Ridge**. A continuation of the Allied offensive on the Western Front which had begun two months earlier at Neuve Chapelle. The battle has been described as 'an unmitigated disaster' for the British Army, which incurred heavy losses and gained no strategic or territorial advantage at all.

May 15th–27th: **Battle of Festubert**. Also part of the same Allied offensive. Many of the men interviewed by Jock fought at Festubert, with the 1/4th Black Watch, all volunteers from Dundee, suffering particularly heavy losses.

September 25th–28th: **The Battle of Loos**. As the stalemate on the Western Front continued, the Franco-British alliance began a major offensive towards the end of September, undertaking their heaviest attack of the year on the German lines. This was the first major test for the volunteers of the New Army, and Loos is sometimes referred to as the 'Scottish' battle, such was the weight of representation from north of the border. Around 30,000 Scottish troops fought there, with half of the infantry battalions having Scottish titles, and Scottish losses were correspondingly heavy. As Trevor Royle points out, of the 20,000 or so names on the memorial to the missing at Loos, probably around one third are Scots.[7] The 1/4th Black Watch, known as 'Dundee's Own', having already suffered huge losses at Festubert, were all but wiped out at Loos: 19 of their remaining 20 officers were killed or wounded, as were 230 of the 420 men. The battle also marked the first use of chlorine gas by the British. However, a change in wind direction blew the gas back over their own troops, and so both sides suffered many casualties as a result. The battle was another disaster for the British Army, losing just short of 60,000 men, with German losses at less than half of that number. Sir John French was blamed for having failed in his tactical approach, and was soon to be replaced as Commander in Chief of the BEF by Field Marshall Douglas Haig, who remained in post until the end of the War.

1916

July 1st–November 18th: **Battle of the Somme**. In December 1915, the Allies had agreed to begin plans for a joint offensive on the Eastern, Italian and Western Fronts. The French were to lead on the latter, with British support, but when the Germans attacked at Verdun in February 1916, the French had to move large numbers of troops to defend their own positions there. The plans had to be adjusted, therefore, with the British stepping up to take the lead in the offensive which was set to take place on a front of some 16 miles in an area of the Somme valley in Picardy, France. The original BEF – the 'Old Contemptibles' of the regular Army – had been greatly depleted in the opening two years of the War, and so it was now largely the Territorials and Kitchener's volunteers who moved into place to ready themselves for the attack that Haig felt confident would lead to victory. What actually transpired was one of the bloodiest battles in human history, around one million men being killed or wounded by the time hostilities ceased there in mid-November. On the first day alone, 1st July, the British suffered 57,470 casualties, 19,240 of whom were killed. At no time before, or since, did the nation lose so many men on a single day. Three wholly Scottish divisions fought on the Somme, the 9th, 15th (Scottish) and the 51st (Highland), and so the majority of the men who shared their stories with Jock Duncan were in action there. One site which features particularly strongly in their memories is High Wood, scene of a long, bloody and exhausting series of offensives and counter-attacks, with the 51st playing a key role throughout. Another place name with great resonance for many of Jock's men was Beaumont-Hamel, a village which was situated just behind the German lines and which was intended as a key target from day one of the Somme offensive. Like so many of the other objectives, however, it proved impregnable for months, until it was eventually taken on November 13th by the 51st Highland Division. The whole Somme campaign resulted in the Allies advancing only six miles.

1917

April 6th: **USA declared war on Germany**.

April 9th–16th May: **Battle of Arras**. Following the relative stalemate of the Somme, the Allies planned for a new offensive, while the Germans shored up their defences by establishing a heavily fortified front known to the English speaking world as the Hindenburg Line. In early April the Allies attacked, with a significant Canadian and Scottish presence, once again including the 9th, 15th (Scottish) and 51st (Highland) Divisions. The initial push met with a good deal of success, with the strategically important heights of Vimy Ridge falling with comparative ease. However, despite some further success in an offensive around the village of Bullecourt, once again it proved impossible to follow through successfully, and another stalemate ensued. British casualties numbered 159,000, probably around a third of them Scots, and with a higher daily casualty rate than was suffered on the Somme.

31st July–6th November: **Battle of Passchendaele (Third Battle of Ypres).** Eager to reach and destroy the German submarine bases on the coast, Haig decided to mount another push on the Ypres Salient in the late summer of 1917. Within a few days of the start of the Infantry assault, torrential rain had turned the flat plains of Flanders into a stinking quagmire, and conditions within the trenches there were amongst the worst of the entire War. Over the 105 days of the battle, the British suffered 275,000 casualties and the Germans 220,000.

20th November–4th December: **Battle of Cambrai.** Towards the end of 1917, the British decided to mount an attack at the town of Cambrai, a key railway intersection and German garrison on the Hindenburg Line in the north of France. Although tanks had been used on the Somme the previous year, this was to be the first time they played a key role in battle. While once again the offensive itself proved ineffectual, and resulted in huge loss of life, lessons were learned on both sides which were to prove important in the months to come.

1918

March 3rd: **A peace agreement between Soviet Russia and Germany was signed**, ending Russia's involvement in the War.

March 21st: **The Great German Push** or **First Spring Offensive** began. With 50 divisions freed up following the peace treaty with Russia, Germany committed to a concerted offensive on the Western Front, realising that this would be the last chance for victory before USA troops arrived in large numbers.

April 9th: Germany followed up with the **Second Spring Offensive** against the British sector in Armentière.

May 27th–June 4th: **Third Battle of the Aisne (Third Spring Offensive).** Germany attempted to split the British and French forces, again before USA troops arrived in larger numbers.

July 15th–August 6th: **The Second Battle of the Marne.** The final phase of the Great German Push, but their troops were exhausted and numbers depleted. The British counter-attacked on the 18th of July, seizing the initiative and laying the foundation of the final phase of the War.

August 8th: **Battle of Amiens** began, marking the beginning of the Allied Hundred Days Offensive. The Allies succeeded in breaking through German defences.

October 4th: **Germany requested an armistice**. The Allies soon had control of most of France and part of Belgium.

November 7th: **Negotiations for an armistice began.**

November 9th: **The Kaiser abdicated.**

November 11th: **The armistice came into effect at 11am,** marking the official end of the War, and victory for the Allies.

These events, then, served as the theatres of war for the men whose stories feature in this book. The summaries I have provided above give the bare facts. But they do not – indeed cannot – even begin to give us an insight as to what it was like to be there. Of course most of us can never really imagine that, but in the pages that follow we can perhaps catch just a glimpse of what these men experienced a century ago. They are just 59 individuals among many million who fought on all sides in that war which was supposedly going to end all wars. But as a group, they share one thing in common. They all came home.

    We are usually told that veterans of the Great War seldom spoke about their experiences and rarely 'opened up' to anyone. For whatever reason, they opened up to Jock Duncan. They are Jock's Jocks. By knocking on their doors, he gave them the chance to tell their stories, and through dozens of hours of interviewing, and thousands of hours of typing, he has allowed us to share these stories with you.

    And that is a very fine thing indeed.

Gary West
European Ethnological Research Centre

Work continues to digitise the original audio recordings on which this book is based. It is hoped that these recordings will be made available online. Please check: https://edin.ac/2IBDIo2 for updates.

List of Veterans

This list of the men whose experiences are represented in this book was compiled by Jock Duncan himself.

Alec Wilson, 7th Cameron Highlanders
Woodside, Aberdeen. Conscripted into the 7th Cameron Highlanders, Mr Wilson was two years at the Front and was taken prisoner in the Great German Push of 21st March 1918 by Marines who were singing a song that he knew in English: 'There are many brave hearts lie asleep in the deep …'.

George Stewart, 5th Gordon Highlanders
Sunnyside of Lethenty, Fyvie. Farmer, was called up into 5th Gordon High-landers and was three years away. Was badly gassed but rejoined in time for some of the worst fighting of the War.

George (Dod) Carrol, Private, Machine Gun Corps
Gallowhill, Gight. Trained at the Gordon's depot in Aberdeen. Mr Carrol was later sent with another 80 men to the Machine Gun Corps. Later he was drafted to the Transport Service as they were needing good horsemen. Remembers at the start of the War, when the gig shafts were commandeered at a Fyvie Kirk service.

Jimmy Reid, 6th Gordon Highlanders
Cults/Alford. Was 3rd horseman at Whitehouse of Alford when War was declared. Mr Reid joined the 6th Gordon Highlanders at Alford with another two from the farm, and was in all the major battles. Wounded twice, he always refused promotion, unlike the pal he was in with from the start. This Sergeant Gilbert had a peculiar saying: 'He was a lucky man that was killed at Mons!' Sergeant Gilbert was killed on the last day. Mr Reid's description of Army life: 'We jist hid on the kilts, nae bliddy pants or onything and a jersey that wis as loosy as hell'.

Jimmy Milne, Private, 2nd Gordon Highlanders
Roseharty. Farm servant at Mid Ardlaw, whose entire complement of single men tried to join up when Kitchener's call came through. Mr Milne had to wait until

he was old enough in the spring of 1916 and joined the 2nd Gordon Highlanders after the Somme and wished it was the 5th when he saw all his local pals passing through on the march with the 51st Highland Division. Mr Milne was in the 7th Division.

Robert MacRobbie, Private, 1st Gordon Highlanders

New Byth. Was horseman at Backhill of Bonnykelly when he was called up, but not until the hairst was finished in 1917. This was a bad one and the kirk congregations were given leave to work one Sunday, when a winnin sough of wind had arrived to dry the stuff. Mr MacRobbie was wounded at Cambrai where his pal, Peter Cheyne from Cuminestown, was killed by his side.

hairst harvest, *sough* strong breeze

John Webster, Royal Field Artillery

Muirs, Briggs Farm and Deershill at Millbrex. Third horseman at Swanford, Greens. When War started he was one of the 30 men that cycled from Millbrex to Peterhead to list in answer to Kitchener's call. He joined the Royal Field Artillery and served in all the fronts in France and Belgium. He describes Passchendaele as the worst.

Bill Minty, 4th Gordon Highlanders

Woodhead, Fyvie. Was working in Aberdeen where he volunteered in the Aberdeen's own 4th Gordon Highlanders. He met Sergeant (Postie) Pratt from Woodhead when he first arrived in France. Postie called him all the silly buggers for joining up. Mr Minty was wounded.

Sandy Simpson, 5th Gordon Highlanders

Woodhead, Fyvie. Belonged to Millbrex originally and was another one who cycled to Peterhead along with his pal, Fred Duncan, among the 30 volunteers. Both joined the 5th Gordon Highlanders, where Mr Simpson survived High Wood on the Somme and was wounded at Beaumont-Hamel. His pal was killed when he was sent to the Machine Gun Corps, and whose name is among the 34 inscribed in the Millbrex Memorial who perished in the Great War.

Donald Petrie, 5th Gordon Highlanders

New Deer, Asleid. Was in the 5th Gordon Highlanders along with Sooter Wilson from Lethenty, Fyvie. Mr Petrie tells of his sergeant's reaction at finding Gordon badges in the pocket of a German prisoner.

William Angus, 2nd Gordon Highlanders

New Deer. Joined up at 17 and was in the 2nd Gordon Highlanders. Was severely wounded and lost a leg.

Bert Gow, Royal Field Artillery

New Deer. Joined at 16 at a recruiting drive at New Deer in the Royal Field Artillery and was in the 51st Highland Division. Mr Gow was an apprentice tailor but never went back to it. He also enjoyed entertaining the lads when they were out for a rest and could still remember the songs he composed, many years later. When Bob Boothby came to New Deer electioneering in the thirties, he always parted with ten bob to Bert to hear him sing 'Boothby on my back', a famous election song he made up.

2. Bert Gow. *Leopard* magazine

Albert Napier MM, Royal Field Artillery ('Taggart's Own')

New Deer. Was working in Aberdeen and joined Taggart's Own Artillery.[8] Provost Taggart undertook to raise a battery and did so within a week but when they got to Bulford Camp they were ordered to take off the ribbon with the title 'Taggart's Own' on the shoulders of their tunics. From then they were Royal Field Artillery and given a battery number. He describes leaving the

3. Albert Napier. *Leopard* magazine

battle of the Somme as like going from hell into heaven. Was awarded the Military Medal.

A. Smeaton MM, Sergeant, 5th Black Watch

Coupar, Angus. Was in the 5th Black Watch where the battalion was in the 8th Division at first before becoming part of the 51st Highland Division. Was promoted to sergeant. Was wounded at Festubert and was awarded the Military Medal.

Davie Stewart, Piper, 4th Gordon Highlanders

New Deer. Went to France with the Aberdeen's 4th Gordon Highlanders and was a piper. His brother, Robin, was a regular and was a Sergeant Piper to 2nd Gordon Highlanders, and already had been decorated with the Distinguished Conduct Medal and the Russian Order of St George when he was killed at Loos with 13 pipers of the band, and where seven others were wounded.

Alec Nicol, Lance Corporal, 7th Gordon Highlanders
Kildrummy. Joined up at 16 when he was at a farm near Rhynie. He trained with the 7th Gordon Highlanders at Bedford and was sent to France with them. Was present when the quartermaster shot the cheese – a famous incident that they never lived down. Was wounded three times.

4. Alec Nicol. *Leopard* magazine

J. Fowlie, Corporal, 7th Gordon Highlanders
Turriff. Foreman at Pots of Rayne when he was called up into the 7th Gordon Highlanders. He liked the annual Lourin Fair.[9] He tells about the officers that were more like themselves out there, that spoke the braid tongue. Mr Fowlie lost an arm in action.

5. George Bryan. *Leopard* magazine

George Bryan MM, Sergeant, 12th Highland Light Infantry
Cairnie, Huntly/Bogniebrae/Forgue. A grocer at Bogniebrae of Forgue, he joined up in the Highland Light Infantry when he failed the medical in the Royal Field Artillery. Promoted to sergeant at Third Ypres when his battalion was decimated by shellfire. Mr Bryan was awarded the Military Medal. He was badly gassed in 1918, and was months before he regained his voice and sight.

John Russel, Private, Royal Field Artillery
Farmer, Gamrie. Joined the Royal Field Artillery at the outbreak of War and was in the 51st Highland Division and later the 8th divisions. The latter was sent down to near Paris to recuperate from their mauling

6. John Russel. *Leopard* magazine

during the Great German 21st March Push and were promptly attacked by another offensive. This time Mr Russel said they lost all their guns. This became known as the '2nd Battle of the Marne'.

Jimmy Scott, Sapper, Royal Engineers

Tifty, Fyvie, later Turriff. Royal Engineers. Wounded at the Somme. A bad conscience made him enlist, he and his pal, Wullie Webster, having been publically shamed by the minister for being drunk. Jimmy tells about the gigs and shults that were commandeered at Fyvie Kirk service and having to walk four miles for a replacement for Mrs Coburn, South Monkshill.

Alec Meldrum MM. Sergeant.

Whitehills and later Banff. 8th Gordon Highlanders and later 1st. Promoted to sergeant. Wounded at Vimy Ridge. Mud and more mud, hail, sleet and snow were Mr Meldrum's memories of the trenches in the winter. He also knew Pipe Major G. S. McLennan well.

7. Jimmy Scott. *Leopard* magazine

John MacRae, Private, 18th Battalion, ANZAC

St Katherine's, Fyvie and New Zealand. Mr MacRae operated a steam mill in New Zealand and was a sheep shearer. 'When we stopped off at ports on our way to England, we were told to behave ourselves and show

8. John Macrae. *Leopard* magazine

how more civilised we were than those wild Australians. Of course the Australian officers said the same to their men about us.' Mr MacRae chose to remain in his native Aberdeenshire after the War.

Norrie Cruikshank, Private, 6th Gordon Highlanders

Keith. Was in the 6th Gordon Terriers and went out to France with them in 1914 to the 7th Division. Mr Cruikshank was a Lewis gunner who was badly gassed in 1917. He describes life at the Front: 'The English – I didna care for them afa weel – they wid ate as much as you and me thegither and then plenty mair. Oh my heavens! I widna like it ti be their cook – na mighty na! The French ate horses, puddocks and snails – they ate aa that kine o dirt. I widna blame onybody for rinnin awa; they barkit at ye aa the time and treated ye like a dog'.

puddocks frogs

Alec MacHardy MM, Sergeant, 7th Gordon Highlanders

Banff. Joined Aberdeen at 17. Promoted to sergeant on the Somme by his major who drew three stripes on his arm of his tunic with a blue pencil. Awarded the Military Medal and wounded four times, Mr Mac-Hardy was posted missing after the Great German Push of 21st March 1918 but came back to take part in the 2nd Marne with the 51st Highland Division near Rheims. Mr MacHardy describes some activities: 'Some o oor game lads acquired ferrets – gweed kens farr fae – and they turned the craters louse. Man they fairly killed the rats and they in turn bred like hell tee. Oh you've nae idea fit gaed on!'

gweed kens farr fae goodness knows where from

9. Alec MacHardy. *Leopard* magazine

Lea Birnie, 1st Gordon Highlanders

Broch (Fraserburgh). Joined up into 1st Gordon Highlanders the day War was declared. Mr Birnie was 4th horseman at Rathen and wanted excitement and joined the 1st after they lost heavily at Le Cateau. He was taken out of the trenches for a while when his legs 'foonered' standing up to his hips in water.

foonered gave way

J. Burnett, Private, 8th Gordon Highlanders

Fraserburgh. Was 2nd cattleman at Woodhead of Cairness when called up at 18. Was in the 8th Gordon Highlanders. Was wounded severely at Third Battle of Ypres.

John Rennie, 5th Gordon Highlanders

Balmellie Farm, Turriff. Was in the 5th Gordon Terriers and mustered at Turra Show when the officers of the company came round telling them to go home and get all their kit and report to the drill hall. They were then sent to Peterhead, Perth and finally Bedford for training. Mr Rennie was taken prisoner in the German Push of March 1918. Was near Colonel Sir Arthur Grant of Monymusk when the colonel lost an arm in the front line (17 June 1915).

Albert Connon, Private, 5th Gordon Highlanders

Turriff. Another Terrier called to the colours the day of Turra Show 1914. Was only 16 and kept back at first, Mr Connon eventually wangled his way out in 1915. He was captured at Beaumont-Hamel along with a few more 5th Gordon High-landers and taken into the huge German underground cellars. Then their captors in turn became their prisoners, when the Black Watch appeared at the entrances. Was wounded at Third Ypres and carried back by German prisoners he had taken. Mr Connon said that Slater Eddie of Fyvie was his sergeant major for about a year in France.

George Barclay, Bombadier, Royal Field Artillery
Turriff, later Auchterless. Was fe-et at Pitglassie, Auchterless, when he joined the Royal Field Artillery in 1915. Sent to Mesopotamia to fight the Turks, he describes the food: 'The rations were nae great dale. Maistly hard tack and fin we biled them, the weevils aa cam to the tap o the watter and were scooped aff. Weel nae them aa maybe.' Mr Barclay came back to fee at Auchterless where he was grieve for 30 years.
fe-et employed *dale* deal

Wullie Gavin, Private, 5th Gordon Highlanders
Longside, later Turriff. Was fe-et near Ellon and went off with 5th Gordon Terriers at start of the War. He describes musical interludes: 'I played the melodeon oot there and eased ti fizzle awa weet nae bad.' About High Wood on the Somme: 'What a lads gid doon on wir first attack. The barbet weer wis never broken in front of their lines.' Mr Gavin was severely wounded at Third Ypres and later invalided out in time to fee home to Logie as hairst man in 1918.[10]
barbet weer barbed wire

Alec Sim, 7th Gordon Highlanders
Farmer Auchterless. Joined the 7th Gordon Highlanders. His pal, Speed, who had been called up called him a fool for volunteering. Mr Sim was badly wounded when he went to the aid of his fallen comrade during an advance at Third Ypres August 1917.

Andrew Finnie, 7th Black Watch
Forglery, Turriff. Was called up into the 7th Black Watch and was wounded.

Robert More MM, Sergeant, 4th Seaforth Highlanders
Black Isle. In the Terriers at 14 while working in the wood near Perth, he requested back to 4th Seaforth Highlanders in the Black Isle and went out with them to join the 1st Division in 1914. Of the Christmas Truce: 'We came out to meet the Germans and the celebrations lasted all day. Nobody turned on anyone; we were all quite happy. It only lasted one day and we exchanged souvenirs like buttons and envelopes with stamps.' Mr More was awarded the Military Medal and Bar and was wounded three times and promoted to sergeant at 16.

Alec Barlow, 1st Gordon Highlanders

Turriff. Was conscripted because he refused to accept too low a fee from a farmer to go home as foreman. He was sent to 1st Gordon Highlanders and found he enjoyed it and was never really afraid. Mr Barlow was shot through both cheeks and regretfully gave his fags away because he couldn't smoke – he was 'ower sair'.

ower sair too sore

Dave Pitkethly, 4th Seaforth Highlanders

Newburgh, Fife. Called up into 4th Seaforth Highlanders but always hankered to be with his mates in the 7th Black Watch. He went many miles to visit them. His sergeant once said to him, 'I have you in for a medal Dave'. To which he replied: 'If I come out of this with my life, that's all I need.' Mr Pitkeithly was wounded in both arms in the German Push on 23rd March 1918. He also suffered effects of gas all his life but had never gone sick at the time. He sang five verses about the 51st Highland Division that they had sang in the trenches.

Donald MacVicar, 1st and 2nd Queen's Own Cameron Highlanders

Uist/Perth. A member of the Cameron Company 'Special Reserve' (3rd [Special Reserve] Battalion The Queens' Own Cameron Highlanders) since 1912 when he joined at 16, and as their champion shot was picked out by Lt Colonel Cameron with a few others to join the 1st Battalion at outbreak of War. He was wounded in November 1914 and was sent to Dundee Royal Infirmary. Then to convalescence at Glamis Castle where he met the 14-year-old future Queen Elizabeth. Mr MacVicar was then posted to the 2nd Cameron Highlanders where he was wounded badly a second time. He didn't get back to Glamis that time, he regrets.

Donald MacLeod, Pipe Major, 4th Black Watch

Dundee. Was in the 4th Dundee's Own Black Watch as a piper. His father's people came from Skye during the evictions. At Third Ypres he piped a company into the attack but they didn't get very far in the mud. Mr MacLeod knew the famous tutor John Stewart, the uncle of G. S. McLennan. G. S. composed the tune 'Pipe Major John Stewart' after him.

Jim Duncan, Gordon Highlanders

Forglen/Penelopefield/Turriff. In the Derby Scheme[11] he was called into the Gordon Highlanders but did not see much action before the War finished. Has great memories of schooldays walking to school 'barfit', and about the Sunday when one of their number was ordered to go to Bootie's Well to get holy water for the christening of a bairn at church, but as it was miles away they just filled the bottle at a roadside ditch.

barfit barefoot

Frank MacFarlane MM and Medal Militaire, Corporal, 1st Black Watch

Forfar. Joined up in the Black Watch at Forfar in 1912 because he scunnered of being in a bothy alone – drying his clothes and making his own food. He said that it was 'nae life ata'. One of the few survivors of the 1st Battalion, he was at Mons and at the 1st Battle of the Marne where he was the last man to see Lt Colonel Duff, when the Colonel asked him to show him where D Company was and they parted in a beet field. The Colonel was never heard of again. Mr MacFarlane was promoted to corporal and awarded the Military Medal and Medal Militaire.

scunnered fed up

Jonathan Taylor, 9th Gordon Highlanders

Gight, Fyvie. A gamekeeper, he was called up into the 9th Pioneers, Gordon Highlanders where he got on for groom to the colonel. 'They were near all ferm servants and could fair use a spade at digging trenches,' said Mr Taylor.

got on for was appointed

John Will, 5th Gordon Highlanders

Cotburn, Turriff. 'I jined up with Peter Taylor, a lad Ord and a Peterson at Turra. That three were sent to the Machine Gun Corps. I wis a ferm servant afore I jined up and sae were the lave.' Mr Will was in the 5th Gordon Highlanders and tells about the musical fun when they were out of the trenches. 'Some played the melodeons and mouth organs ... . Een made a mandolin fae a petrol tin.' He was wounded and had to go back in again when he wasn't quite well because the Germans had started the Great Push of March 1918. It wasn't quite long before he heard them coming over singing and – in his words – 'Boozed'.

lave rest

Wull Dryden, Gordon Highlanders

Forfar. Called up into Gordon Highlanders from shepherding in the Angus hills, he took his motor bike with him which was promptly confiscated on the promise of £10 for it. The bike was never seen again, nor the £10. Overstaying leave with two other shepherds – Geordie Stewart and Geordie Smith – they were nabbed by MPs who took them to a Cockney officer who couldn't understand a word they said.

Alec Robertson, Sergeant 5th Gordon Highlanders,
Captain 1st Yorkshire & Lancaster Regiment

Buchan. The last school attended was Cairnorrie when his father was 2nd cattler at Baldies, he left at 14 and fe-et for £4.15 the six months at Turnerhall. Mr Robertson was in the 5th Gordon Terriers at 16 and in the War rose from private to captain, being wounded twice. A lassie in Southampton pressed a good luck charm – a black cat badge – into his hand as they embarked for France and he had it all through the War.

Jock Murray, 1st King's Own Scottish Borderers
Hawick. A member of a Lewis gun team, Mr Murray served in Gallipoli in the 1st King's Own Scottish Borderers, 29th Division. Later the Division was transferred from Egypt to take part in the Battle of the Somme, where he was wounded. Captured out in front of the line in the German Push of March 1918, he was saved from the bayonet by a Gerry NCO. As a Machine Gunner – according to Mr Murray: 'You never stood a chance.' He spent the rest of the War working on starvation rations, going down to 6½ stone.

Tom Rearie, 5th Gordon Highlanders
Newmachar. Was buried by a shell at Arras with the 5th Gordon Highlanders and suffered from concussion. Mr Rearie was unable to speak for six months but was still sent back to the Front before he was well. He said, 'It was jist a case of, if ye could waak, if ye ken fit I mean'.

Peter Baigrie, 7th Cameron Highlanders/6th Black Watch
Peterhead. A carter, he supplied the steam trawlers with coal from the station with horse drawn cart. He wanted to join the Cavalry, due to a dislike of wearing the kilt. They told him at the recruiting office that there was the Lovat Scouts, so off he went fine pleased; only after initial training, he was switched to the Cameron Highlanders. Mr Baigrie was wounded and nearly died from loss of blood. Was carried back to dressing station by German prisoners.

Albert Edwards, 5th Black Watch/Machine Gun Corps
A Terrier in 1913 Montrose, he went off with the 5th Black Watch in November 1914 to the 8th Division. The boat they sailed in was the *Architect* which had just unloaded a cargo of live cattle from the Argentine and had stunk of sharn every-where. After Aubers Ridge Attack on the German lines there were only 85 men answered the roll call. They always said they would see each other in Caird's restaurant on Saturday as a joke, before going over the top, but got the zip-zip of bullets laying them low instead. Wounded at Schwaben Redoubt, he joined the Machine Gun Corps at Rippon, a unit they actually termed the 'Suicide Corps'.
sharn manure

Jim Burgess, 2nd Cameron Highlanders
Montrose. Called up to the Cameron Highlanders he served in the Balkans with the 2nd Battalion, after being diverted from Calais where he'd landed with a batch for the 5th in France.

James (Jimmy) Smith, Sergeant, Royal Field Artillery
Logie Coldstone/Fettercairn. Employed at the shop at Inverden of Towie, Strath-don, on the lorry and van – both horse drawn. He joined the Royal Field Artillery

in 1912 and was in India when War was declared. At Gallipoli from the first day to the last, he was sorry when they had to shoot their last remaining horses on the beach after they had taken down the guns for loading aboard. Mr Smith was badly wounded on the Somme and left for dead at a casualty station a whole day until the doctor took another interest in him. Mr Smith was promoted to sergeant.

Charles (Charlie) Smith (brother of Jimmy), 7th and 4th Gordon Highlanders

Tarland. A taxi driver at the Station Hotel Ellon, he also drove the horse lorries and buses. Mr Smith found that the taxi tended to lair on the Aberdeen road after frost. Mr Smith at start of the War went up to Tarland and joined the 7th Gordon Highlanders after the Army had commandeered seven fine beasts, leaving just five. He served with the 7th and 4th at the Front.

William Shearer, Royal Field Artillery

Banff. Joined the Royal Field Artillery at the Plainstones recruiting office at Banff. He remembers the day they got their uniforms issued: 'A gie ragtag kine o lad skedaddled weet aa neist day an wis never seen again.' Mr Shearer remembers when they objected after the War finished to having to undergo severe drilling and marching up and down the square. Most had joined up for the duration of the War only, and wanted home.

A. MacEwan, 6th Gordon Highlanders

Banff. Was fe-et at the famous Dallachy Farm and went off and joined the 6th Gordon Highlanders at 17, as a change from the 'humdrum of farm work'. Was in the same company as Private McIntosh who took a machine gun post at Third Ypres and won a Victoria Cross for his bravery. Mr MacEwan remembers the German ace the 'Red Baron' being shot down beside them and regrets not taking away a souvenir from the plane. Wounded twice.

Willie MacGregor, Corporal, Lovat Scouts

Pitlochry. Was a gamekeeper on Glenferness Estate and in 1911 was in the Ferness troop of Lovat Scouts at 16. Their horses came off the estate and they rode them all the way to Beauly when War started. At Gallipoli, Lord Lovat ordered them to get the Turkish sniper dubbed 'Percy' that had caused many casualties to other troops. The expert keepers who had taken their own telescopes to War soon located and killed Percy that night, dragging his body back. In Salonica they threshed the grain off the abandoned farms and had their porridge – what the Herefords described as 'The Jocks eating poultice!' Promoted to corporal.

Harry Nicoll, Royal Engineers

Milltimber/Maryculter. Learning the blacksmithing from his father at Lumphanan, he went off to War at 17 to the Engineers. A keen fiddler, Mr Nicoll got a fiddle made for him from a biscuit box in Mesopotamia to entertain his comrades. When he was posted away, he left strict orders for it to be flung into a shell hole. Years after the War it was presented to him by an ex-Army mate who called at his hotel in Rothienorman. It then took pride of place with his other fiddles.

George Dick, Sergeant, Black Watch

Dunfermline. Describes the difficulty of their CO at the training camp trying to understand one of the sergeants who came from Aberdeenshire who was describing his young recruits as 'geets'.

John Brown, 5th Gordon Highlanders

Cruden Bay. Joined the Navy at first but was invalided out when he got a bad chest after a severe chill. He then promptly went off to the 5th Gordon Highlanders. Wounded at the Front. Mr Brown's hospital ship was torpedoed in the English Channel and sank with high loss of life. He minds the terrible conditions at Passchendaele when the water was up to their waists.

Alec Pratt MM, (known as 'Postie'), Sergeant, Royal Horse Artillery

Woodhead, Fyvie. A veteran of the Boer War and years of service in India, he was on the Reserve list and got a telegram to report for duty when playing football for Fyvie in the local league. He was in the Royal Horse Artillery and in France was promoted to sergeant and awarded the Military Medal. Wounded in the German Push of March 1918, Postie came through the worst from start to finish but mostly spoke about the funny incidents.

A. Smart, 5th Gordon Highlanders

Blackhill, Fyvie. Joined the 5th Gordon Highlanders and was wounded with them and was disappointed to get sent to the 8th after convalescing, as he wanted back to his pals. Maintains many good men got killed coming in and out of the front line.

William Mowat, 1st Scottish Horse and Lovat Scouts

Scone, Perth. Employed by Lyndoch Estate, he was fencing with a squad in Strathbraan in Logiealmond hills and bothying in tents. Coming off the hill one Saturday to Maggie Miller's pub and for supplies, he heard that War had started. Making his way out by train to Dunkeld, Mr Mowat joined the 1st Scottish Horse. He was nearly engulfed by a torrent of water and mud in the trench at Suvla Bay by the 'great storm', but he was pulled out in the nick of time and given rum and shelter in a small bivouac further downhill by two Rannoch lads who sang Gaelic songs – defying the storm and their misery.

2

Pre War:
Life before the War

I fe-et at Blackhillock wi Peter Will fin I left the schweel – and Blackie's wis a gie scrapehard bugger o a place. I didna see ma sax month there though – I got the chance o learnin to be a gamie at the Braes o Gight, wi Lord Aiberdeen. Of coorse it wis wi a sheetin tenant. I eence to skive the schweel to help oot onywy – so that's the wy I got the chance.

In the mossin time they let me aff to help a contractor, fa ciest peats in the Millbrex and Swannie Mosses. This wis to tenants that peyed us by the barra load. A barra load wis 16 peats to the barra.
Jonathan Taylor, 9th Gordon Highlanders
fe-et employed, *schweel* school, *sheetin* sitting, *eence* used to, *fa ciest* who cast/cut

I wis brocht up on a craft this side o Strichen and wis fe-et at the ither side o Strichen for sax pound ten the half eer.
Jimmy Milne, 2nd Gordon Highlanders
craft croft, *eer* year

I wis fe-et fin I left the schweel at Foveran as orra loon. Then neist place I wis strapper lookin efter clips and shalts.
Tom Rearie, 5th Gordon Highlanders
orra loon odd job boy, *neist* next, *clips and shalts* small horses.

My first wages as a tailor apprentice was a few coppers the week for just sweeping boards and keeping the irons hot. I was still learning when I was called up. Sitting sewing was nae my cup of tea anyway and I was glad to leave it.
Jim Burgess, 2nd Cameron Highlanders

I started the schweel at Tarland and shifted to Logie Coldstone far there was 80 pupils an three teachers there. Aa the ferms an hooses are noo awa, it's a gie shame fin ye think aboot it. Afore I wis 14 eer ald I wis fe-et hame to a place doon at Alford. Afore that there was a mannie fae the Brae o Towie cam ower to see my fadder an midder and he wintit to fee ma. Onywy he spent the hale nicht newsin and sayin he could dee wi a gweed loon; but he was ower grippy an widna cam oot o fower poun the sax month. I telt ma fadder I wisna gan near him for that an the mannie widna raise his offer an he left withoot feein me. I later met in wi this fermer fae Alford that speired fit I wis needin an I said 'Sax poun'. He thocht a wee filie an said 'Aa richt, aa'l gie ye that but you'll hae tae work dashed hard fort!' There wis jist the foreman an masel. He was mairried and bade in the cotter hoose. I got aa ma mait in the hoose wi the fairmer an his wife an bade in the chammer at nicht. Noo this chammer hid nae fireplace an I bade my sax month an left at the Martinmas term fin it started getting richt cauld.

I neist fe-et hame tull a fermer mannie an his sister an there wis only masel there. I didna need to ging to the feein markets – I aye got a fee withoot that. I wis fine pleased to see there wis a stove in my chammer an I got on fine there, bidin three terms.

Then I gid hame for second horseman to a bigger toon an bade anither three terms – plooin, harrowin, dreelin, an deein aa the ferm an horsewark withoot ony bother. Of coorse I could ploo at an early age onywy. I pooed a lot o neeps in my early days on the ferms and gie frosty eens tee. Weel I didna hud on tull em ower lang if ye ken fit I mean!

gweed loon good lad, *grippy* mean, *speired* asked, *filie* while, *bade* lived, *mait* food, *chammer* sleeping accommodation, *bidin* staying, *toon* farm, *dreelin* drilling.

…

For aa the siller ye got, it was easy spent; at the first toon I wis at – Milky Braes o Alford – I eekit oot my fee wi snaring rabbits an hares. I got saxpence for a rabbit and one an sax for a hare. I likit the horse and yokin the couts tee. Ye jist got eased wi them and got them eased wi you by handling them, oot an in o the loose box, tull they wid get to like ye, then they were easy to yoke. The staigers cam roon in the simmer and spring wi staigs to serve the meers.

Fae that toon I hired hame to a different job to drive a motor car at the Buchan Hotel at Ellon. This wis jist afore the War and the lad that left learned me to drive it afore he gid awa.

The hotel hid twelve horses and twa horse buses as weel as a horse hearse. The beasts we used for that were jet black wi lang tails. Weel the War started and the Army cam oot and commandeered siven o wir best shults leavin us wi just five.
Charles Smith, 7th and 4th Gordon Highlanders
couts colts, *eased wi them* used to them, *staigers* handlers of stallions, *staigs* stallions, *meers* mares

I wis brocht up aside Clochandichter hill there and wis fe-et roon aboot. There wis ae place, I crossed the brig at five o'clock in the morning wi the milk cairt. I wis at puckles of places: I wis awa up at Strachan wi my first pair o horses. Fin I wis there I plooed at a plooin match, bit the mannie I wis wi got drunk. He wis supposed to help set up the ploo and help me oot. Onywy I got the rochest rig and that didna help things. I wis only 14 eer ald at the time. I learned to dreel and I dreeled iver since.

Fin I wis at Broad Hill I caaed milk to Aiberdeen – aye there wis a puckle os ye ken. We hid nae lichts in wir cairts and gie early mornins. That wis my fadder's job I got; he took rheumatism an wisna fit. I wis nae very shooted weet though.

Then I fe-ed at the hame ferm o Whitehoose as second horseman. My brither wis a gairdener there. It wis a laird's toon and the lovliest place it I wis iver at: there wis even a harness room and blinds in the stable windows.

Jimmy Reid, 6th Gordon Highlanders

puckles lots, *rochest* roughest, *caaed* transported, *shooted weet* suited to it

There wis a dancin maister came to Pots of Rayne when I was fe-et there and taught a class in the loft. There was also some fine barn dances too in the summer. I was cattle loon there till I started on the horses at 16. There were six beasts there. Fullin the muck was all hard graip work at that time. I was first horseman there, when I was called up.

Lourin Fair was held annually at Old Rayne. It was a horse market as well and a great affair. I used to enjoy going to it when a loon.

J. Fowlie, 7th Gordon Highlanders

My first fee at Kincorth wis £5 the sax month. The chammer wis up a stair abeen the stable.

Jimmy Reid, 6th Gordon Highlanders

abeen above

I've been here aa my days and my fadder fermed it afore me. It wis aa vrocht wi horse at the time. We bred em oorsels. They say that the rent comes oot o the stable fae the sale o beasts and it mair or less did. The staigers were great lads – I kent Geordie Geddes – he wis an afa lad and spak a sooth twang. On Seterday nicht some os waakit to Turra. I got a shillin fae my fadder to spen. For aat you got a nip for tippence, a bottle o beer for thripence. Then we gid to a wifie it hid a shoppie aside the Oak yonner and got a feoy baps wi corn beef inside them for three hapnies. We waakit back nae bother efter aat.

Jim Duncan, Gordon Highlanders

vrocht worked, *spak a sooth twang* spoke with a southern accent, *yonner* yonder, *a feoy baps* a few bread rolls

I wis at Steinmanhill schweelie an there wis aboot 40 pupils er, wi twa female teachers. Een o them bade in the hoose. I fe-et hame to the jiners Coburn place at Monkshill as loon the wick afore I left the schweel. The chammer wis up a laft stair and there I bade wi the foreman wi nae heatin ata. Ye jist put a puckle bags ower yer legs in the wintertime.

My boss's grandfadder wis a gie ald man wi nae teeth so the hoose folk bakit his breed wi mair fat int so he could chaa it easy. Doon aneth the chammer wis the meal girnil an the bread wis keepit on top o the meal, so I got a notion to risin throwe the nicht fin I wis hungry an atein the ald boy's breed – it wis best. Bit then a new foreman lat the pinchin ging oot o han fin he fun in wi the mealie Jimmies happit hine doon in among the meal. Weel the umman folk jaloused fit wis goin on an put a stop to that.

My boss the jiner niver sorted his ain wark it needed deen – like the byre barra that needed a new wheel an I eased to speir at him 'Fan are ye gan to mak a new wheel?' Weel it was past rowin. At length he got a bit cankered kine at telt me 'If ye wint a new wheel, then mak it yersel!'

That wis a challenge to me although the mannie didna mean it an I set aboot an made een an got the smith to pit on a ring. I took a lang time aboot it but I managed an fin the jiner saa it – he scrattit his heed an speired fa made the barra wheel so fin I telt him he had a gweed look at it and congratulated me on makin a fine job.

Weel, weel, the term wis comin on an I hid never been socht to bide an I wis gettin a bittie fidgety kine cis ilkey body wis socht weel afore the term if they were pleased wi ye an wis needin ye to bide on anither sax month. Onywy I aff and fe-et hame to a mannie at the Backhill o Fetterletter. I gid roon an telt ma fadder that I wis shiftin at the term, and then I telt jiner Coburn and he telt me at eence that he wis needin me to start my apprenticeship an that I hid better tell the mannie at the Backhill that I wisna comin.

Noo that's fit makin a barra wheel did for me – got me started as a tradesman.
Jimmy Scott, Royal Engineers

lat the pinchin ging oot o han let the stealing get out of hand, *mealie Jimmies* white puddings, *jaloused* worked out, *cankered* angry, *kine* you know, *socht to bide* asked to stay

I wis born at Hungry Hills o Alvaa far my fadder wis foreman. There wis sivin os in the family. I attended the schweel at Blairmaud and Ordiquill.

I left the schweel at 13 eer auld and git ti St Marnons Fair at Mairch, there wis a feein market er at aat time as weel as a horse fair. The horses warna roupit – it was aa private deals. Onywy I fe-et hame to the Braes o Marnoch for sax poun the sax month as orra loon to help at aathing there was a going.

We hid a thrashin mull caaed wi watter an it hid a piket drum ont. It could only thrash up tull twa loadies at a time as the dam gid dry bit we got the stem mull in aboot for a gweed day's wark to gie us a bit store an seed corn an that.

Then my neist fee wis ti Mains o Baldavie as orra loon again, then I gid hame to a place at Ordiquill as little cattler. My neist abode wis to caa my first pair of horse at Scatterty far I bade a sax month; then I fe-et hame ti Tochieneal o Cullen far I bade a hale eer an a half as horsemen an likit it fine.
William Shearer, Royal Field Artillery

roupit sold at auction, *thrashin mull* threshing mill

I was born in Cawdor in 1893 and had two brothers and one sister. My father was a cattle dealer and was in great demand when the small farmers had beasts going away. 'Gregor' that was his name would be called on to come down and see their beasts and estimate what they were worth and he'd tell them to the nearest penny – whereupon the crofters would decide whether to sell them there and then or try the cattle markets. Anyway he would buy here and there and sell them for a profit.

He dealt among sheep as well but he wasn't quite so successful as with cattle. He mostly went off to the north country and bought cattle – from the land of my mother – Rosshire, and dealt with the crofters. He had a good eye for cattle and it was only the one eye he had as he had lost the other one at the stone masonry trade. He was a mason to trade and this chip of stone which he was hammering came up and damaged one eye so badly that it never recovered. He and his brother built quite a few houses in fact – big lodges as well.

I went to Ferness Public School, a two teacher one – a lady infant one and Jock MacPherson the headmaster who belonged to the Moray coast. He was a damned good teacher – if it was there – he could take it out. He wasn't too bad with the strap either although he occasionally went to Nairn or Forres for a drap o whisky and we got a very canny day on the Monday after it.

Jock MacKenzie was with me at the school at Ferness and he wis a great big sclyte of a loon bigger than Jockie the dominie [headmaster] and he used to say to me – 'Watch his neck'. If the dominie's neck was red – then we were for it. But it was usually gie easy in the Monday after he'd a drap and then by Tuesday he was getting into the swing and by Wednesday he was back in full form again. He was a little wee mannie but by gad he was clever.

That same Jock MacKenzie wasn't blessed with brains – well he was clever learning in his own way of doing things. The dominie had a job driving the learning into him and once in exasperation gave big Jock a bang on the head with his slate. Well after that, Jock never came back to school – he was 14 anyway and such a hefty lad that he got started with Kennedy Brothers, the coal merchants who had extensive business in the north – even Skye. He was acquainted with the district and got a lot of trade for them. I mind he came back once – he was about 20 then and had joined the Glasgow Police – oh a big strong hefty lad. We were fine pleased to see him and do you know – he went to see wee Jockie the dominie and got a great reception. Of course he took a wee drammie with him. At Ferness schoolie we got taught singing, Latin, drawing, arithmetic, algebra, mathematics, English and geometry. Jockie was a wee covie but he had it all there. I stuck in and got a bursary – one of two awarded the school but I couldn't take it up as it was a terrible hardship on my parents as a bursary didn't cover all the cost.

I went to the keeping – I liked the open air. I was fine acquainted with the keepers and was good at the fishing as I was always with them when I wasn't at school. Trooties were always welcome in our house. I joined the Lovat Scouts in 1911 when I was 17 at Glenferness drill hall. Lord Leven was in charge. One officer was young Brodie of (Cameron Highlanders) Lethem. The sergeant major was called Cottel – an ex-regular.

The Melvilles had a lot of grand Highland strong ponies on their estate and they supplied us with some of them for our troop. The price I mind was £3 each for which the Army funds payed. They had a lot of these ponies running wild so they had to be broken in. After a while we took into our troop the lads from Tomatin.

Our shooting range was at Glenferness and there was some great shootin at 600 yards with the Lee Enfield Mark 6 with rounded nose bullet. One had to know how to handle it as the trajectory rose quite highly with those bullets. When War begun we got issued with Lee Enfield Mark 7s which fired pointed bullets with a much flatter trajectory. We gamekeepers liked those second rifles – they were grand.

William MacGregor, Lovat Scouts

sklyte large/clumsy

I was born on the Hill of Dudwick. My fadder had the place o Hillbrae o Arnage, a placie o near a hunner aacre.

I hid twa bridders an twa sisters, an A'll tell ye there wis nae wint o wark tulls aa – na, there wis nae sittin doon for us! There wis aye plenty o nowt ti sort, neeps ti pu and of coorse the nowt ti muck and row up inti a midden ootside. Then there wis rucks ti thrash wi wir horse mull that took twa horse ti caaed. Roon and roon I caad them for aboot the twa oors it took ti thrash a ruck. Anidder bridder trailed by the strae wi a sister ti tramp the strae and the neist bridder forket the shaves aff the barn fleer on ti the platform for ma fadder ti feed them inti the piket drum. The mull rollers trailed in the shaves after he cuttit the band and spread the shafies oot.

Noo efter the thrash wis by we a helpit ti fan the caff oot o the corn wi the winister. Ye fed the corn inti the happer on tap and caaed the hannle o the machie. Sheelocks cam doon the spoot at ae side, the feenished corn cam doon anidder een an the caff gid oot the back.

We aa gid ti Arnage schweelie. The dominie's name was Calder bit I cannae mind fit ye caaed the Missie. We hid a mile an a half o coorse road tult an cam oot at Allans' shoppie at Fitecairns.

We took a piece wis o kebbik an breed ti the schweel. The breed wis made fae wir ain corn: a puckle ot wis teen doon ti the Mullert and fin the meal cam hame it was putten in tull the girnel to dee the hale eer roon. Then ma midder made aa wir ain butter and kebbiks aff the twa coos' milk.

In the simmer we jist gid ti the schweel barfit bit did hae beets fir the winter.

We did aa wir cutting o corn wi the reaper wi the scyth for cutting lying holes an for reddin roads roon the parks. Bit the reaper only left giddered shaves that hid ti be bun an we aa war yoket ti aat job. Then we stookit the shaves.

Hairst wis a lang draan oot affair wi a lot o aacres ti dee.

I got richt weel up ti the scythe fin I wis a loon an it steed ma in gweed steed ever since.

I left the sqeel at 14 an fe-et roon till I was near 18.

John Brown, 5th Gordon Highlanders

nae wint o wark tulls aa no shortage of work for us all, *rucks* stacks, *nowt* cattle, *sheelocks* grain dust, *caff* chaff, *kebbiks* cheeses, *beets* boots, *giddered* gathered, *bun* bundled

I was born at Lumphanan an gid to schweel there. The dominie was caad Jimmie MacLean. I left at 14 and vrocht at ferm wark. My fadder hid the blacksmith's shop.

My first fee wis £5 the sax month an I hid ti work like a slave fae five in the mornin ti sax at nicht. I got nae holidays or onything and I hid tae bide in a cauldrift chammer up a laft stair abeen the horses in the stable. There wisna a fireplace, an it wis an afa job keepin yersel het – ye jist hid to craal in aboot the blankets. Weel there mith hae been a bit o heat risin aff the horse – bit yi wid niver hae kent it. The place wis Tillyduke.

There wis a horse mull there. Ye yoked the horse on ti this lang pole that wis attached to this gearin and jist caad the crater roon an roon till the thrash feenished. It only did a loadie at a time – it wisna a big place.

I then gid an saired my time as a smith wi ma fadder.

Fin War started I left at 17 and jined the Royal Engineers.

Harry Nicoll, Royal Engineers

cauldrift chilly, *mith hae been* might have been, *saired* served

I wis born at Corrichree near Tarland, an attended the schweel er till I was nine. Then ma folk meeved up to Logie Coldstone far I wis schweeled till I left at 14.

I was the first sax month wark at a grocer at the square in the village there, caain the shult and deein the messages. Efter aat I fe-et hame till Mains of Tilly-pronie far I bade a hale eer.

Another lad an me bade in a chammer up a stair with the stable below, an could hear the Clydesdales chappin aneths at nicht.

I wis the cattler and pooed neeps and that for them – a gie kittle job in a frosty mornin.

We took brose at half sax in the morning (half past five). Wir feet was on the door steen deed on time ilkey morning and the kettle wis aa ready bilin ready fors. Then the foremen billie gid back to the stable and I gid stracht in among the nowts to neep and muck them.

The fermer didna turn oot till half seven (half past six). There we threshed wi the water mill – a hale ruck teen in at a time an a puckle deen every day.

My neist place wis bigger and I wis there sax month. There wis a horse mill there that nought fower horse to caa her. This wis my job caain them roon and roon in a circle; the foreman took by the strae wi the grieve feedin the shaves and his wife did the forkin.

We thrashed a ruck aa forneen, eence the wick. This ferm wis caaed 'The Newk'.

The beasts pulled the main pivot wheel wi swingletrees, bit efter the thresh wis by, we yoket the bruiser in the efterneen and it only nought twa horses to caaed. It wis there I learned ti ploo a bittie.

I then fe-et at hame to a grocer – fermer at Inverdon o Towie on Donside.

I worked on the ferm on Monday and Tuesday, Wednesday I wis on the ferm on the foreneen an oot wi the grocers' van the efterneen. Thursday – the same, and Friday wis the day for caain in stock fae the stations at Dinnet and Alford. Setterday I was oot wi the grocer van again.

This horse grocer van I took up the braes of Glenkindie and Strathdon and Glenbucket and there wis plenty o folk there at at time.

The snaa in the winter wis a problem and bade a lang time – bit I did manage up sometimes wi the sled van. The folk jist traivelled door ower the wreaths o snaw for their provisions fin we couldna wun.

In 1911 I wis wannerin the streets o Aiberdeen an met wi a recruitin sergeant fae Castlehill. I stoppit him and had a wee newsie aboot listin an that and he seen got me roaded up to the recruitin office to enrol me.

Jimmy Smith, Royal Field Artillery

aneths beneath us, *kittle* hard, *nought* needed, *swingletrees* part of a harness (see glossary)

Fin I started wark, I rase at five an vrocht tull nicht. Then I fed my beasts again at 9. We aa took an interest in wir wark tee, an a pride in wir beasts. They were maistly aa bred on the fairm – the horses. I've vrocht aa ma life and still dee.

Tom Rearie, 5th Gordon Highlanders

I was on the farms at 14 at a fee of £6 the half year, bothied. We did six days work and took turn at Sunday toonkeeper.

I bade a year and a half at this first place and then fe-et at Forfar feeing market to another farm on the outskirts of Forfar. We lads in the bothy took turn on the pannie week about at making the food, kenneling the fire, biling the kettle and making the porridge.

We took turns at the fanners in the morning till daylight come in. The corn was on the loft floor.

Most of the farms had a water mill. The first one I was at – Baderyvie had a horse mill. You yokit the horse on and he kept going roon and roon a hale forenoon. We threshed two stacks or so at a time.

The last farm I was at, there was nobody to mak the bed and just two of us in the bothy. Noo the other lad gid aff and got married and there wis me aleen to sweep oot the bothy and look efter mysel.

There is naething waur than biding yersel in a bothy with aathing to dee and yer claes weet at times. Its company ye need ye see. Roon aboot Feb I said to myself 'This is a hellava life – I'll hae to get oot o this'.

At that time there was a lot of emigration to Canada. There was an agency here in Forfar and every month there was a draft went off; quite a few of my own age.

With the idea of emigration in mind I landed doon in the Cross at Forfar but instead I landed up joining the Army. Well if only there had been another lad in the bothy – I would maybe stuck her out but it's a hellava life yourself.

Frank MacFarlane MM and Medal Militaire, 1st Black Watch

on the pannie preparing the food

I was born at Hill of Hatton, Auchterless. My fadder hid a 45-aacre placie up there. My fee wis £5 the sax month fae my first job wi Captain Chalmers o Pitglassie. I gid hame to pu neeps and sort the coos. There wis sax os there: twa married men – the 1st bailie and grieve; a foreman; a second and third horseman and masel – the little bailie.

I wis there tull 1915 fin I jined the Royal Field Artillery.

George Barclay, Royal Field Artillery

At aat time aabody got off for the Turra Show.

I wis in the Terriers, and wis telt to report to drill hall by oor sergeant. He wis gan roon the show tellin aa the lads that War hid been declared; so I gid hame for my kit and that wis me for the duration.

John Rennie, 5th Gordon Highlanders

I jined the Terriers at Turra wi a lad caaed Jimmy Finnie. He wis 16, I wis 17. That wis on February 1914. We war fee-d at Haremoss at the time. Fin we cam oot o the drill hall after jinin, Jimmy says to me, 'Fit will we dee if there's a war?' I just looked at him and we baith luch.

We were caaled up on the day o Turra show. Oor officers telt us: Jack Ledingham fae Fintry, a man Lyall a schoolteacher, and Frank Crutchman fae Auchmill – he wis oor captain – gid roon tellin aabody in the Terriers. They said 'Go home and get your gear and report to the drill hall at once!'

Albert Connon, 5th Gordon Highlanders

luch laughed

Do you see the Marchial College there, well I was at the biggin o a bit o that place. I bade in digs in Aiberdeen at the time.

…

My regiment gid fae the South African War to India. When out there I got typhoid fever. They sent me up to the Himalayas to a hospital to recover and do ye ken, aa it I got to tak wis fye water. It was fower month afore I coured that; and it wis a lang time afore I got onything substantial to ate. I wis doon to sax steen.

I felt richt sorry for the peer natives; the craturs hid naething. I'll never forget seein the warnin flags the peer things put up in ae village, to lat folk ken that there wis cholera in the place.

Up near the North West Frontier they war a different race o folk. I mind twa lads fae an English cavalry regiment gan missin in ae village. It had been oot o bounds onyway.

The place wis searched and the twa men were fun killed and hung up, up on posts. They were an afa mess apparently, although I never saa them. It wis their ain mates that fun them.

That nicht that regiment gid fair mad. Their officers could dee naething to stop them. They charged through the place on horseback and slashed the natives on aa sides.

Apparently there was an afa rumpus aboot that affair. I think some landed in the clink and the regiment wis sentenced to dee anither nine eer in India. This wis a gie sair thing seein it they hid already deen nine eer and were due to ging back hame onytime.

Alec Pratt MM, Royal Horse Artillery

fye water whey

When I was in New Zealand I drove bullocks and in the end was driving a steam engine on a threshing mill. I also did some sheep shearing.

At one shearing shed the owner was an Englishman. We didn't like his manner. He called us by our second names and spoke down to us.

At the next one we did, was owned by a fellow Tom Duncan. He would greet us with 'Morning Jake', 'Morning Bill'. Different altogether!

I joined up and trained a little out in New Zealand, but we did the most of it when we arrived in England.

John MacRae, 18th Battalion ANZAC

I wis fe-et at Rathen as 4th horseman. Twas weemin milked the coos. A gran foreman wi the name of Minty was there. He cam fae Langside. This wis a place o fower hunner acre wi fower cotter hooses.

Lea Birnie, 1st Gordon Highlanders

I was brocht up on a croft at Wartle. I started work at 14 at Pike of Insch at £6 the six month. There were the two farmer's sons and myself. I was well fed there. From there I went to Pots of Rayne for a while, then Braeside. Like all farm servants, I didn't stay long at any place. I liked to be on the move all the time, and went from Braeside to Overhall of Insch as horseman. I attended feeing markets – that's about all the holidays we got.

It was hard work in the ferms but being brought up on a croft I was used to it.

I was called up in 1916 and trained at Bridge of Allan.

J. Fowlie, 7th Gordon Highlanders

I was born at Montrose and went to the school at Hillside. There I won a bursary to go to the Academy where I studied and was getting ready for the exams when I took scarlet fever and that was me finished with schooling at 16.

I came down here to Perthshire wanting a job as a forester on this estate and was engaged by Mr Frank Scott – a university learned man.

There were six of us in the bothy but didn't make our own food; there was a woman did that for us – our breakfast and piece dinner and came in and made a meal at night. There were a lot of bothies round about on the farms then with a lot of folk on the places.

We had to look after another estate at Logiealmond called Lyndoch. Some of us including myself went up there to cut and process the vast acres of timber blown down during the great gale of 1913. Most of the forests suffered from that big blow.

We operated a steam-driven saw and portable traction engine for hauling the wagon loads of prime trees to the railway station at Luncarty.

Six months before the War I thocht I would like a change of job and asked to be put on to fencing. I landed up with the fencing gang who were installing paling from Strath Braun over to Logiealmond. There we camped out in tents and made our food from Monday to Saturday, coming down for more supplies on Saturday and taking off on Monday mornings.

Anyway when we came into Maggie Miller's pub this Saturday night they were speaking about the War that had been declared. On the Sunday I went into Perth to see the Black Watch Terriers going off. I did another week's fencing on the hills and when we came down I said to old Jimmy our foreman 'Ach all awa and jine the Army'.

William Mowat, 1st Scottish Horse and Lovat Scouts

I was born on the island of Grimsey in the parish of North Uist. I went to school there and Grimsey Public School was absolutely packed. There was a schoolmaster and a pupil teacher.

When I left school I worked on a croft with a Mr John MacLean for little of anything. I was keen on getting on a boat and Mr MacLean's brother was captain on a ship. I didn't manage that however.

I used to help my mother to process the wool – carding, teasing, dyeing, spinning, weaving and waulking of the finished tweed.

The dying was done from the lichen we gathered off the rocks. Crottel we called it. We had a big crottel pot that sat on stones outside the house. Into this pot was put a layer of crottel, then a layer of wool, followed by a layer of crottel and wool time about. When it was full, water was added to the mixture; a fire was lit beneath the pot.

This was brought to the boil and simmered for a certain length of time. The result was a nice brown coloured wool.

Donald MacVicar, 1st/2nd The Queen's Own Cameron Highlanders

My father started the chanter with John Stewart in Dundee – he was G. S. McLennan's uncle. G. S. composed a tune after him – Pipe Major John Stewart. John Stewart had a band in Dundee.

My father later went to MacDougal Gillies in Glasgow for tuition on the pibroch.

All my father's people came from Skye during the evictions to find work and a lot of Gaelic was spoken in Dundee then.

I was 19 when War broke out. I was in the Terriers but was not sent to France till 1916.

Donald MacLeod, 4th Black Watch

The schools I was at were New Deer, Ellon, Savock, Drumwhindle and Cairnorrie. My father finished as baillie at Baldies, a big ferm toon. Then he spent the rest of his days at Burnside croft at Howe of Gight.

My first fee was with Jimmy Birnie at a sma placie at Turnerhall for £4 15s the six month. My second place was with Greig at Toddlehills of Auchnagatt for £8; looking after cattle and working one horse up to my knees in mud and out in wet weather. We were allowed to sit in the house kitchen till 9 o'clock at night, then off to the chammer without heat except when we were allowed a fire on Sundays. The maid worked from morning to night – Miss Taylor – I was at school with her.

I went from there to Pitzies. He was a fat man and drank. There I was six month on the cattle. I got £12 and then £13 when I took over the horses for the next six month. I was 16 and was ploughing, harrowing and drilling.

I was in the Terriers at 16. Colonel Grant held the Terriers camp at Monymusk before the War so I knew him pretty well. I think he was in the South African War. His horse, which he took to Bedford, had a mark on its neck where it had been wounded in the War there.

Alec Robertson, 5th Gordon Highlanders

I gid hame ti Forbes o Dallachy as third horseman. His breeder had the great ferm toon o Rettie famous in sang.[12] I wis there fin the War started an bade there only sax month, feein to Newton o Mountblairy doon the Turra wy – ach we aye liket a change. I wis still on the horse bit left there and jined up the Army at the Plainsteens o Banff far there wis a recruitin office.

William Shearer, Royal Field Artillery

breeder brother

42

I wis twa eer at Fitehill Schweelie wi Gavin Greig as dominie[13]. He wis a great lad. He just lat us see the tag; he niver gid ye the strap.

The hairst o 1917 wis the warst in livin memory, wi the stooks grouin green and rain ivery day. Then aboot the begginin o November a dry sooghin gale started aboot a Friday and by Sunday the shaves wis comin hame theresels ti the cornyard.

Folk at that time didna work on a Sunday and aabody gid to kirk tee. Onywy the ministers gid them a dispensation to gang hame and lead. We started on that Sunday and vrocht 20 oors a day wi fower cairts at the park, twa at the rucks; the mannie's ain twa dothers biggin the cairts. Mysel and an ither lad biggit the rucks and the mannie kept us richt roon the foons. We feenished 105 aacre in fower and a half days and the rain cam on fin we war at the last twa load.

Near aa the fook cam oot o Byth, jist ald men and weemen except his ain dothers. The horses jits ate hie at the side o the ruck.

Noo I niver seen this kine of thing deen before or since, bit we war the only eens that got feenished afore the widder brak. At nicht we vrocht wi the licht o the finest moon oot. We niver winted for mait, itherwise we couldnae hae deent.

I wis deferred wi Hackett there, but wis called up seen after.

Robert MacRobbie, 1st Gordon Highlanders

dothers daughters

We hid to behave wirsells at the Sunday schweel. It wis a lang waak ti near Turra, bit there wis aye plenty o company. There wis a family o nine Alexanders and the youngest een wis gettin baptised ae Sunday. The aalist hid the orders to gang doon to 'Booties' wall, hine awa in the Connin Howe – a gie bit oot o the wy to the kirk – and get this bottle of holy waater for to christen the bairn. Noo the loon wis richt thrawn to ging aa that distance oot o the wy and he jist filled the bottle at the nearest burn, wi aa us looking on. Noo the een that wis christened wis nae neen the waar o gettined deen wi ordinary waater – he's aye livin to this day onywy!

Jim Duncan, Gordon Highlanders

aalist oldest

The sergeant wis fine pleased to jine me up as he got a shillin for ivery body he listed. I was needin to the Artillery as I wis keen on horse, bit failin aat – the Cavalry wid hae deen fine.

Noo the adjutant wis keen that I jine the Gordon Highlanders – I already hid a brither in them bit I telt him that if I didna get among horses I wid jist gang hame again. The adjutant telt me that he would keep me there for another twa days an see if I changed ma mind.

Weel, I didnaa and he accepted the fact and listed ma into the Artillery. The sergeant gid me an Army greatcoat and put me on the train that nicht at Aiberdeen Station for Liverpool, at eicht o'clock that Friday nicht.

In this cairrage aabody smokit pipes o bogie roll and I couldna stan tobacco reek ata and wis iver sae pleased to arrive at ma destination there at ten neist morning. I wis met wi a sergeant and teen up to a barracks in the toon. I felt a bittie strange an hamesick there for a file, niver bein far fae hame afore. I wis trained at marchin and drill for three month. There wis some horses there and a lad gaed us lectures aboot them, bit he didna kensa muckle as me.

Efter aat I wis posted oot to Kildare in Ireland where we – the new eens – got into real Artillery training. This wis a fully fledged battery o 18-pounders. They warna a gweed gun in the Waar; fin we were quick firin – they het up and the spring brake. The 25-pound that cam later wis a better een.

Oor battery shiftet fae Kildare to Aldershot and didna bide lang there – gettin orders to go to India. We embarked at Southampton withoot horses or guns – ither eens were there aa witin us fin we got er at Secunderabad in the sooth.

We sailed throwe the Suez Canal and only took three wicks at wy.

In early 1914 we meeved fae the sooth to Allahabad in the north of India.

Man, I likit India – oh aye the climate agreed wi me fine.

James Smith, Royal Field Artillery

I was a beater when I was nine to 15 years old. I left school when I was 14 and went to the Haugh to serve my time as a grocer.

My father was a charge hand labourer at Blairmore Estate beside Glass. I was a grocer later with Donald MacGregor at Bogniebrae. He had the farm of Gibston which he later sold. He finished up with a hotel in Inverness.

George Bryan MM, 12th Highland Light Infantry

I wis signed up in the Derby Scheme and wis caaled up into the 7th Gordon Highlanders. I didna get a chance to jine fit I wintet. In France oor Company Commander wis Colonel Dalone – a Frenchman.

Alec Sim, 7th Gordon Highlanders

In the Terriers before the War we had a Sergeant Smith from Strichen. He was a Christian and a very fine man. He told us never to shoot a man if he wanted to be taken prisoner. I liked that, and that's what I did all through the War. They were a great bunch the Terriers with a lot of good men like Sergeant Smith.

Alec Robertson, 5th Gordon Highlanders

3

Training

Aboot 30 os biket ti Peterheed to list efter Kitchener's appeal cam through. I wis fe-et at Swannies as second horseman at the time.
John Webster, Royal Field Artillery

I jined up wi ma pal Fred Duncan efter the leaflets cam oot fae Kitchener needin a hunner thoosan men. We biket wi a lot mair fae Millbrex ti Peterheed ti jine up in the 5th Gordon Highlanders. We wis teen richt awa ti dee wir trainin an gid oot ti France fae Bedford in the Spring o 1915. Fred wis teen wi a lot o idder volunteers to the newly formed Machine Gun Corps that eer, bit he wis killed on the Somme.
Sandy Simpson, 5th Gordon Highlanders

We met Alec Pratt in the main street of Poperinge fin we arrived at the Front. He caad us aa the silly buggers for volunteerin.
Bill Minty, 4th Gordon Highlanders

I telt a lee aboot ma age fin I jined up and telt them I wis 17 fin I was only 16.
…
Efter training I wis sent oot at eence an jined the 2nd Gordon Highlanders.
William Angus, 2nd Gordon Highlanders

Ah weel War broke oot and the cattleman and my brither and me listed at Alford. We were first sent to Keith and then stracht doon to Bedford. We hid nae uniforms and jist hid to weer wir ain claes. We wis there for sax wicks, dreelin in aat, afore we got some uniforms. In fact we only got kilts the nicht afore we left for France. I aye mind we were inspected by King George IV and we could hiv seen him in hell. It poored the hale damned time and he kept us witin for oors afore he cam roon. So we got a kilt on a Sunday and gid awa on the Monday. We crossed on the *Cornishman*: a great big boat that took horses, transports, box cairts ana! We gid up to Bethune and we drappit sae much there then back to Sainte-Mère and bade a wick. Then we marched awa up to Estairs and than to Fleurbaix far we gid in to the trenches.

10.   Gordon Highlanders, France, 1915.
Courtesy of D. J. Johnston-Smith

That wis a wick in and a wick oot and there was nae billets fin we cam oot and this wis in November ye ken. Fin we were in, we niver saa a het drink or naething. We were in the 7th Division with the 2nd Gordon Highlanders, the Scots Guards, the Grenadier Guards and the Border Regiment. The 8th Division were on the idder side o us. They had a brigade o darkies, Sikh and aat!
Jimmy Reid, 6th Gordon Highlanders

We hid Andy Cattanach fae Auchterless – a great character. He gid back to the railway efter the Waar, bit I lost trace.

We gid oot in April 1915 and laaned at Le Havre and gid stracht up to a place caad Morval; a guid 30 oors run on the train. Fin we gid aff there we merched to a little village and bade there a filie. Then fae there we gid in to oor positions and fired oor first shot in action on the 8th May 1915.

We took aa oor ain horses, guns, cairts and baggage oot wees fae iss country. Some o the horses were Taggart's ain. Later on the beasts cam fae abroad. They were maistly aa licht beasts ye ken!

We crossed in convoy fae Soothampton. Or first guns were Boer Waar eens: 15-pounders. Later on we got the new 18-pounders.

I wis a gunner, bit fin we got oot there I wis putting on to drive. Auld Sergeant MacPherson, an ald Boer Waar man, tried a lad Sangster first, bit he said 'Try that lad ower there – he drave horse!' So MacPherson cam ower to me and speired 'Hiv ye iver vrocht horse?' I says 'Aye – I've vrocht horse at hame on the ferm!' So he says, 'Weel, eel, jist tak a pair cis were afa scarce o drivers!' So I dreeve

aa the time I wis in the 51st; bit nae in the 8th Division: I gid on to aa kine o jobs in it including trench mortars and aat kine o stuff.
John Russel, Royal Field Artillery

We were at Ville Chapelle first then a filie at Festubert and then spent the first simmer up at Flanders.

Some days we didna fire mony shells – the neist we wid a been goin aa day; it aa depenned fit Gerry wis sayin tult.

I'll tell ye, there wis an afa lot o rifle fire in the beginning: they wir crackin on steady. In the end we never heard a rifle for the shellfire.
Bert Gow, Royal Field Artillery
tult to it

I jined up at Aiberdeen fin i wis 17 eer auld in September 1915. Arriving in France I attended a course at the Bull Ring at Etabs. This wis cut short cis the Germans hid broken through at Armentiéres and we were rushed up richt awa.
Alec MacHardy MM, 7th Gordon Highlanders
Etabs (or *Etaps*) the French town of Ètaples in Picardy.

A band came out from Aberdeen and played; after which a sergeant and a team held a recruiting drive. I joined although I was underage. I did my training on Salisbury Plain and went to France into the line during January 1916 at a place called Vin-Chapelle beside Neuve Chapelle. I was in the 35th Division.
Albert Napier MM, Royal Field Artillery ('Taggart's Own')

I jined up at 16 at Rhynie fin the War started. I wis fe-ed and wis fair fed up ot. At iss toon I didna like the wy the best mait gid ben the hoose! We did oor dreelin at Bedford Camp.
Alec Nicol, 7th Gordon Highlanders

I wis in the Reserve fin War wis declared. I wis playin fitba for Fyvie in the Howe fin I wis called off the park and geen a wire which directed me to report for duty. We went to Ireland to muster and equip for France. We hid some gie fechts wi the Irish fin there.
Alec Pratt MM, Royal Horse Artillery

I jined up at Kittybrewster; I wis workin on the line at the time. We were at Aiberdeen and roon aboot at first, until later on we got a lot o Englishmen as reinforcements.
John Russel, Royal Field Artillery

Eichty os were sent ti the Machin Gun Corps fae the Gordon Highlanders to train doon in England. Hardly ony cam back. The lads fae my area war Wullie Horn fae Turra. He was killed. Jimmy Cowe fae Rhynie and a lad Harper fae Rothie were wounded and I dinna think coured it richt and de-et efter the War.

There wis siven Wullies in a class at Woodhead Schweel includin my ain brither. Well do ye ken, neen o them cam hae faet!

Dod Carrol, Private, Machine Gun Corps

Fin we sailed for France I wis put on guard duties. I wis stunnin lookin oot fin aa at eence the ship's hooter started up and michty me I wis stunning aneth her. I got ass great a fleg I nearly jumpit inti the sea.

Jimmy Scott, Royal Engineers

fleg fright

When we stopped off at ports on our way to England we were told to behave ourselves and show how more civilised we were than those wild Australians. Of course the Australian officers said the same thing to their men about us.

Our officers came aboard ship at Cape Town when we were due to sail, with tea chests full of booze. I remember hearing the skipper shout – 'What you got there?' They replied, 'This is brandy! This is beer! This is whisky! 'This is …' and so on. The skipper said to them 'Well, you had better take it back up town; there's no liquor coming aboard this ship. What's good enough for the men stands good for the officers too!' I will never forget that.

…

We got five shillings a day to the Tommys' one.

…

There was an architect with me when I joined up, an educated man, he had designed some fine buildings in New Zealand, including the freezer works in Wanganui. He wouldn't accept a commission when it was offered him, preferring to serve in the ranks.

John MacRae, 18th Battalion ANZAC

The first nicht oot in the front line we were laying a cable and in the dark we lost 32 men. My hat wis knock'ed aff and I didna ken at the time, bit there wis a bullet hole richt through her. This wis lang range machine gun fire the Germans hid targeted on No Man's Land that hid deen the damage.

Jimmy Scott, Royal Engineers

I wis enrolled in the Derby Scheme, but got exemption till I was 19 eer ald, when I wis caaled up to the Gordon Highlanders.

Jim Duncan, Gordon Highlanders

The maist o oor men were ferm servants and gey hardy lads, bit I mind there wis ae time we got some recruits that were diverted fae the London Scottish and by God it wis surprising fu good they got and neen o them hid ever seen the country-side afore. They were gey saft bein city lads, bit seen made wunnerfu guid sogers.
Alec MacHardy MM, 7th Gordon Highlanders

I wis fe-et at Backhill o Bonnykelly wi Hacket fin I was caaled up. I did my trainin in Advocates Road in Aiberdeen.

I got leave for twa days to get married but overstayed it, so fin I got back I wis shoved inti the guardroom.

Neist morning we hid to rig for France and boarded a train for Dover. From there to Calais and into bell tents. Aye ye ken! Yall sleepet wi yer feet to the pole.
Robert MacRobbie, 1st Gordon Highlanders

I wis fe-et at Jock Mackeisick at Muirton fin I jined up. I wis 18 eer auld. The twa ither eens on the place belanged ti Elgin and they gid up there and jined the Seaforth Highlanders.

Do ye ken some were that keen that they bocht their ain kilts. We jist got a rifle bit nae ammunition at first. A lad MacLaren that wis janitor at Keith – he made the kilts.

We aa gid tae Bedford to dee wir trainin.

Fin we laand in France we mairched a hale wick up to the Front.
Norrie Cruikshank, 6th Gordon Highlanders

I wis at Mid Ardlaw fin the War started wi Robertson, as fourth horseman. Fin Kitchener's appeal sheets cam roon the fairms, oor mannie widna dish them oot to oor chammer; I suppose he didna want to lose his men. At Mid Ardlaw there wis fower horsemen; three baillies; a shepherd; a strapper and a grieve.

Wishart Massey the shepherd was a great character; he hid gotten hud o a feoy o this pamphlets and lats see them. He says 'Weel, fit aboot pittin doon yer names?' He pit doon the names o fower o us and himself.

So it laand up that the five os got a rail pass in to Aiberdeen to jine up. Do ye ken, Wishart even gid the length o sellin his twa dogs at Kittiebrewster Mart that morning on the wy to jine up. Ye see Wishart hid been atein neeps wi his flock ootside Strichen at the time we got word tae gang in, and I biket oot on a Sunday to lat him ken. Weel, weel! Fin we laand up at the Castlegate recruitin office the second bailie and me were dismissed as being too young. Noo Massey and the rest o them hid geen for a dram, and fin they cam in Massey got up to his usual ill tricks and started to torment the sergeant major and ither folk there. He wis fairly going for them and efter a filie they lost the rag and threw them oot.

The second horseman gid back on his ain neist day and I jined the Transport. I wis determined to jine, so I gid to Peterhead to jine up in the Gordon Highlanders, bit they widna tak me there either. The 5th were jist leavin there to ging to Bedford. There wis naethin else for me bit to bide oot my time till I wis auld eneuch. This I did at Ardlaw, Hillheed o Crimond and Bogenjohn, where I got my papers.

Wishart hid to gang up afore the medical board, farr they turned him doon on accoont o haein a double rupture. He wis a great lad; an afa character, bit richt handy at carvin wid wi a knife, like ploos, horses and dogs. Do ye see this here o a pair at the ploo; that's his.

Jimmy Milne, 2nd Gordon Highlanders

I jined up in 1914 and trained in Aiberdeen. This wis on 4th August for a fower eer engagement and gid inti the 1st Gordon Highlanders.

I wis pairt o a lot that gid oot fae wir billets in Torry at end o October that eer, as reinforcements to the regiment that hid lost a lot o men at Mons.

That first winter wis terrible; the bolts all froze on oor rifles. Colonel Fraser of Saltoun was oor CO. He wis a rich fine chiel.

I wis eence teen oot o the trenches and teen to hospital fin my legs founered wi stannin up to my hips in watter in the trench. They war aa swalled up and they took wicks afore they coured it. That's the wy they are sic bad noo ye ken!

Lea Birnie, 1st Gordon Highlanders

founered foundered

I wis called up at 18 and wis workin at Woodhead o Cairness at the time as second cattler. This wis a pair a three and orra beast placie. We were aa chammer lads.

I wis in the 8th Gordon Highlanders, 15th Division.

J. Burnett, 8th Gordon Highlanders

I joined up in 1912 on the 20th February, I was 17 years old and five feet nine inches tall. I saw a Forfar lad who was a trooper in the Life Guards and I thought I would like to be in them because he was very smart in his uniform. He was tall and handsome and braw. In I went to the recruiting office and said I wanted to join the Life Guards. The recruiting sergeant said, 'Ye canna jine that her. Youll hae to ging to London for that'.

Beside him was a placard on the wall of a Gordon Highlander; so I pointed to it and said, 'What about them then'. So he said, 'Ye canne jine that either, youll hae to ging to Aberdeen'.

'Well,' I said, 'what can I join?'

'The Black Watch of coorse. I'll jine you up right away.'

So that was me joined.

Frank MacFarlane MM and Medal Militaire, 1st Black Watch

11. Troops of the 8th Battalion, Black Watch making a bayonet attack at Bordon Camp, 1915.

Imperial War Museum

I wis caaled up as I wis in the Terriers at Langside.

We aa mustered at Peterheed and then gid doon to Perth far I slept in the St Ninians Library for a fortnicht. Fae there we gid doon to Bedford Camp far we trained; then gan oot to France on May 1915.

Wullie Gavin, 5th Gordon Highlanders

I wis in the Terriers at Perth. With their Black Watch Battalion. I was mustered when War started, I went to my officer and told him I wanted back to my own lot in the Black Isle. I was granted my wish and sent back up north to join the 4th Seaforth Highlanders at that time still at Nigg. I was only 14 years old.

We went from there to Inverness and stayed there a while, then later entrained for Bedford Camp. We were sent to France in October 1914 and joined the 1st Corps, 1st Division, 3rd Brigade.

Robert More MM, 4th Seaforth Highlanders

I did my training in Perth and passed out as a first class recruit. I joined my regiment in Edinburgh Castle at a place where the National War Memorial now stands.

At the time there were six companies. We were sent down to Aldershot and the Cameron Highlanders who were there, changed places with us: going to Edinburgh.

We were now part of the 1st Guards Brigade, 1st Division, 1st Corps who had a commander by name of Douglas Haig. He lived in Government House.

Within a short time we were under intense training with the rest. The regiments were the 1st Coldstream Guards, the 1st Scots Guards and the 2nd Munster Fusiliers. The Brigadier General Maxie. Our six Companies were doubled up.

In early 1914 we had King George IV appointed as Colonel-in-Chief. He came down and inspected us at Aldershot on a terribly rainy day which finally faired off. We were paraded in Buff order with white tunics. We marched past him standing with General Haig, Brigadier General Maxie, Lt Colonel Sir Hugh Rose of Kilravock and Lord George Stewart-Murray of Blair Castle in attendance.[15] He was a brother of the Marquis of Tullibardine. Lt Colonel Rose – an old man – was changed as CO by a Lt Colonel Grant Duff. We knew then that something was happening.

There was a Captain Dalgluish attached to the military attaché in Berlin. He was in the Black Watch and came home about three weeks before the War and was appointed Second-in-Command of my Company. He knew the background working of the German Army from A to Z. We got lectures from him on how they operated: the type of rifles and weapons they used and the tactics on the field of battle. We found out later that he was wrong in one case. He said that when they were advancing in open order – that they fired from the hip indiscriminately. We found out later in real, that they didn't – they took aim the same as us.

When War started we had to return all our ceremonial kit into store; white tunics, feather bonnets, scarlet tunics, sporrans, white gaiters; all marked with our name and number. We were told that they would be returned at the end of the War. [This equipment we had to buy ourselves then got an allowance of 30 shillings the quarter to keep them on.] We waited a few days till the Reservists were called to the colours, after which our mobilised strength of the 1st Watch was 1033 other ranks and 29 officers. When we returned on 7th May 1919, there was only one officer and 29 other ranks left of the originals. We that were left were never offered our ceremonials back.

Frank MacFarlane MM and Medal Militaire, 1st Black Watch

I jined up at Turra wi three idder lads. A lad Steven fae the Teucher Howe enrolled us. Wi me wis Peter Taylor and a lad Ord and a Peterson. That three were sent to the Machine Gun Corps. Mind ye – they aa cam back. I wis a ferm servant afore I jined and sae were the lave. I gid oot to the Front in 1915.

John Will, 5th Gordon Highlanders

lave rest

I served my time as a linoleum printer. I was called up in 1916 to the Cameron Highlanders and trained at Stirling after which I was sent to Canterbury for further training. From there to France and immediately was sent to 4th Seaforth Highlanders, 154 Brigade, 51st Highland Division. This was after the Battle of the Somme.

Dave Pitkethly, 4th Seaforth Highlanders

I joined up in 1912 in the local militia which was later named 'The Special Reserve'. I spent the first six months full time training in a company of 3rd Cameron Highlanders.

When War started we were mustered to Inverness. I was put in charge of a Lewis Gun team. We were now in the 5th Battalion Cameron Highlanders. Lt Colonel Cameron of Lochiel was trying to get the 1st Battalion up to strength at Aldershot. He, and Lord Seaforth came up and inspected our battalion. We were all drawn up in ranks, hoping to be picked of course.

When they came up my line, Lt Colonel Cameron stopped and asked me my age. I replied that I was 18 but he didn't believe me. I was happy to see my name on the list later on for going to Aldershot but not so pleased that my pal was left. He, Angus MacDonald was 17 but was much taller than me. Maybe it was because I was the company's best shot, having beaten the 55th Battalion's previous best – Colour Sergeant Bain. I remember looking at the board with the results of the shooting competition on it, when he came up and said, 'I see you have beaten me MacVicar. You are 21 points better'. Well, I was brought up with a gun in my hand!

From Aldershot I was sent out with a bunch of lovely men as reinforcements to the 1st Cameron Highlanders. Landing at Saint-Nazaire, we were convoyed by train up to Hooge beside the Menin road at Ypres. The trenches were in poor condition there.

It was all rifle fire in the line at that time and I got on to sniping. I liked the Lee Enfield – most accurate at any distance. You could put ten rounds in the breech, but we didn't as it was inclined to jam.

Donald MacVicar, 1st/2nd The Queen's Own Cameron Highlanders

When we landed first at Boulogne the Tommies on the quay said to us, 'Any money Jock? It's no use over here!' Some of the lads were giving it away – they didn't know any better.

At Bedford Camp a batch of London Scottish joined us. They were in civvy dress. They were great lads. Some wanted a kilt to go home for a weekend in and we gave them kilts for hire at half a crown a time. They went off fine pleased.

Robert More MM, 4th Seaforth Highlanders

We left camp and marched to Aldershot on the 13 August 1914, where we entrained to Southampton. From there we marched to the docks where a big boat was waiting to take us aboard, called the *Black Prince*. The whole battalion went aboard; followed by cookers, store wagons, transport wagons and water carts – each company had one.

The horses were slung aboard in slings.

Apart from us, there was a battery of Artillery and detachments of Service Corps and Royal Army Medical Corp.

We loaded in daylight but sailed about midnight escorted by destroyers round Spithead and Isle of Wight. French destroyers took over when we were about halfway when it was near daylight. The destination Le Havre.

The ship docked at midday on a beautiful sunny day. We started disembarking at once and I noticed the dockyard absolutely thronged with French people of all ages cheering and waving their arms.

One incident I remember well relates in particular to a lovely young lady with stunning blonde hair who started to distribute drinks of absinthe from a 'grey-beard' container. This charming lass was smiling away and dishing it out to our men as they were coming off the ship. All at once Lt Colonel Duff let out a roar – 'Get that woman out of there!' I happened to be standing next to him and he ordered me, 'You go and stand beside her and stop her at once!'

Now here I was beside this braw woman feeling like a muckle gosling in my kilt, trying my best to restrain her and nae kennin a word o French. The lassie couldn't understand what I was trying to do. She was guttering away but I couldn't make out a word.

The battalion formed outside the harbour and marched to a camp in the boiling hot day and then into bell tents – ten men to a tent.

That night it came on a hellava night o thunder and lightning.

Frank MacFarlane MM and Medal Militaire, 1st Black Watch

We were nearly aa ferm servants wi an odd counter louper amang us.
Alec Nicol, 7th Gordon Highlanders
counter louper shop assistant, often a draper

I was conscripted when I was herding sheep up the Glens. I had about 600 in my charge with two fine dogs.

I did my training at Perth and Stirling, and was puttin into the Gordon Highlanders. I took a weekend leave to Wemyss Bay with Geordie Steward and Geordie Smith, both sheep lads like myself. We overstayed our leave and were teen by the MPs. I remember bein teen in front of a cockney officer and we didna ken a word he wis saying and he didn't ken a word we were saying.
Wull Dryden, Gordon Highlanders

We left this country from Southampton on a big boat which took the whole of the 5th Gordon Highlanders aboard. When we came off the train there, we marched to the docks, and all the ladies and fine girls came out to wave us goodbye. One lassie came and pressed a small black cat badge in my hand as a good luck charm. I still had it years later, when I lost it – after the War. I was very sorry about it and searched for it without success.
Alec Robertson, 5th Gordon Highlanders

I trained at Invergordon and at Stirling and when I finished I got ten days embarkation leave. When I came back I joined a draft for the 5th Cameron Highlanders in France being sent out to Calais from Dover by boat and into camp bell tents there.

Three days there, we were ready to move when some of us were picked out from the group of 5th Cameron reinforcements and diverted on to another boat at Calais which sailed later in the day for Salonica in the Balkans. We were informed that we were to join the 2nd Cameron Highlanders at present fighting there.
Jim Burgess, 2nd Cameron Highlanders

When we left Aberdeen we had the emblem 'Taggart's Own' sewn on our shoulders but when we got to Bedford Camp we were ordered to rip them off. We were told we were strictly Royal Field Artillery.
Albert Napier MM, Royal Field Artillery ('Taggart's Own')

As I had went off in 1914 when I was 14 years old my folk tried to get me home a few times. I always refused when I was called in front of the CO. I suppose I liked it though it was rough at times.
Robert More MM, 4th Seaforth Highlanders

I caa-d coal ti the steam traalers at Peterheed hairbour wi horse cairts fae the station. Ilkey een too 60 ti 70 ton. There wis ony amount o them at at time. There wis hardly ony fishin deen, in fact the maist o em were commandeered by the Navy.

I jined up at Castlehill and a feoy days efter I got a ticket ti gang back for my medical. Efter I got aat deen, a mannie saye ti ma, 'It's the Gordon Highlanders for you!' I says, 'Na faith ye – nae bloddy fears. There's eneuch adee wi ma fadder and bridders in em. Na, na, am nae gan in em: there's nae kilt gan roon my erse.'

Fin they tried ti persist I jist telt them, 'Ach – all awa an jine the Navy then!' The mannie then said, 'Hold on then – what would you like to do?' 'I'd like ti jine the Cavalry!' Weel, I was a horseman and thocht I wid like ti get in amang horse. The mannie telt me he didna think he could manage so I telt the crater, 'A richt an – all awa ti the Navy'.

'Hold on,' he said, 'Here's the Lovat Scouts. They are needing 200 men!'

I speired at em! 'Fits aat – the Boy Scouts?'

'No – you damned fool, have you never heard of the Lovat Scouts? It's a Highland cavalry regiment!'

I said, 'Na na, bit they soon aa richt; jist pit me in em!'

So I wis sent awa up ti Beauly, their heedquarters, by train. I reported ti a sergeant – aa that there wis er. There wis naething bit me and iss bliddy sergeant for three wicks. Christ! I wis lost aa thegither, wanderin aboot in civvies. Some bliddy waar! I felt like catchin a train hame mony a time.

Finally I was sent awa doon ti Beccles in England and reported ti the guardroom. The sergeant in charge telt ma he'd niver heard anything aboot ma, as he caad aboot among some papers and lookit. 'In that case,' I telt them, 'I'll awa doon ti Yarmooth!' We war only 40 mile fae there and I was acquaint. 'Oh no,' he said, 'You had better stay here and see the colonel in the morning!'

In the morning, the colonel speired fa I wis, faar I'd been and fit wy I jined the Lovat Scots. I telt him as best I could and said I thocht noo I'd cheenged ma mind and wid like ti ging hame. 'Oh no, you're in the Army now and here you'll stay!'

I did some trainin there for sax wicks an at the ine ot, got a wick's overseas leave for France. I could hardly ken the richt side o a rifle bit aat wis it!

Back I cam fae leave and witin me wis a Cameron kilt and aa us recruits war telt we war gan inti the Cameron Highlanders. So there wis naething for ma ti dee bit pit on a kilt efter in aa – a thing I wisna sickin ti dee.

A puckle o us recruits war sent awa oot ti the Front and landed at Boulogne. We war er a filie tull a sergeant cam doon fae the Cameron Highlanders ti tak charge os.

I mine, he took us oot and telt us ti faa in, cryin oot, 'One, two, three, fowr!' and stannin lookin at's dumfoonered like, fin we didne meeve: we jist steed an lookit at him. He said, 'What the hell's ado with you lot?' He speirs at me, 'Do you know what your doing?'

Another sergeant lookin on telt him, 'I don't think you know yourself; if you had any sense you would see these men are all Cavalry trained – they don't understand Infantry orders!'

Peter Baigrie, 7th Cameron Highlanders/6th Black Watch

They didn't take me for the Artillery as I had a bad foot at the time. So I tried the Infantry and had more success. I was sent to Cromarty to train with a battalion of the Highland Light Infantry that were being formed there.

George Bryan MM, 12th Highland Light Infantry

I joined the Terriers in 1913 in Montrose here. When War commenced we were sent out to the Front in November 1914 to the 8th Division, 48th Brigade.

We had many Egyptian and Boer War men in our ranks and on the 28th October we joined a cattle boat called *The Architect* at Southampton. It had just unloaded a cargo of cattle and the conditions on that ship were terrible with stink and sharn everywhere.

We sailed that night when it was dark and landed on the 2nd November at Le Havre.

After one night in camp there we entrained – in a cattle train and steamed up to base at Saint-en-Marie, where we were inoculated before we bedded down for the night.

Next day we marched up to a place called Estaires near the La-Bassée road where we were reviewed by General French. He sat on horseback and I can remember fine what he said. 'Men and young lads. It's not the bravest and boldest that is going to win this campaign but the flyest and the cutest. You are up against a clever enemy … !' After saying some other words of advice, he gave his horse a kick and away he went.

We went into the trenches that night at Neuve Chapelle – La-Bassée Road section into Reserve.

Albert Edwards, 5th Black Watch/Machine Gun Corps

sharn manure

On the Monday morning a few of us that had got thegither took the train up to Dunkeld where we had heard that the Marquis of Tullibardine had two regiments of Scottish Horse mustered and was looking for more men to form a third regiment. This would make a brigade.

When I came off the train at Dunkeld, a whole stream of lads came off as well to join up and were laughing and joking as we walked up the streets to jine up. Well – of course we had no idea what this War was all about – we were young and in search of excitement. I was 21 the day that War broke out.

We trained as Yeomanry at a camp at Scone Racecourse where we were involved with horses all the time although we got Infantry training too. We moved to Ingham where we continued training. We were all richt keen and eager to go where the fighting was.

William Mowat, 1st Scottish Horse and Lovat Scouts

I mind fin I was in India meetin in wi a lad that wis eence foreman at the Ord o Dinnet – Jimmy Hunter, a gweed man wis.

Fin War brak oot, the hale lot os wis putting back to England bit iss time takkin back wir horses and guns and landin at Plymouth in December 1914. We war sent into canvas at Mornhill Camp and stracht awa the maist o the lads gid doon wi illness caased wi the change o climate fae India. Onywy they laand in hospital. It didna touch me – I must hae been ower hardy, bit efter this happened they shifted us aa inti billets and began trainin as part of the 29th Division.

The 26th and 22nd got issued new guns bit wir batteries that hid sax guns to a battery, war noo reduced to fower a-piece, wi sax horses to a gun. This wis becis they thocht that sax guns wis ower muckle for ae commander.

James Smith, Royal Field Artillery

I got a bittie restless masel and an ae Sunday a feoy os got a hire car an gid up to Tarland toon far they were recruitin men at day and we jined the 7th Gordon Highlanders. We were puttin stracht doon to Banchory here and got kilts and uniforms bidin there tull Wednesday an sent on doon to Bedford Camp by train to jine the battalion trainin there.

…

We got nae training at Banchory an got the kilts to pit on an I spent the caalest nicht in my life wi damn all in aneth them. The lads were aa big strong men aff the ferms an do ye ken, we war aa in gran fettle thinkin waar wis the greatest thing on earth an feart that it wid be aa ower afore we got er.

We hid to wite a gie filie as we did a lot o trainin at Bedford Camp and didna get awa till May neist eer in 1915, sailin fae Dover an landin at Calais in the dawn. There wis jist stunning room on the ship I mind.

There we gid into bell tents at the heed o a hill then oot neist day an aff on a train up to the front line far we got shotties in the trenches noo in an.

Charles Smith, 7th and 4th Gordon Highlanders

I jined the Royal Field Artillery and did my trainin at Maryhill Barracks.

Fin there, the fairmer o Newton o Mountblairy applied for me to the Army to get me for a hairst man and de ye ken I got a fortnicht's leave an it wis extended to five wicks to get it finished.

Fin I got back I wis sent oot to France into 123 Brigade of the 41st Division. I canna mind oor battery number. Onywy we hid 18-pounder guns. This wis at the hinnerine o the Somme Battle fin I jined them.

William Shearer, Royal Field Artillery

hinnerine the hind end/far end

I wis fe-et at Dallachy when War started and gid doon to the Plainstones at Banff where I was recruited into the 6th Gordon Highlanders. I wis only 17 and thought it was a great adventure and a fine chance to get away from the humdrum of farm work.

A. MacEwan, 6th Gordon Highlanders

It wis funny min the wy I jined up. I wis in Methlick ae Setterday nicht an met in wi my pal Wullie Webster fea the jiners there. We laand up in Cobet Smith's a grocer that selt porter ale. We baith hid a bottle ot or maybe twa and were thinkin we were gie cheils and caperin aboot in the street makin a bit o a din, fin the minister cam wakin by. On the Sunday he preached a sermon aboot the degrading exhibition the twa os put up feenishin up sayin we would be better employed in the Army fighting for King an Country than making fools of ourselves with strong drink.

The twa os didna ken if we wis worthy o a sermon or nae aa to wirsels an maybe felt a bittie honoured, bit we took him at his word an hired the hotel man fae the Temperence hotel to tak us into the toon o Aiberdeen to jine up. Wullie gid into the Army Service Corps and I jined the Royal Engineers.

Jimmy Scott, Royal Engineers

In October 1914 there wis a toss up atween the 5th and 6th Gordon Highlanders, to see fa wis gan to France becis there wis a battalion needed oot there at eence.

Onywy the 6th won and there wis a gie lot o lang faces wi us I can tell you. So the 6th gid oot richt awa.

Aa them that wis ower young were then teen oot and sent back to Aiberdeen so that wis me back there wi a lot mair to wite till we were auld eneuch. Then ae time they were pickin oot men for a draft for France to get their medical, a feoy o us lads that were ower young slippit in tull a side door and jined them. Efter we passed oor medical as near aa did, naebody tried to stop us this time: they jist turned a blin ee or something and aff we gid to France as pleased as could be.
Albert Connon, 5th Gordon Highlanderss

I was called up the night before War was declared against Germany. The black-smith's son came over from Glenferness on his motor bike to inform me. We mustered our troop at Glenferness and set off for Beauly our headquarters, riding our ponies of course and when we were walking them through Inverness we heard the War had been declared. We had young Ian Melville then as a troop leader from the estate at Glenferness. He was a great big strapping laddie of six feet four inches with fair hair. I remember once when we were riding down the streets of Blairgowrie with Ian at our head when a big tinker wifie shouts out – 'Hey mosh, look at that muckle fair haired loon … !' That was all good fun to us but Ian blushed to the roots.

When we arrived in Beauly our seats were damned sore I can tell you. That distance was the farthest we ever travelled but we enjoyed the whole affair – this War was a great adventure for us and I remember when passing through Inverness we were saying that we hoped it wouldn't be over before we were there.

At Beauly we were billeted at Wellhouse Farm which belonged to a Mr Birnie – it was beside the railway line. The horses were strange to one another and were far from pleased at being in a strange place far from their home pastures. One row was tethered up one side of the shed and another row down the other side. They were too near each other and some lashed out with there hind legs at one another and when one was on horse picket, it was a terrible hazard attending to them. Those flying hooves were like facing machine guns. In no time at all there were a couple with a broken leg. Old Logan, the vet from Inverness had a hellava time with them. He was very lame himself and I remember he shot one horse when I was helping and made a poor job of it. It was still alive after the first one and he had to repeat it another twice. I was at the burying of that damned beast. The ground was solid red clay at Wellhouse Farm and there were ten of us darging the hole and this stuff just clung to our shovels – we were taking back as much as we were taking out so we didn't go far down and left a big mound.
darging digging/working
…

After ten days at Beauly we – the whole regiment of the Lovat Scouts – went off down to Blairgowrie to camp and I was among some that were billeted at a factory building there. Ian Melville, our troop leader, had succeeded his oldest brother Jack who had died before the War of injuries caused by a fall from a horse. The injury to the head was treated by a surgeon but he couldn't save him. I was at his funeral.

William MacGregor, Lovat Scouts

Efter my trainin I jined a battery that were bein sent oot to Mesopotamia. I gid oot on the liner *Dunvegan Castle*. The crew aa gid doon wi dysentery, so they asked for volunteers to shovel coal and that wis my job till we got to Durban. There, we hid the time o wir lives wi the finest folk I iver met. This wis folk fae the toon that cam doon to spear if there wis onybody fae Scotland on the ship. Weel do ye ken! They couldna dee eneuch for us, and mind ye, we hid the 1st Seaforth and the 2nd Black Watch wi us, so they hid a gie tac on, bit man, fit fine folk.

George Barclay, Royal Field Artillery

I wis fe-ed at Dr Wilson's farm fin War stated aside Ellon. He fe-ed ma at Langside feein market. I wis in the Terriers at the time. Twa days efter that we were mustering at Peterheed. We were there a wick and gid fae there to Perth far we bade a fortnicht and wis in billets aa ower the toon. Then it wis aff to Bedford and into civvy billets.

Wullie Gavin, 5th Gordon Highlanders

I min fin I jined up, the first feoy days at Maryhill Barracks – there wis a gie rag tag kine o a lad cam in as a recruit. He got his medical examination an passed aa richt an then of coorse he got issued wi a hale rig oot o uniforms – quite an that and skedaddled weet aa neist day an wis niver seen again.

William Shearer, Royal Field Artillery

quite coat

When I was called up I was up at Glenurquhart herding sheep. I was called up to Perth and took my motor bike. The Army commandeered it at once and promised me £10 for it but I never got it, oh no!

Wull Dryden, Gordon Highlanders

I wis in the Derby Scheme and wis fe-ed at Wester Melrose at the time. Fin term cam I wis spiered to gang hame to another place as foreman bit I stuck oot for £33 the sax month. The fermer widna offer mair than 31.

I says, 'Oh no, am nae for that!'

'Weel,' he says, 'You'll jist hae to gang to the Army. I could get total exemption for ye, ye ken!'

'Do ye think am feart at the War?' I says tull the mannie. 'Na na! Nor your threats either; so ta ta chiel and yer fee tee!'

Alec Barlow, 1st Gordon Highlanders

Sir Arthur Grant oor CO said to us at Bedford, 'All those who wish to follow me to France, take one step forward'. Weel of coorse we aa steppe't forrit.

Sir Arthur then gazed at us and said, 'I am proud of you! I am proud of you!'
John Rennie, 5th Gordon Highlanders

I was called up to the Gordon Highlanders and trained at Tillicoultry and wi drafted to the 9th Gordon Highlanders, 15th Scottish Division.

We were aa ferm servants and could fair use a spad at digging trenches. I got on for groom to the Colonel.

There wis ae lad wi us he wis ae deein fatigues, aye, shit hooses and the like. There wis nae deval for him – as seen as ae job wis feenished there wis aye another een laid on. Wi aa that shot and sotter – the peer lad's claes wis aye an afa track and onywy he couldna tidy himsel up ataa; so he wis aye on a charge for that and for the fact that he niver saluted officers either. He hid jist cam clean aff the hills o Sutherland. Still he jist plitered on and didnae seem to care a damn.
Jonathan Taylor, 9th Gordon Highlanders

Provost Sergeant Findlater wis a great character. At Bedford he eenced to tak aa us wrang deeirs on parade at nicht and dreel us up and doon. Fin he halted us he then telt us some gran stories and made us lach like hell. Then he wid say, 'Stop aat bloody lachin – yer nae supposed to lach here! As you we......er!'

A great lad he wis, we aa liked him.
Alec Nicol, 7th Gordon Highlanders

12. Gordon Highlanders leaving Bedford, 9 November 1915.
Gordon Highlanders Museum

I jined up on Skippy Fair day in New Deer. Skippy Fair Market wis a horse fair. The horses werna roupit – they war aa selt wi private bargain.

There wis recruitin staff oot fae Aiberdeen at it an I left my apprentice tailoring and listed at 17. I niver gid back ti the tailoring.

A great crowd jined up at day, apparently a helluva number o ferm lads ti answer Kitchener's call for a hunner thoosan men, an they war a lot o great big stoot chiels.

Bert Gow, Royal Field Artillery

roupit auctioned

13. Soldiers awaiting the train at Huntly Station, *c.*1914. Troops are lined up on the platform awaiting a train. Towards the right a group of young well-wishers are on hand to wave them off.

Image © National Museums Scotland

4

First Time in the Line

The War started an I attended a recruitin meetin at Hatton far a great lot of ferm billies turned up. Maist o the lads jined the Gordon Highlanders bit I jined the Naval Division.

I was caaled up at eence – this wis in August 1914 an wis putten doon ti Crystal Palace an started dreelin. We sleepit on hammocks an I canna tell ye fit wy min, bit I took ill wi flu or something an laaed up in hospital far I wis later discharged. Noo I niver wis a day nea weel in ma life, and hid ti gang ti London ti get it. Onywy they didna like the look o me an sent ma hame.

Fin I got hame, I fe-et hame to a mannie at the Ellon Martinmas feein market an gid hame to Springhill o Langside as foreman. Gweed men war getting scarce by iss time, but then aa the billies I kent an wis eence fe-et wi war awa in the Gordon Highlanders so I only stuck it tull the Whitsunday term an gid doon ti Peterheed an jined the 5th Gordon Highlanders tee. I wis teen awa doon to Rippon Camp ti dee ma trainin richt awa.
John Brown, 5th Gordon Highlanders

We had a long wait for action and were not required to move till nearly a year later, when we were moved without our horses to Devonport on to a troopship for Egypt where we were supposed to receive horses that were there. This was the troopship *Transylvania*. This troopship was dirty and our food was practically non-existent. We were crowded into quarters between decks, sleeping in hammocks above mess tables. There was a boat drill every day and sentries were posted to look out for submarines. There were also other troops aboard besides the Scottish Horse. Among them were several military prisoners doing field punishment. They were tied up to the wheels of field guns for a while each day.

The ship berthed at Gibraltar to pick up supplies of coal. There the barges came out and labourers carried coals up the planks into bunkers in the ships side – a hard dirty job. I was mess orderly that day and had a great feast of bacon and eggs and other meals of the same quality – a great change from the plate of thin porridge I ate normally.

The ships then sailed for the island of Lemnos where they dropped anchor. Apparently we were now destined for Gallipoli instead of Egypt. I remember

seeing a Russian battleship there which had five funnels which we promptly named 'A packet of Woodbines'.
William Mowat, 1st Scottish Horse and Lovat Scouts

Getting up to the front line the first time was a trying time for recruits, but you see that was the safest place of the lot except during a German push. Most of the shelling went away over our heads to the rear.
A. MacEwan, 6th Gordon Highlanders

I wis called up richt awa and trained wi the 3rd trainin battalion at Aiberdeen, jist getting oot in time for the last battle o the Ancre. I aye mind fin we occupied trenches that wis fu o deed. Wi the shellin they were maistly aa covered wi the earth faain in, bet we kent wi the spring in wir feet that it wis bodies we were stannin on. We couldn meeve for dubs there.

This wis my first taste o the War and do you ken iss, I wisna nee feart. I canna tell ye fit wy that wis.
Alec Barlow, 1st Gordon Highlanders
dubs mud

I went to Etabs first and went through the mill there. The Bull Ring was a hard case.

I was posted to the 8th Gordon Highlanders at first but sent to the 7th later. At the end we became a composite 6/7th Battalion.

I was a lance corporal before I went out and was put in charge of a machine gun, shortly after my mate on the gun got killed by a bullet through the neck.
J. Fowlie, 7th Gordon Highlanders

I mind on a new batch of recruits started scuttling up and down the trenches in fear when the enemy shells started to fall near us. This was their first taste of it and they soon started to settle down when they saw us old hands smiling away quietly and reassuring them that the shells were quite far off, and telling them they were in the safest place. One lad told them, 'Oh you cannot run away from that you know!
Albert Edwards, 5th Black Watch/Machine Gun Corps

New men were never much good for a while.
Robert More MM, 4th Seaforth Highlanders

When we were due to go into the front line for the first time, I was sitting on a log beside Captain More, an architect from Methlick, and Captain Walton, a teacher from Dollar Academy, when a bullet struck the log right between mu fingers. This was a spent bullet, but it fair made me jump.

Captain More was killed about the last day of the War but I think Walton came through.

We proceeded into the communication trench up to the line about a mile and a half up when a shell or two started to explode around us. I crouched down in fear and found myself peeing. This is what fright does – I had no control. I was all right after that – it never happened again. Later when I had the job of taking up recruits into the line, I knew what they were going through. I tried to calm them – well laddies of 18 and 19, although I was not much older, I would say, 'Its all right, that shell is far away'.

…

Two years later Boulogne. When there I reported to the Railway Transportation Officer (RTO) who then arranged that I be put in charge of recruits to the Highland Division. Next day we entrained and that night got off at a place where my orders stated the division was. This was wrong, as they had moved a bit. I then looked for shelter for the lads for the night.

Next day I got them all sorted out and we set off on the march to join their intended units. We marched and walked a long way and it was night before we got to the place where we had to split up and join our various battalions in the line. We were tired and hungry and first timers and I knew what they really felt.

Alec Robertson, 5th Gordon Highlanders

14. Gordon Highlanders at the Battle of Mons.
Gordon Highlanders Museum

When I went into the front line for the first time it was in the dark. When I arrived in the trenches I was detailed with another new arrival to do some digging on a position out in front. While engaged on that task a shell came down and exploded right there. I was buried and my mate who came up with me was blown to bits. I was dugout and saw his leg lying some distance away. That was my baptism of fire.

Later on I heard the company sergeant major say to somebody, 'Remember that young white haired fellow I took up this morning – well he has been killed!' I then said to him that I wasn't killed it was the other fellow.

A. McEwan, 6th Gordon Highlanders

We were gan inti the front line for the first time. It wis pick dark. We were waakin up this road makkin for the trenches, fin the Gerry shells cam crashin doon. I got ass great a fleg ma heed jerkit and the chin strap o ma tin hat nearly hanged me. We aa lay doon in fear – that wis a hellava nicht that I mine on. Efter a file i gat eesed tult, I even got eesed to seeing the heaps o deed – wir ain and Gerry that lay in front os aa the time. I never saa sae muckle deed as lay oot there at Arras.

Peter Baigrie, 7th Cameron Highlanders/6th Black Watch

fleg fright, *tult* used to it

5

Mons to the Marne

Mons to the Marne and back

I wis sent oot ti scout ti see far the Germans lay in front o us at Mons. I got richt up amon them and listened ti them newsin – bit I didna ken fit they were sayin of coorse. I slippit awa fin it wis still dark to wir ain lines. Fin I got back there wis naebody there – they hid pulled oot.

De ye ken, I cam throwe the War an niver got a scrat.

Alec Pratt MM, Royal Horse Artillery

On the morning of the 16th August 1914 we entrained on to cattle trucks – 40 men to a truck.

We travelled all that day and finally got off at a place called Le-Nouvion. From there we marched to Boué and stopping in a farmer's field. After a quick breakfast we began a route march up to meet the German Army. Each brigade battalion took it in turn to be the vanguard. The routine was to march for 50 minutes and rest for ten, with so much food in the haversack. Then the company cooker trundled along with the stew. The countryside never looked better – it was bonny; just in the middle of harvest. We stopped all night and slept in the open every night. On the 22nd August we stopped at a place called Bold-Baige for the night but suddenly were ordered to commence marching all night. That was a march of 23 out of 24 hours. We crossed the Belgium frontier at midnight, stopping shortly after at a place called Grand Rennes. Everybody was completely exhausted and we were glad to just lie down on the bare cassie stones in the street. It was warm weather and we fell asleep at once after eating hard biscuits and cheese.

The inhabitants were not to be seen, being all in bed by this time. Still there was one old wifie came out with a coffee mill and made some coffee as thick as tar and it tasted like nectar.

We were alerted to move after three hours. Apparently B Company had been sent forward without sleep to do picket duty a half mile ahead.

They had raked about and found a few farmers' implements to block the road, prominently a binder among them.

At about 3am they heard the sound of horses hooves coming clip-clopping

15. The Royal Scots Greys practising a charge in France. The officer is riding in front
with his arm raised to start the charge. The horses wear double bridles to give
greater control. The men are in field uniform with steel helmets.

Reproduced by permission of the National Library of Scotland

towards them. Suddenly in the dim early morning light they saw a troop of
German Ulhans, one of which spurred his horse forward and sailed over the
cutting bar of the binder.

The order was given to fire and during the encounter most of the enemy were
accounted for including the first one who turned out to be an officer.

On the 23rd we were ordered to retreat and we adopted the reverse tactic of
battalions taking the rearguard in turn. The Royal Scots Greys were bombed with
darts by German planes and also got a nasty doze of Artillery fire. When we passed
them they were washing their white horses with Kondies fluid. It turned the beasts
almost khaki.

I remember one day the butchers slaughtered a cow in the field. That made
great stew. Then it came on a thunderstorm. The rearguard that day was the 2nd
Munster Fusiliers. The 2nd Infantry Brigade was away on our left, their rearguard
was the 1st Gordon Highlanders.

The stew was dished up and we were sitting eating at the side of the road – it
was grand this freshly killed beef all stewed up, we were fairly enjoying it – when
we heard the sound of a battle with heavy machine gun and rifle fire. We didn't
know at the time but this was the 1st Gordon Highlanders ambushed and
surrounded at Le Cateau.

We crossed to the south of the river Marne within 12 kilometres of Paris, and
could see the spires in the distance. This was about the 30th August 1914. All of us
were absolutely tired out, the Reservists being in the worst state, having been in

civvy street and not entirely hardened up to the marching: their feet went all to pot.

I saw the French Reserve Army coming up in buses and taking the field on our front, successfully stopping the Germans.

The Germans retired and we re-crossed the Marne on the 7th of September. Our opponents on the other side was the Pomeranian Guards. Big heavy men who wore a shikole type of helmet. They were entrenched in foxhole shelters. In the attack on their positions, we killed and captured a lot of them but lost a lot of our men ourselves. Lieutenant Wilson was killed, Captain Dalgluish was wounded and died later and Captain Drummond was also wounded and taken away.

We advanced to the river Aisne and came on the vineyards with the grapes looking their best. When we ate them, they taster bitter. We learned that they were sprayed with sulphur to deter bugs or such like. This was supposed to wear off by the time to pick them came round.

When we crossed the river it was on a dense foggy day. The water was low after a dry spell but there was a ruined bridge where it was possible to cross single file. After waiting while the whole brigade was assembled we then advanced up a steep incline to the village of Run Dresse. Before long we came under shellfire from huge Jack Johnson 9.2s. It was obvious that they had our range even though we were obscured by mist. We were ordered off the road and landed into a field of sugar beet. Moving across it we came under rifle fire; the bullets were whistling over and around.

At last we came to a building which loomed out of the mist – this turned out to be a sugar beet factory. This was fortified and protected by barbed wire.

The Cameron Highlanders were on the right of us and the 2nd brigade were still further on their right. D Company attacked at once and suffered a severe mauling from machine gun fire.

Colonel Duff's headquarters had been established by this time at our rear, on the face of a hill. I was sent back as a runner with a message detailing our position by our captain. Colonel Duff asked me about where to find D Company but that was not easy to describe in that terrible fog. He suddenly grabbed a rifle and bandolier and asked me to show him the way. I was returning to my company anyway and he accompanied me part of the way till we heard the sounds of battle coming from the factory which was hidden from our view in the mist.

We parted company in that beet field and that was the last time Lt Colonel Duff was ever seen again. No one had seem him killed – his disappearance remains a mystery to this day.

That night – the 14th September – we were issued with shovels and were ordered to dig ourselves into the ground. In our kit was a standard small pick and shovel which we used to scrape a small shelter, but this was now real shovels and from then on we dug trenches and strung out barbed wire which had been carried up. This was the first time I had seen it erected, and some lads hung tins on it to sound alarm. From that day on the line became static.

Several attacks were made on us for the next few days to throw us off the escarpment but were easily broken up with 15 rounds rapid fire, causing the Germans heavy loss of life.

The Souves relieved us in the third week of October, but not for a rest. We entrained at the rear and landed up at a place called Hasbrouk. From there the brigade formed up and marched to a peaceful looking town which was undamaged, named Ypres. Up to that time it had only been attacked by the Ulhans.

…

There was a lot of bayonet fighting at first especially at the Marne and the Aisne crossing when there was a lot of close-quarter fighting for positions held by the enemy. The only thing bad about ours was they were too young. I would say of all the bayonets used on the field the French ones were the best, it was like a dart and grooved down the side while ours was like a sword and could be used as a hand sword, but on the whole the question of charging with the bayonet en masse with flags flying was not on.

…

Even after the War Lt Colonel Sir Adrian Grant Duff was never found. His brother made a search for his body but found no trace of him. I was apparently the last man who saw him, when we parted company in that beet field at the Battle of Ainse.

That was the first time we experienced the Jack Johnsons which we nicknamed the 'Coal Boxes'. He may have been blown to smithereens with one of them – for the Germans were using them against Infantry in the field. They were so demoralising that we lost an officer and a few men from shell shock: they just went stark raving mad.

Frank MacFarlane MM and Medal Militaire, 1st Black Watch

Ypres and Contemptibles

We marched through Ypres and through Hooge right on to a village of Gheluvelt on the Menin road. The Gerry attacked here and his strength was so dominant that we gave way. The shelling was ferocious. Retiring through Pilkem, we saw the corn ricks and houses on fire. At night, our company sergeant major fell in a midden and his uniform and kilt was an awful mess. His temper was none too good I can tell you.

We retreated back about six miles to a wood which we fortified with the 2nd Gordon Highlanders on our left and the Scots and Coldstream Guards on the right.

Round about the end of October 1914, the German Artillery started firing early one morning. This barrage was particularly vicious and made us keep our heads down. It stopped suddenly and we were amazed to hear German bands playing military music away in the distance.

We didn't know it at the time but the Kaiser had been visiting the Front and had issued orders to his troops to smash Sir John French's 'contemptible little Army'. So this was why the bands had been playing – to encourage their assault troops to do just that.

Well, the attack started with the Prussian Guard that morning, marching shoulder to shoulder with the bands sounding and playing away to their rear. This was a misty morning as they loomed into vision. What a spectacular scene that was: these men marching towards us in immaculate lines, with their brass spiked helmets, bravely singing 'Deuchland Uber Alles'. Their greatcoats nearly touching the ground, they swept remorselessly towards us.

At last we were given the order to open fire and the result was absolute devastation for them. Our rapid rifle fire and the Lewis guns reaped a dreadful toll of their ranks.

We stopped them and they tried again at midday. The same thing happened although a few did break through and had reached our headquarters tent. Lt Colonel C. B. Stewart – who took the place of Lt Colonel Duff – was accosted by a German, who fired his rifle at him. The bullet grazed him in the forehead. Sergeant Redpath happened to be in the tent at the same time and he quickly shot the German dead on the spot.

After that incident all personnel were rushed into the line that could shoot a rifle, including a welcome force of Life Guards. They were great big rangy men who could use themselves well.

That week we were joined by the Territorial London Scottish. These lads were a great asset.

That was the start of the Ypres Salient and when we came out of there the town was in ruins as we passed through to the rear for a rest.
Frank MacFarlane MM and Medal Militaire, 1st Black Watch

Ypres kept going like a mull aa the time: the shells kept crashin doon on us day an nicht!
Wullie Gavin, 5th Gordon Highlanders

Christmas 1914

In 1914 we cam oot ti meet the Germans. In No Man's Land in Christmas Day 1914. We got on great an swapped presents an fags an that. I gid a lad a tin o Maconnachies and he gid me a broon loaf – bit I didna care fort. Baith sides took the opportunity ti collect aa the deed bodies an beery them. My certie that wis nae picnic, some were jist bits and hid ti be collected into bags an the stink beat hell. There wis nae fechtin till we were relieved an sent back bit that wis efter the New Year.
Jimmy Reid, 6th Gordon Highlanders

16. Soldiers celebrating Christmas in the trenches, Western Front. Men sitting in the mud in a trench have laid some white paper on a crate and set out some slices of cake, a tinned pudding, a packet of raisins and what looks like an orange.

Reproduced by permission of the National Library of Scotland

17. Members of the 2nd Battalion, Gordon Highlanders fraternising with German soldiers on the Rue de Quesnes sector of the Front, Christmas 1914.

Imperial War Museum

We partook of the Christmas truce, we came out to meet the Germans that day and the celebrations lasted all that day. There was a big noise about it because we still had our numerals and battalion identifications on our uniforms. The truce with us only lasted one day and we exchanged souvenirs like buttons and letters with stamps on.

It was a good day: nobody turned on anyone; we were all quite happy. We were new there and did not have any casualties up to then.

The trenches were in a terrible state. When we jumped down off the parapet we were up to our hips in mud and water.

Robert More MM, 4th Seaforth Highlanders

Fin the Christmas truce was on; a lad fae Lumsden and me gid awa inti No Man's Lands far we saa the ruins o a sheddie. There we come on some sand bags, fit we made a horseshoe cover oot in the open. This wis becis we couldna bide in the trenches, they were fu o watter!

What a sotter aathing wis in. We tried aye to red up the trenches. We never participated in the Christmas truce and took a dim view of those that did.

Jimmy Reid, 6th Gordon Highlanders

sotter mess

6

Neuve Chapelle, Festubert
and Aubers Ridge

At Neuve Chapelle Colonel MacLean wis killed; Smith o Pittodrie wis killed; Lt Colonel Uniacke o the 2nd got killed. Colonel Stansfield[16] wis a richt gallus kind o cheil – he gid ower the top wi a pick shaft. There wis nae CO wi MacLean bein killed, so oor captain got on for CO.

We still had nae full equipment at the battle o Neuve Chapelle. I got issued wi size nine beets and I only need sevens. Fin I aboot turned I nearly left ma feet ahin!

Gan ower, I took shelter fae machine gunfire in an orchard among heaps o muck. Fin I looket at the idder folk on the grun – there wis naebody livin – they war aa deed.

Jimmy Reid, 6th Gordon Highlanders

Our brigade were involved in the Battle of Neuve Chapelle. This was the first time I met the Meerut and the Lahore. They were Gurkhas, Pathans and Garhwalis.

I remember taking a message from the colonel of the 1st to the colonel of the 2nd Black Watch. who was part of the Meerut Brigade. When crossing over in the pitch black night I was challenged by a Dogger and I couldn't understand him, nor him me. I was fired at but his aim wasn't good. The battle was a disaster. The 4th City of Dundee lost Colonel Walker. Festubert was worse for us. That was in May 1915, we were that short of officers and the supply of regular ones had dried up; so they invited any NCO that wanted to apply for a commission, to do so and they would be considered.

Nine applied and were promoted. On the 9th May we attacked the German line which was heavily fortified; by nightfall, out of that nine, only one was left alive.

The wire was all uncut due to our weekly Artillery not destroying it.

We retired and were due to go in again at four in the afternoon but the order was cancelled. We lost 400 men, our worst loss at any time. A lad named Burns from Forfar was killed. He had done some fine deeds that day and was recommended for the VC but got the DCM instead posthumously. We stayed in Givenchy area all that summer. The Guards were taken out of our division and formed into one of their own.

Frank MacFarlane MM and Medal Militaire, 1st Black Watch

My pal Charlie [17] wis killed at Neuve Chapelle. The lads I wis wi there were neer aa deed fin the War feenished.

Norrie Cruikshank, 6th Gordon Highlanders

I was wounded in the leg at the Battle of Festubert. Heavy casualties were caused among us. Many of my mates were killed, although my brother came through all right.

Later they called for horsemen to man our transport and munitions wagons and I volunteered. Most were from the farms and could handle horses and mules well enough. So I went on to that.

A. Smeaton, 5th Black Watch

We didn't lose too many men at Neuve Chapelle. We were still not fully equipped. The Artillery did not know what to fire at for a start – they lacked direction and they just battered away at short range. Of course they were short of shells at that time. Sometimes we went into our own barrage.

…

One Sunday in March 1915, the whole battalion went into the front line at a village away to our front held by the Germans called Neuve Chapelle.

At the back of us were batteries of field guns dug in wheel to wheel; for about 300 yards which were bombarding the enemy trenches all night. In the crack of dawn those guns raised their sights and the village of Neuve Chapelle went up in flames and smoke. We went over the top and advanced on the Gerry trenches and found the Gerries coming forward giving themselves up. This was the Prussian Guard. The shellfire had softened them up and they didn't like it a bit. They were so used to having the fire power on their side only. It was all mostly Gerry shellfire till 1916 though. Our lads captured about 200 of them. Their officers wore brass helmets but the rest of the Guard wore ordinary kind.

This was the first encounter with them and we felt quite elated as we handed them over to the French troops in reserve.

The next real attack we made was at Aubers Ridge. The East Lancs went over first and went off over the open ground and started falling right away. Then Gerry released a dam which caused a flood of water to come rushing across the land. This torrent caught the East Lancs and drowned them like rats.

When the water subsided, it was our turn to go and get up on to the water-logged land where suddenly the Gerry machine guns went 'zip-zip!' and the slaughter of our lads begun. There we had to stop and in the end retreat back to the trenches where we started from 1000-strong leaving the most of the lads lying dead or wounded. Which was like a death sentence although some were got in by stretcher-bearers before they perished.

There was no food at all provided that day and at night we were relieved by the Northamptons and went back into reserve.

Next day when we paraded in a field only 85 men answered roll call.
Albert Edwards, 5th Black Watch/Machine Gun Corps

We took ower the line fae the Gurkhas at Festubert.

I aye mind the poem aboot the CO of the 6th that wis killed at Neuve Chapelle. 'Colonel MacLean and his kilted men will ne'er return again … !'

…

We gid oot in April 1915 jist in time for the battle o Festubert. There I wis wounded in the knee fin I wis oot on patrol. Aye michty aye! A German bullet. I thocht I wis buggered for life; it gid through the side o my kneecap. They aa said fu lucky I wis – a Blighty[18] een ye ken! I wis at a hospital in Manchester for three months wi aat.

I eence got mentioned in dispatches for a richt funny thing min. We were oot on patrol, and I aye saa this licht blink-blinkin in the dark. I sent twa lads ae wy and another twa the tither. Weel fin I creepit up on this light, I saa it wis een o wir ain men it had on a luminous waatch. I reported fit I hid seen fin I got back, and do ye ken, a general order gid oot to get redd o aa wir luminous waatches.

For that affair I was mentioned in dispatches and wis sent for by the hich ups to get presented we-et and hid ti wite ass lang on parade fort. Fin I got back my officer speired fu I got on, so I said tull him, 'I wid rather face the Germans than ging throw that again'. He jist gid a guid lach.
Alec Nicol, 7th Gordon Highlanders
hich ups high ups, (i.e. senior officers)

7

Gallipoli, Egypt and Salonica 1915–18

Gallipoli

At the port of Mudros we embarked into lighters and sailed that night for Gallipoli where we successfully landed before daylight on the beaches of Suvla Bay. When morning dawned it was revealed that we were sheltered from the view of the Turks by cliffs. Looking out at sea I saw many warships which were there to provide covering shellfire.

When we were getting our gear organised, a Turkish plane came over spotting and almost immediately shells started coming over and bursting in the air over the cliffs. A shell fragment killed our cook sergeant as he was organising breakfast. He was an ex-Boer War man.

The shelling stopped after a while.

We took over from the English Yeomanry who had been there for a while longer and I remember our first job in the front line was to sap new trenches in the dark to get nearer the Turkish front line. By day we were seen by them from the surrounding high ground. We found the work hard as we were very unfit from the long sea voyage and lack of decent food on the way.

I remember being out with a working party where I was in the covering squad when we had to open fire on a Turkish patrol we heard, that was inquisitive enough to try and find what we were up to. That was the first that the Scottish Horse opened fire in earnest at Gallipoli.

There were a lot of great shots among us what with the large number of stalkers and gamekeepers and the like.

The Turks had excellent snipers and with the advantage of their better observation it was difficult to move about in daylight. To avoid exposing our heads, we used periscopes. One time I was using one when it came under fire from a sniper so I took it away. A machine gun officer came up to me and wanted a look through as he was scouting for a suitable post for to set up a machine gun. I warned him not to as a sniper had got on to it, but he paid no heed and held up the periscope. Immediately it was struck by a bullet and he received a nasty blow on his face by the eye sight.

During the first few days at Suvla we were kept busy digging latrines and dugouts when we weren't on sentry. At night there was little rest and only room to lie down on the fire step at the foot of the sentry you had relieved.

I was asked to be section leader (unpromoted) and I found that meant extra responsibilities. I had to keep a rota and I was asked for a man for this or that duty. I drew the rations for my section which came up at night from the beach. These consisted of Frey Bentos bully beef and hard biscuits, and now and then a bread ration would be distributed. Sometimes there was only a quantity of crumbs left which I laid out in portions and cut cards for first choice and so on.

Dysentery took a terrible toll and the doctors didn't seem to take it seriously and prescribed medicine and back to duty. Although later on when the affected got too weak, they were evacuated to a hospital ship.

We were under fire all the time from the snipers and even at night our men were silhouetted against the sea. One night a covering party suffered a burst of fire which resulted in many casualties.

William Mowat, 1st Scottish Horse and Lovat Scouts

We sailed for Gallipoli and off shore we were transferred on to little boats and came to the beaches of Suvla Bay where we landed quietly. The Scottish Horse were there before us.

One night, the news came though of a great victory at Loos and the Australians and our troops in the front lines started cheering. The Turks thought it was an attack on their lines and started firing across with everything they had. We were well behind the lines at the time and it was pitch dark, but the noise was deafening and the bullets were gong 'whing … whing' around us and over our heads, and we could also hear the patter of spent ones landing on the ground.

This cheering caused a lot of casualties and they started coming down through our lines. One I remember was a Scottish Horse man they were carrying on a stretcher. It was daylight by now. Two hundred yards away from us was a well with a barricade of sandbags round it. When the stretcher party was passing us, down came a Turkish shell barrage and although it wasn't too near – the two stretcher-bearers laid the wounded down and took to their heels for cover behind the heap of sandbags, then we were amazed to see the casualty rise up and likewise sprint off and do likewise.

William MacGregor, Lovat Scouts

We dug the wells in dried up river beds and they were called derries. We didn't get much shelling at Gallipoli, not with the naval guns of the *Queen Elizabeth* at the back of us to answer back. She used to fire a salvo every day from her 15-inch guns. We envied the men on the ships their good food and hot baths and comfortable billets. A parcel from home was a great event and friends aye shared the luxuries like tins of sardines.

William Mowat, 1st Scottish Horse and Lovat Scouts

We weren't allowed to expose any machine gun at Suvla in Gallipoli but many a time my team went out front to give covering fire in the dark while our men were improving and extending out trenches. So one time Willie Calder and myself were away up in front beside the ruin of an orchard in the direction of Chopper hill. After a while in the dark your eyes could see pretty well and this was a really dark night. I whispered to Willie that I could see forms of men lying in extended order out there and enquired at him if he knew if there was a covering party out that we didn't know about. He didn't think so and the more we studied those forms out there the more we argued about it, especially when there was no movement in these mysterious shapes, till at length we came to the conclusion that they were dead bodies. I crawled out to have a look and right enough it was some of the fallen from the British attack on 21st August 1915. They had lain out there a long time and were in a gie state. I stayed out there and removed the identity discs of those corpses who had belonged to the Sherwood Foresters, Manchesters and Notts and Derby. I took them back and handed them in – at least their folk back home would know now the fate of their loved ones.

William MacGregor, Lovat Scouts

At Plymouth a feoy boats arrived to tak the hale 29th Division. We hid this boat that hid offloaded meat at Liverpool fae America, and we didna hae to sling the horses aboard – they jist waakit up a gangway, the same as we took aboard wir guns.

There wis a lot o new beasts fae America an they hid to be yokit, a job I likit weel eneuch, bit they war gie hardy strong wild lads aa the same.

This ship we gid oot to Egypt wi, wis caaed the *Kinstonia* – I aye mind that, and ye hid to waak the beasts aboot ont for exercise. We disembarked at Alexandria and into camp. There we wited for the New Zealanders and Australians to come fae their ain countries. Fin that happened we gid on to wir same ships and sailed for Lemnos. A hale fleet o them congregated there wi a lot of battleships and all, and on the 24th April 1915 we set sail for the shores o Gallipoli. I mind it wis an afa fine nicht.

The beaches war targeted in letters and we were destined to W Beach. The 1st Lancashire Fusiliers gid ashore there first and ran inti a hellava shellfire; that wis in spite o the fact that the fleet o battleships hid been shellin aa nich. There wis even hich raas o barbet weer on the beach an it wisna broken, and sax feet high at aat. It wis nae picnic for them I can tell ye. The Turks was firin at them at point blank range wi machine guns and rifle fire. We hid loaded the batteries inti barges an war witin a gweed bit oot at sea and the Navy's big shells gid howlin ower wir heeds to laan among the Turks along the cliffs.

Eventually the Lancashires captured eneuch o grun for us to come in and fin we laand the hale sea and the beach wis reed wi bleed and the bodies o the gallant Lancashires lay in heaps aawy.

We got dug in and started firin as seens we could. It wis a job getting decent shelter for the horses though.

hich raas o barbet weer high rows of barbed wire

…

The 1st Dublin Fusiliers landed on V Beach an harly a soul got ashore alive. They used the *River Clyde* steamer wi barges towed ahin. They thocht fin the *River Clyde* grounded, that the barges would swing roon on to the beach – bit they didna, na faith, they piled up and that caased mair causalities wi the men aa bein piled in a heap mair or less. They gid ashore aa richt bit suffered fort an it wisna till it wis dark that they got established there. That wis jist neist to far we wis – but then we hid plenty on wir ain plate to deal wi to tak muckle notice.

Wir horses hid a lot o casualties wi shellfire – they war big targets as they war only tied on to wir wagons bit we did tak turns at lookin efter the craturs day an nicht bit aa the same some didna lest lang. Thank goodness the waals werna tampered wi – like bein poosaned bit they werena, so there wis freshwater available though it sometimes got in short supply.

The mait we got wis aa richt – aa depenned on the widder ye ken. There wis bully beef an bacon and files a nippy o rum although I didna drink it. The flees war a gie job – if ye opened a tin o jam or bully beef they war jist black wi them at eence. This caased an afa trouble wi dysentery although it didna affect me at aa – an afa lot gid doon weet. Oor dugoots war into the side o a bank bit files we sleepit in the open jist wi a ground sheet owers. It wis gie het in the simmer time bit by jove it wis terrible cauld in the winter.

James Smith, Royal Field Artillery

waals wells *poosaned* poisoned

The landing at Gallipoli killed a lot of the 1st, but I only joined them with some reinforcements. Gallipoli was hectic at first until things settled down, then we couldn't move and the Turks couldn't either. In fact a Glasgow fellow said to me, 'I'm just writing home to my wife and telling her that if I am killed – it will just be an accident!'

Jock Murray, 1st King's Own Scottish Borderers

We heard the Turks talking all the time and their dogs barking too. They kept them with them all the time.

…

As days and weeks passed, our numbers got fewer and fewer with casualties and sick taking toll and ultimately I was left with only one man left and myself of my section of eight men.

Sleep was the great comforter, we were so tired all the time, but we thought about food and spoke about it often. I remember Jimmy Dunn saying, 'I wish I was at home sitting at the fireside with my mother baking scones. I would just lift them off the girdle and spread them with jam!'

I remember my own mother used to say, 'Waste not, want not, for you may live to say – oh how I wish I had the bread I once threw away!' Well that had come to pass all right at Suvla Bay.

William Mowat, 1st Scottish Horse and Lovat Scouts

The Australians were farrer north than us, bit later on some o them cam roon to oor side an attacked at Suvla Bay alang wi some mair British troops bit they didna get very far er either.

The sick and wounded war teen oot on lighters at nicht to hospital ships bit the majority comin aff were dysentery cases the maist o the time.

The Turks hid a nesty habit o firin their rifles up in the air an the spent bullets cam stracht don on top os in fact we lost a lot o folk at wy. I mind we hid a sergeant blacksmith got een in the chest and fin the doctor wis sittin dressin him with bandages – anither een struck him (the blacksmith) on the airm.

The Turks hid great snipers and there wis an olive tree that they eence ti use a lot although we did clear them oot tee.

We hid aboot 60 men in oor battery killed includin wir ain colonel and adjutant. The twa o them war away up in the front line fit ye caa 'forward obser-vasion' and at the time they was busy telephoning back the range o wir shells we were firin fae oor battery, fin the Turks attacked and overran the position and baith men war killed. They hid only their revolvers ti defend theirsels and the gunner signaller attached ti them, wis fun deed wi the telephone still in his hand.

Fin morning cam we attacked the infiltrators an re-occupied the line again, an that's fin we recovered the bodies an saa the many deed o the 5th Royal Scots. I was a sergeant by this time an I supervised the burial o wir ain folk. At this task, we aye buried them wi their claes on and I niver eence saa a service held aa the time I wis at Gallipoli. Later on I shewed the deed inti a bag. Wee aa took it in turns to go on observation duties bit it was unusual for the commander to go as on this occasion.

Oors an the Turkish deed war jist left awa oot in No Man's Land an I niver seen a truce to beery the deed on oor front at ony time.

James Smith, *Royal Field Artillery*

I don't remember of there being any rain in Gallipoli since we landed, but on the evening of 26th November 1915 at seven a sudden thunderstorm with a deluge of rain came on. I shared a dugout with Jimmy Fraser. He had been in the ration party and had acquired a bittie of cheese which were about to enjoy.

The rain poured in torrents and our dugout begun to take in water. I held my rifle between my knees as I sat there to prop up a waterproof sheet. Suddenly a rush of water descended into our trench from higher up which immersed our dugout and drooking us to the skin.

Jimmy got up first and I found I was too waterlogged to climb out in my weak condition and required Jimmy's assistance to do so. This was dark and there we were stranded in the open cold and wet all night. Fortunately by daylight the rain had eased and the water level in the trench had subsided enough for us to get back in and stand on sand bags. We managed to get an issue of rum and a little tea but as the day wore on the weather deteriorated into freezing cold and rain which turned to snow. The ground froze and so did our greatcoats and wet clothes. My feet were completely numb. As darkness fell, Jimmie and his brother and myself huddled standing in a corner of the trench, our coats like boards.

I started to fall asleep and fall down, continuing to do so until I decided to get out of the trench and try and have a walk to heat myself up a bit. I succeeded getting out with a help from my mates. When I wandered around I noticed many men lying on the ground out in the open sleeping anywhere.

I kept falling down and heard two stretcher-bearers shouting for help to carry a stretcher but I was not able to help. Later I stumbled down to where I heard singing and came on a scrub tree with sheets of waterproofs over it. I looked in and a voice shouted – 'Get to hell out of here!' This was Alan MacPherson from Rannoch who recognised me and sat me down on an ammunition box and put a blanket round me.

They had a jar of rum lifted from somewhere and these two provided me with succour when I most needed it with sheer nectar of tea laced with rum. They were singing Gaelic songs, defying the storm and forgetting their misery.

With the rum inside me I slept till morning when these two took me down to the doctor's dugout to report sick.

William Mowat, 1st Scottish Horse and Lovat Scouts

Word came through that the Turks were going to blow a mine over where the Herefords were so I had to organise two machine guns to go over and dig in at the rear of them to back them up. Now this regiment battalion were all new – composed of young laddies and they had been on their way to India when their ship was diverted to Suvla instead. Just boys! They had reported the Turks sapping but we didn't believe them. We went ahead and picked a good position as well as you could in the dark. The important thing was to keep the equipment and ammunition dry all the time which wasn't easy. We set up our two Vickers – there was another corporal and myself in charge of the two teams and we had to keep alert all night so we divided the watch between us and I was first on. I was just moving between the two positions when the great storm struck.

It was a cloudburst of terrible intensity, just a sheet of water came out of the night skies causing complete chaos and devastation in the lines. This was on the night of 26th November 1915.

Now nobody high up had the sense to realise that if a storm broke, then the water from the high up parts would come swirling down into the low parts where we were dug in and that's exactly what happened. The deluge filling up the trenches of the Herefords in the dark with a combination of mud, debris and water and some of the laddies that were down the dugouts perished. The rest of them had to come into the open and suffered terribly as there was not much shelter anywhere and now the storm had changed to snow and severe frost – a complete change from summer to winter overnight.

The Turks were in the same condition and in fact there were many enemy bodies washed into our lines although many of our lines had ceased to exist.

Still the water drained away in time, the day after the big storm, and there was no shooting at all from both sides going on on account of the terrible conditions, but I noticed an odd shot starting up about eleven in the morning – everybody got back into cover again by that time. In fact the ground was near solid with the frost.

Willie Calder, a schoolmate of mine, was in my machine gun crew – he was a very nice fellow. The day after the storm, Willie was changing his last pair of dry socks in our trench and shouts to me he was going over to the machine gun. This would expose him so I told him to stay where he was or he'd get shot, but I was too late – out over the top he went and got a bullet through the hip here. He got back in and I bandaged him up as best I could and sent word for the stretcher-bearers to come up. Two small mannies came up and had a look at big six-feet three-inch Willie and wondered how they were going to carry all that weight. At length Willie said, 'Look boys I'll just walk and you'll support me on each side for a bit!' Well he felt sorry for them, but it was no use, he had to go on to the stretcher eventually. He told me after in Egypt that they carried him short bits at a time and one chappie kept saying, 'He ain't arf eavy Earb … !' By the time he'd got down to the medical tent he was near frozen.
William MacGregor, Lovat Scouts

The withdrawal from Gallipoli was one of the finest moves ever accomplished in the War. Rifles were all set up to fire an occasional round while we evacuated the place on to ships at night. Then the ammunition which was stored in gulleys was seen to explode with delayed charges after the whole division was safely aboard.
Jock Murray, 1st King's Own Scottish Borderers

Fin we left there the troops fixed up rifles – Turkish eens that they first sue aff the barrels o, to fire a shot a piece an mak the Turks think that the lines were still manned. This wis deen wi fixin the rifles on tripods an riggin up the triggers wi a tow throwe a pulley. This tow was fixed on ti a can into which watter wis drappin an the weicht in time triggered aff a shot. Aa the time we slippit awa on ship back to Egypt.

Fin we got er, we cleaned wirsels up an got new uniforms and some reinforcements o new men and war allocated mair horses. We war then roaded for the Suez Canal to wite the expected attacks o the Turkish Army, bit we warna lang er fin

orders cam to move to the Western Front in France.
James Smith, Royal Field Artillery
sue aff sawed off

Those young boys of the Herefords suffered terribly – they had to leave their positions when they flooded and the frost had played havoc. Then of course the Turks were in the same boat.

When we were being evacuated from Gallipoli we came quietly down from our lines at night, with devices – like candles burning away as timers to set off rifles firing spasmodically. We were tired and I was limping badly with my gammy leg. There was a half mile to go and it was a difficult task making our way down the river beds now littered with dead Turks and debris washed down after the great storm. We were helped aboard lighters after waiting our turn and were hoisted on by the Royal Navy lads standing in the water up to their hips. I had to see that my machine gun crew loaded ours safely aboard too and we left the shores of Suvla Bay to the Turks along with stores and plenty of bully beef and tents. From the lighters we transferred on to a ship. Each received a tin of condensed milk which was very acceptable and we went into her shelter down decks and lay down and slept like logs.
William MacGregor, Lovat Scouts

We war at Gallipoli fae aboot the first day till the last – landin on the 25th April and leaving on the 9th January neist eer.
James Smith, Royal Field Artillery

The Somerset Yeomanry had been out long before us and had suffered many casualties and incidentally some of the gentry shooting tenants we let to, back home were among them – a (Major) Sir Charles Myles and another toff – I forget his name now – I was temporarily their stalker gamekeeper during the shooting season. We renewed our acquaintanceship under a different kind of fire.
William MacGregor, Lovat Scouts

I never had a bath all the time I was there for three months.

With the heat the lice multiplied and we tried to pick them off as best we could. One time we had off our shirts picking lice when the colonel came along and asked, 'Any good catches the day?'

The fleet couldn't fire on the Turkish front line as they would have endangered our own.
William Mowat, 1st Scottish Horse and Lovat Scouts

Egypt

I came back to Dunkeld depot after leave to find many of my friends back there after being wounded or sick from Suvla and we gradually got hardened up again with short marches and the like. One day when we were on parade, an officer came round and asked for volunteers to rejoin the regiment who were now in Egypt.

Bob Gordon who was in my section out in Gallipoli was standing beside me and I said, 'Come on Bob, lets go!' Bob replied, 'No – I'll never volunteer again!'

Bob was later sent back to the Black Watch and was killed on the Somme that year – 1916. Jimmie Wallace was killed with him, another Scottish Horse man. Bob was another man who said that he would not survive the War.

I was sent straight out with a draft in cold wintry weather at home and when we reached Devonport we noticed that spring had arrived with leaves on the trees and cows grazing in the fields. We embarked and the conditions on board were much more pleasant than the first time.

Disembarking at Alexandria, we were taken to a camp called Sidi Bishr where we stayed a few days before transferring to the regiment at Kantara on the Suez Canal.

It was great to be back with my friends. They all looked fit. My pals Geordie and Jimmy Fraser who had helped me in that flooded trench during the great storm at Suvla were in grand form. This was a grand place and we bathed in the Canal and sunbathed on its banks.

One day as part of a large force including the Indian Camel Corps and the Australian Light Horse, we marched up the desert to an oasis called Deodar, on the camel route from Palestine to Egypt. There we dug entrenchments on the higher sand dunes and kept watch day and night for the Turkish Army we heard advancing towards us at the rate of 20 miles the day.

The Australian Light Horse and English Yeomanry struck the Turks getting behind some of them and taking about 400 prisoners into our lines.

These Turks were very tired and hungry and thirsty. They drank the bitter water of the well and we gave them tins of bully. I saw one man using his teeth to open one tin. I also mind on the colonel watching a wizened old Turk sitting with his back to a palm tree with his feet wrapped in puttees and a woebegone look on his face. One of the Australians was standing beside our colonel and remarked, 'Isn't he a quaint old bastard Dad!' Suffice to say 'Dad' didn't reply.
William Mowat, 1st Scottish Horse and Lovat Scouts

I was part of the troop of guards who escorted the Turkish prisoners of war from the Suez to Kantara and that was the last time I was mounted on a horse in the War.

After that trip the whole regiment was marched to Kantara and put on a train for Cairo and later at Heliopolis outside the town. We enjoyed all the amenities of the historical city and although I saw the pyramids from a distance, I never got the chance to visit them.

We were given intense Infantry training and were informed that we were now converted as such – the whole three regiments of the Scottish Horse; we were to be named the 13th Black Watch. The Lovat Scouts who were with us were now the 10th Cameron Highlanders. Some of their stalkers who were predominately Gaelic speakers, had brought their own telescopes to war with them.

My troop was transferred to them so I now became the proud wearer of a Lovat Scout blue bonnet with the motive '*Je Suis Prest*' on it. On October 1916 we, along with my old regiment embarked at Alexandria and sailed for Salonica.

All our clothes were burned except what we had on before we left Gallipoli and we slept on the boat all the way to Egypt never landing at Mudros. We got new uniforms and equipment and were encamped at Sidi Bishr outside Alexandria. It was grand with plenty of sea bathing – a great comfort. My leg that was frostbitten was back to normal in no time; now the only casualties were caused by dysentery and malaria – none by the enemy. I even went a visit to the pyramids and climbed up one. A splendid experience.

I was an orderly and supervised the cleanliness of our quarters which were tents. I noticed a book lying among some junk – it was a paperback and when I picked it up, I read the title *Spies of the Kaiser* by William Lacoe, and when I opened it, the first words I read were '… On the Dava Moor … !' What a coincidence wasn't it – that was where I was born and brought up. My gad, I was into reading it right away.

William MacGregor, Lovat Scouts

Salonica

Then we boarded ship and sailed for Salonica. Landing there we marched up to the Struma Front, stopping at villages on the way. We had a lot of equipment on our back so it was hard going and we were glad to reach the Front on Kilometer 59.

William MacGregor, Lovat Scouts

Our troopship sailed into Malta for coal and there a gang of Maltese as black with coal like the ace of picks – trooped up and down planks with bags of coal to fill the bunkers. When we sailed from there some of us did guard duties and the chap I was on with said to me, 'What if we go down?' Of course we had our boat drill for the occasion which was to man the lifeboats 14 men to each, but what kind of chance had you with 1500 men aboard? The voyage the rest of the way to the shore of Salonica passed without incident and we disembarked next day.

Jim Burgess, 2nd Cameron Highlanders

18. A soldier, wearing the shorts of Mediterranean kit, possibly writing a letter home at a bombing post, F Sector, Salonica, Greece, in 1918. He is of the 12th Battalion Argyll and Sutherland Highlanders.

Image © National Museums Scotland

We landed at Salonica and went into tents at Summer Hill overlooking the town. During the night it rained and it came through the tents and soaked us and blankets through and through.

Next morning we started the long march to the Struma valley in stages of 10–15 kilometres each day with full pack, rifle and ammunition. The Scottish Horse led the way with their pipe band playing at times and we followed and our pipes did likewise to cheer us up.

Once we reached the river Struma we joined the 82nd Brigade of the 27th Division. They were all regular battalions – the 2nd Gloucesters, the 2nd Duke of Cornwall's Light Infantry and the 10th Hampshires [Hants]. This was the village of Nigrita and not a soul was to be seen except a priest in long robes and a tall hat.

After a week we were marched across the country to the front line facing the Bulgarians. Taking over from the Gloucesters we held a line of forts near a village called Kastraki. I was in a farmhouse from which the inhabitants had fled.

I remember there was not much happening except filthy weather which even flooded the bridges of the Struma. This was the place where I spent Christmas and New Year.

When spring came we made an attack and advanced through a wood toward the enemy and they begun to shell us at once. Our trench mortars replied to try and silence their machine guns who were now putting over a curtain of fire. We had casualties already, one shell wounding eight men on my right.

We dug in and were relieved that night by the Gloucesters – a far cry from Gallipoli where there was no relief.

Our attack was not a success – we had 120 casualties and next day our task was to take over from the Greeks who were guarding a ford, but when we arrived the Greeks had fled.

William Mowat, 1st Scottish Horse and Lovat Scouts

Donald Finlayson was a fine shot. He was a piper and came from Plockton. Before the War he was a keeper at Letham Estate beside Nairn and was a big chap. He was a crack at the broon hare shooting and was my head keeper at Letham. In the Scouts I was his corporal. Once he and a lad Jock MacKenzie from Whitewell of Aviemore were out on patrol and met in with some Bulgars. They shot two of them before the rest slipped away. Next day I was detailed to take out a burial party and bury them. A magpie had the eyes out of one. We busied ourselves digging and I noticed that they weren't as well-equipped as us.

Oh ay! Donald was a crack at the hares – if one popped up at 200 yards it was as good as dead. That's with the rifle of course.

The mosquitos were a pest – in fact there were two men detailed to spread creosote on to stagnant pools – that killed the fry.

…

The Bulgarians had the Germans 9.5 gun and you had to seek cover in a hurry if it got going.

They gave us a hellava doing up one Sunday morning when we were at our porrage. There was more sand than meal amang them that morning.

When summer came we left the plains and occupied the hills. We made a raid on a village in the dark and it was going quite well when the whizz bangs got in amongst us and we went to ground. We infiltrated later round the back of them and when daylight came we attacked the village and about 100 Bulgars surrendered. Coming back from there we were pinned down when they began to shell us with 9.5s. I remember the Glenurquhart boys took shelter in a hollow about 50 yards from where I lay. A shell landed in amongst them and got five of them. I remember there was a wee chappie with them – and it's remarkable when things were serious, how the comical side comes to the fore. 'Wee Mannie' we called him – he had no neck – a wee short neck, like this. He had pointed lugs and was comical to look at. Well he came out of there like a shot, reminding me of a rabbit bolting from a ferret in a hole.

Two of the killed had only joined the day before as reinforcements. They were number five platoon I remember fine. Also many of our prisoners were casualties by this time.

While we were pinned down there, I noticed a large cloud gathering in the hills and moving our way and if it did the rain behind it would provide cover for

our retreat the long way back up the valley. It did, that's what happened! It was just like the hymn – *I to the hills will lift mine eyes!*
William MacGregor, Lovat Scouts

It was there in that village of Salma that we captured the Bulgars' fancy lady. Dr Fraser Lee got her out of our road quick. As a matter of fact he was my doctor in civil life and was in partnership with Dr Cruikshank at Nairn. He attended my Aunt Margaret when she was ill too.
William MacGregor, Lovat Scouts and William Mowat, 1st Scottish Horse and Lovat Scouts in conversation

Brigade Headquarters came to the conclusion that the Lovat Scouts were giving valuable information of enemy movements – well they composed of many stalkers and the like from the Highlands, so our commander, Colonel Bailie, was asked to start a scouting school to train the other brigade troops in the art of observation. These were the 2nd Gloucesters, 10th Hants and the Duke of Cornwall's Light Infantry. Of course spying out the enemy was a pastime with our lads – even any time we were on the march and stopped by the wayside – out would come their telescopes (which were their own), and they would scan the horizons. So this was a tribute to the valuable information devolving from this asset.

In this foreign country, there were many interesting facets to study in the mountain villages which had been evacuated in some haste. At the centre was a large farm with the workers' houses clustered around it with another solid-looking one more prominent than the rest. Within this conglomerate of buildings was a church which was of course the principal building in each village. I always took a special interest and visited as many of them as I could. On the inside walls were painted pictures of saints and biblical scenes. One picture I shall never forget was painted on the gable of one, showing hell as a fiery furnace with poor sinners being forked into the flames by devils – as a vivid warning to all as they entered the door.

There were many small skirmishes all that summer but towards the autumn we were involved in fairly large engagement. Our brigade planned to capture three villages which formed a triangle of land held by the Bulgarians. One of them, called Salma, we had evacuated in early summer to get clear of the mosquitos and it was the furthest away village of the three objectives.

Our Scouts noticed a line of outposts and redoubts in front of Salma about 300 yards apart and it was planned that we would move to the attack between these. The 2nd Gloucesters and 10th Hants were to do the same on their fronts and meet up with us behind Salma about 5am.

We moved out at sunset with each man carrying a number of Mills bombs and 100 rounds of ammunition. No mess tins or trenching tools were taken or such, that would make a noise. As we approached their lines we heard firing break out on our left. At this time we were between their outposts and we lay there and waited for the enemy firing to die down. This was the rest of the brigade troops being spotted and fired upon.

When we continued to advance again we immediately encountered a Bulgar patrol. The vegetation was fairly high and in the darkness they could not really make out where we were. We slipped by them while they continued firing to their front and as we approached Salma, our objective – dawn was beginning to break and while we were crossing a road behind the village, a Bulgar came running towards us shouting. We took him prisoner when he came near – he thought we were reinforcements of their own men coming to their assistance. He got a shock and surrendered at once. All this time a battle was developing on quite a scale away on the side of the rest of the brigade attack. We attacked and were shouted a challenge by the Bulgarians. Given no answer they opened up with a machine gun and I saw the bullets hitting the ground in front of us until someone threw a grenade and the resulting burst put an end to that as it ceased firing.

We went right through the village from the rear and attacked their entrenchments on the other side. We lobbed bombs into their trenches and they immediately surrendered. As we collected the prisoners into a group their own people in the entrenchments further up started shelling us and caused shrapnel casualties among their own men and ours.

...

The object of our raid on Salma was to take prisoners only but not to hold the position so we took 200 prisoners back to our own lines and our casualties too – they were 30 men. Coming through our wire we were greeted by our padre and Colonel Bailie, our commander, who commented, 'Well done, there is a double issue of rum awaiting you!' We had been on the move since early evening of the previous day and it was now midday. It was a relief to be back in our own lines again with a meal all ready and a welcome tot of rum which went down well after the excitement.

The Gloucesters and the Hants attacks had been pinned down and we – the non-professionals – came out with great credit; many of our officers and men getting decorated for their part in the affair, the only successful attack of the brigade.

William Mowat, 1st Scottish Horse and Lovat Scouts

When we landed on the shores of Salonica we were hurried up the country to our various regiments. I joined the 2nd Cameron Highlanders and it wasn't long before I was out on patrol among the scrub to search out the enemy. There a lad Fletcher got a bullet through the elbow. I remember later I assisted him to a first-aid post to get it seen to. The nurses put him on a table and cut away his clothes to get at the wound.

On the floor was the body of an officer who had died of his wounds. He was a Captain Anderton and he came from Aberdeen. I later helped with his burial.

I never met in with the Scottish Horse while I was there. I later went to machine gun section and by jove you had to plug your ears when you fired on the tripod. The weapon got red hot in a short while.

…

At Salonica the storks nested on the lums and their beaks clattered like a machine gun all the time.

The South Wales Borderers were the first troops to enter Sofia.

Jim Burgess, 2nd Cameron Highlanders

8

Mesopotamia 1916–18

The heat in Mesopotamia wis ony thing up to 100 degrees in the shade so it took a lang time afore we got acclimatised. I aye mind takin the leadin gun team across the Tigris on a brig o pontoons that the Indian Sappers hid laid. I thocht the hale lot os – guns, horses and aa, were gan to sink to the kingdom come. The pontoons aa sank alow the watter a bit, bit I jist kept goin. To show fear wid hae caused a hellava [.........]. I jist keepit the beasts gan as though I wis at the ploo back hame. The ither gun teams followed suit. This wis a mile aneth Baghdad.

There, we hid the Bengal Lancers, the Australian Light Horse and the Gurkhas.

Fin the Australian Light Horse attacked they got slaughtered by the Turkish machine guns. Our battery then put over a barrage wi shells that we fused to burst 20 feet abeen the Turks' heeds. This HE (High Explosive) shells destroyed their machine gunners to a man – you shid hiv seen the mess.

George Barclay, Royal Field Artillery

We gid awa overseas fae Southampton on an ald boat *Briton*. A richt ald thing infested wi rats. The mait wisna that bad though. We turned at Gibraltar and sailed throue the Mediterranean and headed for the shores o the Dardanelles, bit jist within oors of docking there we were aboot turned and sailed instead for the Suez Canal. Coaling at Port Said we continued doon the canal eventually landin up at Mesopotamia on the Red Sea.

We gid up the Persian Gulf ti Baghdad. I thocht the conditions wis terrible fit wi the flees an the heat. We jist hid ti march on the road an mony a een hid to fa oot, although a lot of supplies war transported wi barges up the river Tigris. Noo it wis sax hunner mile trek fae Basra ti Baghdad an there wis a hell o a lot o troops involved – Gurkhas, The Black Watch and the Seaforth Highlanders war wi us tee and we war the relieving force on wir wy ti Kut far General Townshend's Army wis surrounded by the Turks.

...

We heeded for the relief o General Townsend's Army up at Kut bit the monsoons cam on an man – then we niver got meeved ata. It flooded aa damned thing an we jist cam ti a stop.

Fit happened up at Kut wis that Townsend depenned on gettin his supplies maistly fae the river barges fae the sooth bit then the floods strak – the Turks cam roon this bend in the river ti the sooth an trappit them – Townsend couldna get oot an wi aa that floodin we couldna meeve forrit ti relieve them. Although we depenned mair on mule transportation for meevin wir equipment – the grun wis jist a goorhole and weet an dubs. Oh, na! we couldna brak throue at aa. Weel, Townsend held oot for 83 days or so. Lack o supplies – munitions an mait. They got watter aa richt – oot o the Tigris. Na – they hid ti surrender in the ine.

Oor water wisna great, we got it oot o tanks aa chlorinated an it wis richt coorse. Ye wisna supposed ti drink the watter oot o the river untreated.

Harry Nicoll, Royal Engineers

goorhole mudhole

9

Italy 1917–18

I niver saa a shot fired in France again. The hale division mustered and were entrained for the sooth o France and embarked at Marseilles for Italy (in October 1917).

Fin we landed there we were sent richt into the mountains o the north through the bonniest country that iver you did see; it was like a great holiday to us that hid been eesed to naething bit weet and dubs o Flanders.

…

Fin we finally got up to the Front at the river Piave, the Austrians were dug in on the north side and us in the sooth. We noticed them oot sunning themsels and even dookin in the river. This wis afa funny like efter fit we were eesed tull in France; this wis mair like hudding holidays. Oor T battery were aye wi us and they couldna resist the temptation; they opened up and I'll bet gid them a gie scare. That put a stop to that caper.

…

A lad Jock Aitken wis we me in Italy ana. He cam fae Banff; I aye thocht I wid rin in to him efter the War bit niver did.

Fin we meeved up to wir positions in the mountains it took fae sax in the morning to sax at nicht to get there – it was richt hard wark. Fin the Germans broke through in France in 1918, there wis fower o oor divisions in Italy. Twa hid to be rushed back at eence. I heard that they jist picket cards and the result depenned on the eens that got the twa hichest cards bein sent back.
Jimmy Milne, 2nd Gordon Highlanders

10

Battle of Loos

At Loos, I mind Colonel MacQueen sayin, 'Come on men – it's hard!' Oor fire-step wis eicht-feet deep. When the whistle blew – the first lad up the ledder wis aye mintin and mintin and the divots fleein fae the heed o the ladder; this wis machine gun bullets. The first sax men up the ledder to ging ower the top, fell back deed. I wis neist, and my tunic and kilt were jist riddled.

The new lads in oor company widna charge at Loos and we were left up in the air and hid to stop. We ran a great dead and folk were bein shot doon aawy and hingin on the German barbit weer. I flappet and a lad fell on my legs. Fin I turned roon I saa his heed wis split richt open and his brains were aa ower my feet.

We took the German guns aa richt at Hussey and dug wirsels in, bit then hid to come oot again at night. We got a damned good hidin! We gid in wi 600, and 89 answered the roll call neist day. Of coorse some o them come back later on – haein got mixed up wi idder lots. We took the guns aa the same.

Jimmy Reid, 6th Gordon Highlanders

mintin attempting

We assembled for the Battle of Loos – a village in a mining area. This was in September 1915. Our objective was a place called Hulluch. We had a lot more Artillery by this time, and a large amount of gas as supplied to release on the Germans.

The gas was released in the night preceding our attack but the wind changed and blew it back to our lines, making it imperative that we wore masks. These masks were primitive affairs from what we received later on, and were just a face mask and a tube from it into a filter.

The 15th and the 47th Divisions went right through Loos and beyond it. We were held up by terrible fire in front of us at Hulluch. Holding on to the ground we did gain; nightfall came and there was no sign of the relieving divisions coming up as promised. In fact it was 48 hours before they made their appearance and without their Artillery; it was still lying at the docks. This was the 21st and 22nd Divisions. We pulled back from the ever-mounting counter-attacks as it became impossible to hold out any longer.

We saw the Germans moving about in Hulluch but it was impossible to take it. The lads of the 15th Division were reputed to have got furthest forward with

Dundee's 4th having reached beyond the rest. All had to pull back in the end.

Up to then we wore the Glengarry. After Loos we were issued with Balmorals.

Everybody were growing moustaches and beards; just before Loos we were ordered to shave clean and get our hair cut to the bone. This was from the surgeon, Major General Strickland.

It was the Germans that wore the tin helmet at first, followed by the French and then us. There was no lining or anything at first, until they issued a rubber ring to rest against the head. Finally there came a more comfortable issue of a padded fitting.

Frank MacFarlane MM and Medal Militaire, 1st Black Watch

At Loos, there wis an afa storm o thunner and lichtnin the nicht afore.
Norrie Cruikshank, 6th Gordon Highlanders

There we were in support only at the Battle of Festubert.

At the Battle of Loos we were only in reserve again.
Wullie Gavin, 5th Gordon Highlanders

19. Letter sent by Corporal George Buchanan of the 8th Seaforth Highlanders to his sister, dated 4 September 1915. He was killed in action at the Battle of Loos three weeks later.

Image © National Museums Scotland

11

Battle of the Somme:
High Wood and Beaumont-Hamel

We marched to the Battle of the Somme from far away, it took days. It was dark when we got there but still away back from the actual front line. The shelling from both sides went on non-stop. I tethered my horses in what I thought was a safe looking place – among the remains of a copse – and fed and watered them, after which we lay down and slept, dog tired as usual.

Early in the morning a terrible salvo caught them. It came crashing down and killed the most. What was left were injured so badly, that they had to be destroyed – what an awful sight, some with their bellies hanging out.

A. Smeaton MM, 5th Black Watch

20. Soldiers washing at the edge of a flooded field in the Somme. The mud up to the thighs on their trousers shows how wet the conditions were in the trenches.

Reproduced by permission of the National Library of Scotland

21. Feeding the troops on the Western Front, Ancre. In the background men are
lining up for their ration, while in the foreground others are sitting or standing
and eating soup or stew from bowls and tins

Reproduced by permission of the National Library of Scotland

There was a rumour than an officer had led his men into battle the first day of the
Somme carrying a riding crop and supplying footballs for his men to kick in front
of them. If that's true – then he was a bloody idiot! That's all I can say; he knew
nothing about warfare if that was the case.

Frank MacFarlane MM and Medal Militaire, 1st Black Watch

When we marched to jine the Battle o the Somme, it took 21 days. We fell oot for
ten meenits ivery oor and stopp'ed aa nicht of coorse, sleepin jist far we could. The
cookhoose bilers keep'it hottern aa the time aye ready to dish oot the stew fin the
time cam, and by God we war aye ready I can tell ye. The bilers were like the tar
eens the roadmen kept; ye ken fine.

Weel that wis the warst thing that they iver did to us: oor feet niver coured it
for a gweed file I can tell ye.

Alec MacHardy MM, 7th Gordon Highlanders

I wis on the Lewis gun team wi a lad Logie Duncan. We war jist plunket wi
ammunition awa oot in front and telt to dee wir stuff, they daared us to come oot
o there or they wid sheet us. Logie wis a gie cute lad and aye managed to acquire
rum. He wis a helluva lad and didna care a damn for naething.

I mind ae time the Germans attacket, there wis naethin bit blue uniforms as

far as yer ee could see: it wis jist like a blue sky. Oor gun got ass het we could hardly
hud her. The Germans were hinging on the weer away.

Norrie Cruikshank, 6th Gordon Highlanders

We marched to the Battle of the Somme from a long way off; just camping by the
wayside at night. A lot fell out with bad feet. The last stretch was done by buses.
We went off the buses and straight into the attack at High Wood in the early
morning. The corn was still standing and the Gerry wire was still intact. We got
up the length of the Gerry wire and our wire cutters got busy. The casualties were
so bad that we had to stop and go to ground.

Robert More MM, 4th Seaforth Highlanders

We wis at Arras fin the Battle of Somme started. Three wicks efter, we were
ordered there. It was a fower-day march bit we were telt to dee it in three. That we
did and then wis stopped and hid to wite anither three days at a place caad
Dernancourt. We wis in kent grun doon there was we hid been afore. We then
proceeded into action by Albert far the Virgin Mary hung upside doon, ye niver
saa sic a desolate scene; what a bloody place it wis!

At nicht there wis naething bit the countryside lichted up aa roon; and the
noise – fit wi oor side firin aa the time and the Germans huddin them in tee. We
were dug in at the side o a cemetery and I noticed a colonel and an adjutant o the
Gordon Highlanders hid been beeried there.

John Russel, Royal Field Artillery

kent grun known ground

I jined up in early 1916 and trained at Rippon Camp; gang stracht oot ti the 5th
Gordon Highlanders.

In July we marched a lang wy ti jine the Battle o the Somme, fallin oot ivery
ten meenits and lyin in bivvies at nicht.

The 5th war aa lads fae Buchan – Maud, Ellon, the Broch and so on: gran
stoot cheils the maist o them.

Tom Rearie, 5th Gordon Highlanders

the Broch Fraserburgh

When we came back from Gallipoli we landed off the boat at Marseilles. From
there by train to the Western Front. Coming off the train, we marched for days to
the trenches, so much every day, falling out every hour for a rest. That's one thing
– I had a good pair of feet – they stood up well.

Jock Murray, 1st King's Own Scottish Borderers

The hale 29th Division embarked and sailed for Marseilles an war meeved by train
to Flanders (from Egypt).

We still had wir 18-pounders wi us to fit wis noo added some 4.5 howitzers, they war a fair weicht although I hidna neathing to dee wi them.

There wis plenty adee trainin aa wir new men at first bit then cam the day fin we meeved up and dug wirsels into position on the Somme Front an commenced shellin the German line on 26th June – that wis 1916. This wis in support o the intended attack o wir ain division – the 29th, at a place caaed Beaumont-Hamel, a German fort o great strength.

I hid seen an afa lot o preparation goin on an an afa lot o troops witing the word go, so I kent this wis something big aa-richt. The Artillery barrage that oor battery wis pairt o, wis something infernal in intensity and continued and continued day an nicht an ye wid hae thocht that naebody could live throwe er – bit by certie they did: at twa in the mornin o 1st July, oot in front o us – the Newfoundland Regiment 1000-strong, went over the top an as they advanced ower No Man's Land, the Gerry machine guns jist mowed them doon. Wir bombardment for the previous feoy days hid deen nae gweed. The Gerries hid great dugoots weel below grun that wir shells couldna mark an fin we stoppit shellin they jist cam richt oot an started firin. The gallant Newfoundlanders niver got up the length o their lines ata, an war absolutely slaughtered. The rest o wir divisional troops got the same dose – aa the best men tee.

I hid some nerra squeaks on the Somme – een wis fin I wis ordered to bring the gun I wis in charge o, inti action ae nicht. This we did an started firin. I left Sergeant Styles in charge and gid awa to dee something else an aa at eence a Gerry shell laaned and he wis killed, his brains were aa ower my coat that I hid teen aff an left er.

Then I wis strack wi shrapnel masel on September by the burst o a 5.9. Ye didna hear them comin oh na – that wis ae thing aboot them. I got a bit the size o yer thoomb an it did a hellava damage to the sma o my back an I wis cairried doon to a dressin station. The wounded that the doctor thocht wid hae a chance war meeved oot as seen as they were attended till, bit I wis left er to dee I suppose. Weel I lay there and tholed it for a feoy days till he took another look at me an decided I micht hae some chance efter aa: so he got me roaded for this country. That wis a terrible journey mind ye, I couldna mind onything aboot it – I wis that ill, bit I eventually feenished up in a hospital in Eastbourne far I wis successfully operated on and that wis a bad wound.

I mind fin the days I spent in that tent on the Somme – they nae seener war cairryin in casualties than they had ti cairry the maist o them oot again deed.

It wis a funny thing min aboot luck an superstition – I wis aye in 13th Battery an wis born on a 13th day in aa, an niver hid as muckle as a scrat till I wis temporarily sent ower to help the 26th Battery as they hid lost aa their senior NCOs an it wis at that time I wis wounded. Mind ye the shellin we got on the Somme was something atrocious compared wi fit we got at Gallipoli.

James Smith, Royal Field Artillery

22. A laughing young soldier has clearly just washed his hair with the muddy water from a puddle that has collected in the bottom of a shell hole.

Reproduced by permission of the National Library of Scotland

Tashie Young[19] wis a great pal o mine. At High Wood we got up to the German weer bit hid to tak shelter in shell holes an the like as there wis nae wy throwe. Weel I began to get shelled wi wir ain folk. Tashie wis killed we een – I pickit up bits of the 18-punner that did it. They jist kept comin ower for a file and there wis nae wy wi could stop them as the field telephones war in bits. There wis nae easy wy back either as we were pinned doon by the Gerries.

Tashie's folk had a sma placie aside Inverurie somewy.

Jimmy Reid, 6th Gordon Highlanders

On the 1st July, it started. We were at Givenchy Front, then doing the usual grind of trench warfare. We could hear the terrible noise of battle from where we were lying.

Suddenly, on the 3rd, we were ordered to move. So we packed up and marched behind the lines and entrained for Arras. When we got off we were assembled and started on the march to the Battle of the Somme. This was a four-day stint via the Albert with the Virgin Mary hanging from the Cathedral.[20]

We landed into the front line at a place called Contalmaison. The line was static and the reason was German fortifications of great strength. We were sent in against one and took Contalmaison Villa; going over the top at 6am behind a creeping barrage which finally concentrated on the Villa itself. The Villa was on a hillock and whoever held it commanded a view of the whole valley.

I remember when going over seeing the dead of both sides lying four-feet deep in places from the previous few day's fighting.

We took the Villa anyway but lost a lot of men doing it.

Frank MacFarlane MM and Medal Militaire, 1st Black Watch

At the Somme I saa gun crews o anither lot desert their guns fin they took a German barrage. This wis a thing we would never dee.

I wis eence directed by our commander to take up a load o shells to a battery on the Somme. This I did and came under severe shellfire as I took my horse team in as fast as I could. I reached the battery all right and got off my load; then as I was preparing to move back again, a young officer ordered me to lowse aff and yoke into the guns to assist in moving them.

I refused and said that I had been told to return immediately by my officer.

He then charged me wi refusing to carry out an order and I had to give my name and number. He said that this was open arrest and that I would be court-martialled later.

When I got back, I told my officer who gid fair mad wi rage and said, 'Just you leave this to me!' I niver heard another cheep.

Alec Pratt MM, Royal Horse Artillery

We war up at High Wood on the Somme and it wisna muckle o a wid be ony means. We got up to the Gerry line bit could dee naething weet. They did tac it in the ine bit it wisna us, na fegs!

Before we went in at High Wood on the Somme, I mind on a horse team o Artillery pullin a gun comin doon the howe. Ae lad wis sittin on the drivers seat wi the rines in his han. The idder lad wis sittin on the back o the leadin horse. They were chargin doon the road which wis takkin the batterin fae the Gerry shellfire. We were lying awa up the brae a bit witin to ging it to the attack in the early mornin.

'Hold tight, Tommy!' I heard een o them say. Aa at eence a beast fell to the grun of the six-horse team and wi that, the twa lads jumped aff leavin the peer beasts gan gallopin doon the howe, pullin the een on the grun screamin oot ot.

Then efter aat cam a watter cairt wi a twa horse team withoot a driver, cam fleein through the barrage, bit aa na; they were baith strack and fell doon!

We attacked and gid richt up to their trenches and fun the weer aa hale. We jist hid to hide. Somebody tried to telephone back but the lines were aa broken wi shellfire.

Jimmy Reid, 6th Gordon Highlanders

na fegs no fear

Fin we attacked at High Wood on the Somme, the German weer wis aa hale. We were losin an afa men. I flapp'et and keepit my heed doon. There wis another lad at my side and he rase up to get a pirk at them. I says tull him, 'Dinna dee that – keep yir heed doon in to the grun.' Na na! he rase up and shot aff a roon, but nae mair, that wis him feenished.

Noo efter the War, I wis deein a bit o coortin o the lassie thats noo my wife. Ae time she showed me the photograph o her brither that wis killed in the War. I says, 'I ken far aboot this lad wis killed – he wis lyin aside me at High Wood'.

John Rennie, 5th Gordon Highlanders

weer wis aa hale wire was all whole, *pirk* shot

At High Wood we gid ower the top and gid half a mile under fire to the German trenches, we come up against barbed weer unbroken and hid to stop. There wis nae wy through and the casualties were that heavy that we had to tac shelter in shell holes.

There wis five os in the een that I wis in, including the sergeant who cam fae Netherbrae. Aa at eence he rase up and said, 'Come on lads, wee'l hae to dee something'. He fell richt back deed aside me at eence.

We lay there till dark and creepit back only to be ordered oot to get in the wounded. Fin we did that there wis mair casualties fae gunfire.

Fin I attended the graveyairds for the council I can still mind fin looking at the memorial steens, on the lads that wis killed that day and the sergeant tee.

It wis at the Somme, that I mind a sergeant fae the 2nd Gordon Highlanders cam to us lookin for reinforcements. He started to greet and told us that the 2nd had already nearly lost aa their men.

Fin we later went in at Beaumont-Hamel in November, it was a roaring success. We took aa wir objectives although I wis wounded and teen awa. I mind it wis an afa misty day.

Sandy Simpson, 5th Gordon Highlanders

When we went over at High Wood, the corn was still standing with blue and red poppies at their best. I mind fine – the platoon officer looking at his watch before going over.

Alec Robertson, 5th Gordon Highlanders

The Gerry wire at High Wood wisna touched and mony een got hung up trying to get throut. We couldna get back either as we war pinned doon. A colossal loss – murder! I forget fu mony.

Oor pipers a filie war used as runners bit they got afa casualties an war pulled oot in the ine.

Tom Rearie, 5th Gordon Highlanders

At High Wood our shelling didn't break the German wire. It was hopeless. There were three woods I remember more than any other – High Wood, Deville Wood and Matz Wood, because they were all heavily involved. I saw the South African Scots out there too.

Bert Gow, Royal Field Artillery

I wis putting to the 2nd Gordon Highlanders wi a lot mair, tull they got reinforced fae hame. This wis at the Somme. Bit I got back to my ain crowdie then.

Alec Nicol, 7th Gordon Highlanders

Afore we gid in at High Wood we were lyin in a howe aside a wid jist ristin; witin wir turn. We were in battle order wi packs on; jist sittin there in the early mornin.

Aa at eence a lad shouted fae farrer up the hill, that the Gerry shells this pairt we were lyin in every 20 meenits and their barrage wis due ony time. We didna need nae second biddin I can tell ye, bit scised awa up the hill oot o the road. We were jist barely oot o there fin the HL (Haniel Luege) shells cam crashin doon. Fin we were watchin the shellin there wis a horse team o sax beasts pullin a wagon cam fleein through the barrage withoot a driver. Een o the peer beasts fell doon and the ithers cam gallopin by doon the howe oot o sicht o us pullin the peer horse on the grun screamin oot ot.

This was the 30th July 1916, and we were finally sent in to the attack aboot sax in the morning. There wis a gie lang road to ging and we lost an afa lads on the wy up.

I got richt up to the German front line trenches and fun the barbet weer aa hale. It wis that thick I could hardly see through it. I tried to sheet the Germans in their trench ahin the weer bit couldna see them for the weer. I flapped into a hole and a lang time efter the order wis passed to retire. Noo that wis easier said than deen. I mean try creapin back wi a kilt on, keeping yer heed doon pushin yersel back aa the wy tryin to get ony cover that wis goin. Finally I got back ahin a corn ruck.

Albert Connon, 5th Gordon Highlanders

We focht at High Wood. Maist o the trees were aye there. I wis gie feart at first though I seen got eesed weet.

…

I mind three Gerries tried to get me – bit that didna; I shot them deed first.

William Angus, 2nd Gordon Highlanders

What a lot o lads gid doon at wir first attack on the Somme. The barbet weer wis niver broken in front o their lines (High Wood). I seen learned to dodge fae shell hole to shell hole and richt smert aboot it tee. Aa it ye heard wis 'zip … zip' o the bullets ivery time ye made a dive fort.

Wullie Gavin, 5th Gordon Highlanders

The nicht afore the attack at Beaumont-Hamel we were in Mailly Wood; when up cam a runner fa speired at my sergeant – Billy Hay, The Sooter – if he wid look oot a lad to accompany him to headquarters. The Sooter said, 'Tak onybody ye wint!' I heard him say, 'I'll tak Connon'. Fin we cam back in the morning the battalion were aa ower the top. We set aff efter them. The day wis afa misty and there wis an afa lot o shell smoke aboot as weel.

Ower we gid tull we heard sheetin in front o us and we lay doon to see fit wis gan on. Fin the mist cleared a bit, we saa a crood o lads in a trench firin, bit nae oor wy. The runner fa wis in charge said, 'Lat's work oor wy up a bittie and see fits happenin. We'll gang awa ower to the left – there's plenty o room there'.

By diving fae shell hole to shell hole, we cam to within 20 yairds o them. The runner looket oot and suddenly turns to me and whispers, 'Ging back. It's the Germans!' We managed to dook back into anither shell hole in the mist and lay there. Aa at eence an officer wi a machine gun crew o fower men flapper mair or less doon on tap o us. There wis only room for the twa os afore so ye ken the jam up we wis in noo that there wis seven. The sergeant said, 'Right, lets set up the gun!' A gunner replied, 'Nae bloody eese settin up wir gun here – we'll get bombed to hell!' We were in range o Mills bombs. Suddenly the Gerries cam ower at a rush ats oot o their trench – aboot atween 50 or 60 o them, and there wis naething else fort bit hud up wir hands and surrender; we could dee naething against a crood like that.

We laand up in a big dugoot that immense, that there wis a railway line rinnin up the middle ot awa into the distance, as weel as electric. This was us captured and we lay there for twa oors tull we noticed Gerry in a fair pirr aboot something. The German officer surrendered to oor officer; handin ower his revolver an his men aa piled their rifles. We were noo in charge: the tables had turned. Aa at eence we heard a lad bawlin doon the stairs at's and we hid to be bloody smart aboot gan up itherwise they wid o bombed us. This wis some o the Black Watch and we jist made it in time I can tell ye – they hid the Mills bombs aa ready to throw.

I mind fin I got ootside I saa a Gerry rinnin ower a ridge hine awa. I took a pirk at him, bit missed. Of coorse I didna ken the Gerry rifle. Then I made for Y Ravine far I met wi my ain sergeant – Sooter Hay. I'll niver forget ae casualty bein cairried back on a stretcher, he wis huddin a cigar in his moo, that wis the biggest een I hid ever seen in my life – puffin awa fair contented. That hid cam oot o the Gerry officers' stores.

Albert Connon, 5th Gordon Highlanders

pirr fit of anger/panic

The bodies of the enemy and our own people had been lying out in open for a day or two and were distended 'so' high.

This was at Trônes Wood, which wasn't a large wood by any means but it had been the scene of heavy fighting and had changed hands five times.

I was out with the colonel one time and he said, 'Napier isn't this the horrors of war?'

I replied, 'It isn't a very pleasant sight Sir!'

'No, it's a sight we'll remember to the end of our days!'

…

We had two battalions of the Bantams in our division and they put up a great show at Trônes Wood at the Battle of the Somme. They got so badly mauled that they were never used again but only for guard duties at ammunition dumps and such like.

…

When we left the Somme and marched to Arras, it was like going into heaven out of hell. Even there the doors and windows rattled with the sound of battle going on at the Somme.

Albert Napier MM, Royal Field Artillery ('Taggart's Own')

Bit Beaumont-Hamel wis a success. We war in reserve and war richt pleased to see the prisoners comin back, aye comin back. I wis newsin awa to them nae bather – I fun them aa richt ye ken!

Alec Nicol, 7th Gordon Highlanders

Beaumont-Hamel was rainy and misty, but I was too excited to notice. We just went up and over and got on well. The Gerries came out of their trenches and dug-outs with their hands up and surrendered. I remember one big fat fellow that rase up in front of me with his hands in the air say, 'Don't shoot – I am from Inverness too!'

Robert More MM, 4th Seaforth Highlanders

We war getting ready to attack Beaumont-Hamel and Major Milne cam up on horseback. He shouts – 'Heh you!' and pints at me. I thocht, 'Holy God fit hiv I deen wrang noo!' Some o the lads said, 'They're gang to sheet ye min!'

Onywy ower I gangs and salutes. Major Milne says to me, 'MacHardy, you've been a considerable time out here and have seen quite a lot of action. Have you got a pencil by any chance?' I says, 'A pencil – faar wid I get a pencil?' At that the adjutant produced a blue een; so Major Milne niver cam aff his horse, bit jist raxed ower and drew three stripes on my airm. 'Now,' he says, 'from now on you are the sergeant of this platoon!'

Noo I niver really took this cairry on seriously and a wick efter we hid to parade and the sergeant major picked me as 'right marker'. Up comes Major Milne on horse back to tak the inspection. Aa at eence he spotted me and wheeled his horse aboot and shouts at me – 'MacHardy what are you doing in the ranks?' I says 'Marker Sir!' He says, 'Marker my arse!' He then cries on the sergeant major to take me down to the tailors and wait until I had my sergeant's stripes sewn on. He then says to me, 'I've never had a man refuse an order before!'

The sergeant major, I kent him fine – he belanged to Insch – speired fit happened at me; so I telt him. He hid a gweed lach and said, 'Michty it's a winner ye wisna shot for deein aat!' Weel, weel I wis jist a loon ye ken!

I got detailed to take Y Ravine wi my company at Beaumont-Hamel. It was fu o barbed weer and I'll easy tell ye this – the kilt wis nae eese gan though aat. We took it aa the same!

…

An afa place wis Beaumont-Hamel. Fut a stuff we captured: fin we got in amang their reserve lines there wis even weemin in their dugoots – ye widna believed!
Alec MacHardy MM, 7th Gordon Highlanders

raxed reached

At Beaumont-Hamel oor company advanced across a great screed o grun to get to the Gerry line. I think it wis an afa misty mornin. By the time we were up there, the prisoners were streaming back tulls in bunches wi their hands up.

Oor company escaped nae sae bad. We didna dee muckle to tak the prisoners they were comin oot o their trenches aawy, flingin awa their rifles. I wis detailed wi a feoy mair to tak them back, bit on wir wy a Gerry sniper started shottin ats fae a shell hole. He shot doon a feoy o oor men afore they got him and they didna tac him prisoner either – na, no, he got a hellava death; they jist battered him wi rifle butts. Weel it wis his duty to gie himself up wisn't it? It took a filie to get him aa the same; aa that we hid to ging on wis a flash fae a gun – nae sae easy to see in a misty day wi sic a racket gan on.

The Gerry dugoots there were mair superior to wir ain; they were toppers and hid real beds and aathing in them.
Wullie Gavin, 5th Gordon Highlanders

Beaumont-Hamel wis soon like a cairt coupin steens aa the time – ye couldna traivel for the dubs; ye couldna pit ae fit by the ither for the clort.
Jimmy Reid, 6th Gordon Highlanders

clort mud

Our battalion joined the Somme Front in April 1916 before the battle and were involved from the start.
Jock Murray, 1st King's Own Scottish Borderers

We eensed to gang oot afore a big doo and cut the barbed wire aa ready to ging ower the top in the morning. The Germans wid ken fine and hae their machine guns trained on the gaps at the first sign.
Alec Nicol, 7th Gordon Highlanders

Before we went over 3000 shells passed over our heads in one and a half hours.

When I was wounded I came back through an Irish battalion. There were many of them had shell shock and were standing there shaking. Our officers we had by then didn't know much about warfare. They trained us for the Battle of the Somme in a field doing rifle drill and marching to and fro, and nothing about the layout of the German front line. When we went over the top, one of our officers walked in front of us with a walking stick and it wasn't long before he was killed. He was trying to do the old Scottish laird bit!

Jock Murray, 1st King's Own Scottish Borderers

Our lads got cute before an attack on the German lines: they trenched away into No Man's Land during the night as far as they could and lay out in front of the wire. The reason was that the Gerry machine guns were fixed on our trench parapet all the time, ready to bring down their fire at the first hint of trouble.

We went over at Beaumont-Hamel and took their lines. What a booty we found; food and hams and the like. Their dugouts were immense.

A. Smeaton MM, 5th Black Watch

23. Troops crossing the Scarpe, Arras, France. The bridge appears to be partly broken and they are crossing on planks across to the near bank. A flat-bottomed punt in the foreground may be being put in position to form part of a pontoon bridge.

Reproduced by permission of the National Library of Scotland

Fut a job it wis to get up yon hill on the Somme: wi machine gun fire and barbit weer; my heavens! It wis like gan in tulla fire. Aye, Lord be here! We took a lot of guns, bit the Germans hid a hellava men – fin we shot them doon, there wis aye plenty mair to tak their place.
Norrie Cruikshank, 6th Gordon Highlanders

At the Battle of Beaumont-Hamel there wis naething bit dubs but it wis a success. We gid inti the German dugouts and they war better than onything that we hid.
Tom Rearie, 5th Gordon Highlanders

The North-East lads made fine upright soldiers.
Alec Robertson, 5th Gordon Highlanders

We relieved the 51st Division efter they hid teen Beaumont-Hamel in November 1916. We hid mairched for days to get there. Efter we hid teen ower fae the 9th Royal Scots the Germans didna half gie us a roch time.

The Germans hid a generator to licht up aa the tunnels at Beaumont-Hamel, bit they hid blaan them aa up afore they left so it wis nea ees to us.
Jimmy Milne, 2nd Gordon Highlanders

12

Arras: Vimy Ridge, Scarpe River and the Hindenburg Line

Our division was in reserve to the Canadians when they took Vimy Ridge at a place called 'Happy Valley'. We took Greenland Hill beside Vimy Ridge.
Alec Meldrum MM, 1st/8th Gordon Highlanders

Our battalion were in reserve to an Irish one who took their objective – a hill. They lost it fin the Germans counter-attacked. We were sent up and it wis planned that a British plane wid come ower and guide the Artillery's creepin barrage in oor final stormin o the hill, but we were telt to show the pilot far we were by huddin wir rifles up in the air.

We got ower aa richt to far we were gan to assault the hill; at least as far forrit as we could get to wite the airplane. A plane appeared aa richt, an we aa waved wir rifles in the air fae shell holes and cover we were in, and discovered ower late that it wis a Gerry. Doon cam the warst shellin I iver experienced richt on tap os.

The shellin slackened and fit wis left os made a dive for the hill. We got richt up to the tap o her and I got shot through baith chicks: aye the bullet gid in at ae side and oot the ither. I wis knocket doon bit raise up again jist in time to see a big Gerry comin at me wi a bayonet. I looket for my rifle bit couldna see't so I oot wi a Mills bomb, pulled the pin and threw it. I dived doon and looked up efter the explosion and saa the Gerry had disappeared; bit he mith only hae been flappit like masel. We were aa issued wi twa Mills bombs and it wis a gweed job we were, itherwise I widna be here the day.

I traiveled back to the dressin station and got attended tull and laand up in a field hospital. In the neist bed was an Australian. He said, 'What about giving me your fags Jock; you'll be going to Blighty and you'll get plenty there.'

I jist handed him the lot: I wis ower sair to smoke.
Alec Barlow, 1st Gordon Highlanders
chick(s) cheek(s)

At the back o Vimy Ridge we hid railway lines strechin awa back. I mind I wis on ae bogy fit we caaed by han – gan awa back doon for supplies, fin there wis een in front os got blaan to bits wi a shell, and aabody ont.
Alec Wilson, 7th Cameron Highlanders

24. 1st Battalion, Gordon Highlanders Warrant Officers, Arras, France.
Gordon Highlanders Museum

We relieved the Canadians at Vimy Ridge efter they took it fae the Germans.
Alec Nicol, 7th Gordon Highlanders

We heard the bombardment at Vimy Ridge fin we wis lyin ahin the lines at Bulle-court. At the back os were Canadian lumberjacks cuttin doon a wid. They telt us that the Canadians hid suffered there fin they took it.
Jimmy Milne, 2nd Gordon Highlanders

Hindenburg Line[21]

The German dugoots in the Hindenburg Line were great: aboot 80 feet deep but they were nae eese: they were aa facin the wrang wy.
Alec Wilson, 7th Cameron Highlanders

Over the top we went at 4.30am. We hadn't far to go to the Hindenburg Line. A massive barrage preceded us, I didn't think there was any Germans left but by God there were plenty about. At Mont-St-Eloi a shell went through a church spire and it was still standing.
Alec Meldrum MM, 1st/8th Gordon Highlanders

We were shifted to Bullecourt in front of the Hindenburg Line and we were in at the smashin oot in April and May 1917.

I aye mind we were lyin in reserve fin the 62nd Division attacked in front o us. Weel they got an afa smash up. Then we gid in ahin them wi the Australians on wir richt – I aye mind on that. We didna get very far either.

We were in the line at Bullecourt aa that simmer.

I wis eence on a bombing raid there and that wis some cairry on! The target wis supposed to be stables we were attacking. They hid some big lang dugoots in there. I wis in B Company. We were detailed to attack on the left. A Company wis gan in on the right. Royal Engineers cam oot wi us to blow up the targets wi gun cotton. Onywy the Germans must hae got word o us comin, for the lads wi the eagles in their bonnets were witin for us: the Prussian Guard. We saa them fin they sent up the star shells, and it wis jist like day licht ye ken. They gid us fireworks aa richt; there wis hardly ony o oor company left.

Oor officer hid gotten afa wounded and twa os lifted him up to cairry him back, bit he widna lats. His face wis afa damaged, he wis that determined that we leave him.

…

I wis puttin on to the machine guns for three months and I liket that fine cis I hidna to dig or hing oot weer or onything, it wis a fair treet, jist lookin efter yer guns.
Jimmy Milne, 2nd Gordon Highlanders

25. Trench at the Western Front.

Reproduced by permission of the National Library of Scotland

The Germans retired to the Hindenburg Line and fin we gid forrit, we fun them aa weel fortified in deep dugoots and pillboxes. There wis a spring o watter awa oot in front and oor lads aa kept chancing – jist dashin in and oot. Bit there wis an afa lot o them getting killed tee. It wis richt gweed watter and we were richt desperate for it. In the end it wisna worth the risk and wis putting oot o bounds in the hinner end.

Alec Barlow, 1st Gordon Highlanders

We gid ower the top at Bullecourt. I wis on a three-man machine gun team. My pal Glendinnin got wounded and gid awa back. Shortly efter that the ither lad got it in the heed and gid fair daft; so that wis me left on ma ain. I wis lookin for somebody to mak up a team fin I cam on a Gerry hingin on the barbit weer wi baith his airms blaan aff. I got hud o a lad to gie me a hand and we got the peer lad aff and awa wi the stretcher-bearers. It's a funny thing, the Gerry aye hid on their big coats simmer and winter fin they were in action.

We were aa supposed to get a tot o rum fin we gid ower the top. We didna then, bit I saa an officer drunk, so some folk were getting it. Niver mind he got the works niest day!

…

Bullecourt was an underground village. We were jist livin like rats in the grun. The trenches were covered up anaa.

Jimmy Milne, 2nd Gordon Highlanders

We occupied the German dugouts and of course they were facing the wrong way. I remember going up the stair when a Gerry shell burst at the entrance and this blew me head over heels down again.

Dave Pitkethly, 4th Seaforth Highlanders

13

Third Battle of Ypres

Ypres Salient was shaped like a horseshoe and the Germans were shelling you from all sides.
Donald MacLeod, 4th Black Watch

Hill 60 was in Belgium and was held by the Germans. From this vantage point they must have seen us even though we went to the toilet. They always seemed to have the high parts somehow, like Vimy Ridge; he had that you see! Anyway the high ups had apparently decided they would have to capture Hill 60. So the Artillery officers got together and planned the creeping barrage and set their watches. The Artillery began the creeping barrage in front of the Infantry; lifting forward every now and again to let the Infantry forward. If the Infantry went too fast then that was their fault.

Anyway I was sent out to observe the action with a Welsh officer. The troops did not get very far I'm afraid.
Albert Napier MM, Royal Field Artillery ('Taggart's Own')

I saw my first battle at the Third Battle of Ypres (Passchendaele). It was raining hard when we went over the top at three in the morning. We were the second line in the attack and took over from the first line to relieve them. Supporting guns were then dug in at the back of us and began firing. The German guns then started shelling them back and in a short period of time, blew our Artillery and our company to bits. When their shelling stopped we only had 16 men left, and that was out of a 150-strong. Our NCOs were all killed and there were two officers – but they were so much shell-shocked that they were no use for anything.

Captain Gardener arrived and he put me in charge mainly because I was the oldest. He made me acting sergeant, and our depleted company held the line for a week until we were relieved. I was then ordered to take my men down the line to a chateau, where we were ordered to join up with B Company who were depleted as well. Some of the boys I had were 16-years-old.
George Bryan MM, 12th Highland Light Infantry

The warst battle I wis in wis the Third Battle of Ypres. That fin oor tanks cam throwe oor lines. We were oot in No Man's Land hidin in shell holes and do ye ken I wis richt feart they wid run ower the tap o hiz. Bit man it was great seein them efter they did gang throwe: they jist gid in and oot o the shell holes nae bather and we rase up and gid ahin them and got on gran.

They held us in the end: they were aa ower strong for us. Oh mighty me! The shellin – we'd never seen the like ot. No, Third Ypres wis by far the warst id ever seen. I wis wounded again – I wis lookin up fin a shell burst and I got a wee bittie atween the een, it wisna muckle o a wound – jist a bittie o shrapnel gid smack and I felt the bleed comin poorin doon my face. I thocht, 'Oh me, am deed, am deed!' I feel ma brains comin oot no! Bit it wis naething!

Alec Nicol, 7th Gordon Highlanders

The Third Battle of Ypres was started at 3am by a big naval gun sited on the railway away at the back somewhere. Then on a front of 21 miles there were guns firing wheel to wheel over our heads.

George Bryan MM, 12th Highland Light Infantry

Fin the Germans attacket at Ypres my shooder turned aa black and blue wi huddin in the fire; I couldna touch it – it wis ass sair. It wis the American ammunition that did it, it wisna gweed. I mind a mate o mine caaed John Bull hid to ging back to the dressin station wi his shooder. Oh aye! ye hid to hud yer rifle in ticht aa richt. This was at the Third Battle of Ypres, aye the hindmost een.

Norrie Cruikshank, 6th Gordon Highlanders

We gid ower the top at the Third Battle of Ypres: a terrible place – the shellin wis something infernal.

My pal Speed who hid been caad up said to me, 'What a feel ye are Alec Sim, for volunteering!'

In the advance he wis wounded and during a lull I helpit him tull his feet to try to get him to a safer place to get his wound seen tull, fin aa at eence, something took me in here and I fell doon in aa. I raise up again bit I couldna cairry ma rifle so hid to leave it lyin. I wis bleedin bad aneth the oxter bit felt naething at the time and didna ken that the bullet hid jist missed ma hert. My pal Speed and me helpet een and ither back to a dressin station bit it wis a lang time afore we wis attended tull. They had a lot mair on their hands.

Alec Sim, 7th Gordon Highlanders

At Third Ypres een o wir big guns gid 'woof' at zero oor, and then we didna heer een an ither spickin for shellfire. Then the Gerry started huddin them in tee, wi shells that burst abeen wir heed and scattered shrapnel aawy.

Jimmy Reid, 6th Gordon Highlanders

At the Battle of Third Ypres we gid ower the top. A lad fae Cuminestown wis wi me bit fell doon deed afore we got very far. Anither lad and me aa at eence seemed to be on wir ain – we hid geen farrer forrit that the lave. Twa Germans raise up and gid themsels up and the fower o us sat doon in a shell hole and hid a news as best we could.

I put them awa back themsels and the twa os gid awa forrit again and laand up in a shell hole that hid an afa smell o gas. I saa a trench oot in front os that look'et as though it wis teem, so I said to my mate, 'Look lats gang in to that trench in front os'.

Wi that, we made a dash fort and in it were three Gerries fa shot up their hands to gie themsels up. I beckoned wi my hand iss wy for them to come oot; wi that, a hale shoor o them steed up aawy in front os, so I signed on them to dee the same. They startit comin oot o their trenches aawy, until there were aboot 50 or 60 githered.

Then I noticed some mair o wir company hid shown up and were comin to geese a hand. Suddenly ae leg gid worth and I fell doon and my mate fell and aa. We fun that a bullet hid strack us baith in ae leg – it hid geen through his een and lodged in mine. It must o jist been the wy we were stannin thegither. Onywy oor lads flappit and the Gerry prisoners near aa skiddadled back in to their trench. Thank goodness the sniper niver started up again – I got the twa three prisoners I hid left to cairry the twa os back to the dressin station; this they were fine weelin to dee. That wis some freak shot wisn't it – coupin the twa os. I still hiv the bullet in my leg yet.

Albert Connon, 5th Gordon Highlanders

lave rest, *teem* empty, *worth* useless

The airches on my feet collapsed an I wis sent hame afore I hid seen muckle action bit fin they got scarce o folk I wis sent oot to the 4th Gordon Highlanders in time for the Third Battle of Ypres at Passchendaele in August 1917.

It cam on rain fin it started an oh it wis terrible – ye wis widin up to yer knees in goor. The trenches were fu o watter an it wis clay grun makin it a helliva job gan aboot.

It wis an afa job tryin to tak oot casualties in the dark as ye wis pullin an pushin een an ither cairryin the stretcher into shell holes reem fu o watter. Ye see the shell holes were that close thegither that there wis nae wy o escapin.

Wir Artillery were stuck in the dubs ana, there wis nae wy they could meeve aboot.

Charles Smith, 7th and 4th Gordon Highlanders

I aye mind on 4th October 1917 fin we gid in at the Battle o Passchendaele. We were in support at first and oor brigade consisted o the 8th and 9th Devons and the 2nd Border Regiment; and wir ain 2nd Gordon Highlanders.

26. The Cloth Hall, Ypres, Belgium.

Reproduced by permission of the National Library of Scotland

Fin we did advance we met wi the hellavist shellfire oot. It wis terrible, and we hid an afa lot o casualties. The Germans hid pillboxes aawy, and we battered awa at them and managed to tak a feoy. We gid stracht through Passchendaele wid, and occupied a pillbox there. Some o the wounded we got in tult in the dark. In fact it wis gie weel fulled up. Then there wis a feoy os gid roon tull anither een that wis captured and helpet in the wounded again and fin daylicht cam in, we aa saa we'd deen the wrang thing gan in there as the doors were aa facin the enemy. Oh God what a sorrowful affair! The Gerry started huddin in the shells and een that come in to the pillbox knocket oot oor officer and a lance corporal, who had his airm blaan aff. There were a lot mair casualties among them that were already wounded.

Onywy we were in that battle for ten days afore we got relieved, fin we gid back to Dickebusch for a rest.

...

Some o us were picked to gang back to Passchendaele at nicht wi ammunition. So aff we set in the dark wi mules aa loaded up. We first of aa gid by the mine crater at Menin; and that wis some hole I can tell ye. Jist at that time the Gerry airplanes cam ower and sent doon a hale shooer of bombs, bit we got by that aa richt. Then we meeved up through the soss o dubs and shell holes and the pliter o watter that

27. Troops of the 4th Battalion, Gordon Highlanders (51st Division) crossing a trench, Ribecourt, 20 November 1917.

Imperial War Museum

wis Passchendaele wid. It wis a hellava weet time o eer. Onywy it bein sae dark we lost wir wy. A machine gun opened up and we hid to dook. Oor officer turned feart and fin the firing started up again he scised and we were left on wir own. Withoot mair adee we wannered back the wy we cam in the dark far we cam again by luck on the Menin road, bit a section we hidna seen afore.

We cam on twa MPs – it wis near daylicht, I speired at them bit they didna ken. Then some Australians cam up wi a couple o donkeys. I tried them on to see far aboot oor battalion lay – ye see oor brigade wis neist the Australians. A sergeant said he did, and would we jist follow him. This took us through Ypres and richt back to kent grun and far we started the nicht afore.

Jimmy Milne, 2nd Gordon Highlanders

soss o dubs mess of mud

At Passchendaele, we travelled ower the watter filled grun on duckboards. We then felt the hellish smell o corpses an saa the boords war laid on tap o them. Their remains an skulls an that – an afa sicht.

John Webster, Royal Field Artillery

14

Battle of Cambrai

We attacked Bourlon Wood at Cambrai. Fin we lifted wir barrage to lat in the Jocks, the Gerry jist cam oot o his funkers an blasted aathing in sicht. Oh na! We jist hid to come richt back to far we started aff fae that morning.

Man, the cooks brewed up tae – jist tae – nae sugar, nae milk, an that wis the best tonic we iver hid. Aye an on a teem stammack!
Bert Gow, Royal Field Artillery

Our company sergeant and officer went in front of our tanks in the advance at Cambrai. They said the tanks were too slow. They were soon shot dead.
A. Smeaton, 5th Black Watch

A trench we were in crossed the Cambrai-Bapaume road and the road itself hadn't been trenched. Sergeant Gardiner said to me, 'Will you help an officer – he is needing a servant?' I said, 'Well, I have enough to do looking after myself.'

'Dave,' he said 'I want you to give it a trial!' I agreed to give it a trial and I went along to this officer's dugout and was introduced.

The officer told me that he had a message for the Argyll and Sutherlands on the other side of the road and that he wished me to accompany him. Off we went and got right up to the crossing point. We stopped and viewed the road. He then said to me, 'I must warn you that the road has been sniped all morning so I am giving you the option of going first or second'.

I told him I would go first and then flung myself across and rolled down the other side. I turned and looked back, and there was the officer lying prone in the middle of the road, now I didn't know if he was still alive or dead so I went up the trench and met some Black Watch boys – one of them a lad from the village here – I had a good news with him later. We formed a chain and managed to pull the officer in but he was dead. At least we got the message off him.

When we attacked Bourlon Wood at Cambrai, the Gerry snipers were causing heavy casualties. They were shooting at us from up the trees.

There was a poet captain killed. I later helped put a memorial to him at La Fountaine. That was transferred to Dingwall and put up there.[22]

…

I was at the 1st battle of the tanks at Cambrai at a place called Bush. This started at 4am and we went over the top at six. I remember one lad telling me, 'Look Dave, you'll keep as far away from them things as you can. When Gerry spots them, he'll throw everything at them'.

It was as true as he said: we lost a lot of men when they tried to follow the tanks after we made up on them. Cumbersome things they were.

Dave Pitkethly, 4th Seaforth Highlanders

Ae time we gid up ahin tanks, and by God we suffered for it: the Gerry hid up a plane and we got an afa time o shellin.

Wullie Gavin, 5th Gordon Highlanders

At the Battle o Cambrai, King Edward's Horse cam up and began to charge the German lines, bit mighty me! The Gerries wis biggit inti hooses an pillboxes, and they opened up and began knockin the horses an folk doon aawy. They hid ti fling aathing aff their horses an lat the peer beasts go – na na, it wis nae eese ava!

Jimmy Reid, 6th Gordon Highlanders

At Flesquières, wi the 51st, we didna fire ony barrage; the Infantry jist gad stracht into the attack ahin 50 tanks that morning. They hid cut the weer throw the night on a five-mile front wi something like 500 tanks to the hale operation. This wis at Cambrai. Weel at oor gun pits I wis stunnin aside Lieutenant White, fin he jist drappit doon dee. We hid heard the shell comin ower bit thocht it wis gan to burst weel awa, so we didna tak nae notice ot. It exploded in the air a bittie awa and man! Jist a little bittie hid flown ower and got him throw the hert. That's afore the battle started. We followed the Infantry forrit to fit wis to be wir objectives ten miles awa, but we stopped at five.

Oor lads hid teen them unawares and killed aa their sentries and catched them aa doon their dugouts. They widna come oot to be teen prisoner so they bombed them oot o them. Fin the Gerry did come rinnin oot they were aa half dressed. Fin the Jocks got farrer on ower the hill, they cam on mair positions and a battery o guns. The Gerries abandoned aathing and ran – except an officer, who stuck to his gun and kept firing to the last: knocking oot a few o oor tanks afore he wis killed. He wis bayoneted to death. I cam by later on and took his identity disc. That's it there look wi the date, born 1884 ont!

John Russel, Royal Field Artillery

We attacked at Eastercourt. The 6th were first up and didna see a thing. We cam neist and got the warst ot.

The chemical works at Cambrai wis a bad battle. I wis wounded a third time; this time in the back, bit it wis nae Blighty iss time, na na!

Alec Nicol, 7th Gordon Highlanders

15

Great German Push, 21 March 1918 and Onwards

We were in the ald Hindenburg Line a file and then gid up to Monchy-le-Preux aside Vimy Ridge on the Cambrai road.

On the 21st o March the Germans cam ower on's and we were driven oot o there. We were aa disintegrated and mixed up we idder lots in nae time.

I mind I cam on horses tied up. The men lookin efter em hid aa ran awa. They were aa dancing aboot, feart at the barrage. Then doon the road cam a troop o Artillery and as I watched them the shells jist come crashin doon among them. Some o the gun teams were knocket oot and ithers continued up the howe as fest as they could gang. I saa the beasts jist lyin there wi legs broken and that and ithers that were aa richt but couldna get oot o their harness. Oh, an afa sicht! I went into shelter in a huge bunker. An officer was there on a horse. He shouted, 'What are you doing here? Get out of here!' A Gordon officer came rounding everybody up that he could see. He said to me, 'Where is your rifle – I've a good mind to shoot you without your rifle!' I had lost it by this time.

Onywy he got a puckle os rigged to hud a bit o the line and we were nae lang in fin we heard the German attack comin.

They were singing 'Sailors Beware'.

I kent that sang in English – 'There are many brave hearts lie asleep in the deep … .

Oor sergeant in charge said, 'We'r aa feenished: we can dee naething!' He led the wy oot first takkin a Lewis gun and throwin it doon. A Gerry pintit a bayonet at him. I gid nesit and anither held a butt in my face. If ony os hid made a wrang move we wid o been killed – I wid hiv jist got the butt smashed in my face.

Fits courage? Bravery they caad it. We were aa learnt in wir trainin to turn the tables on the enemy, if we were teen prisoner; bit if we'd tried onything we'd jist o thrown awa wir lives.

We were assembled and made to teem wir pooches and lay aathing on the grun. They aa took a gweed look at my boy scout knife. Aa lad speired fit I used the pike ot for and he thocht it wis for killin Germans wi. They aa took a gweed lach fin I telt them I used it for stabbing tins wi.

Alec Wilson, 7th Cameron Highlanders

teem wir pooches empty our pockets

28. Carrying a full kit on their backs, these British Infantrymen are marching in single file to the front line at Cambrai.

Reproduced by permission of the National Library of Scotland

Lt Colonel Anderson was in charge of our battalion. He was the son of Professor Anderson – the Polytechnic.

We were at Ypres when the Germans broke through on the Somme. Our brigade were taken out and rushed by train for two days and nights and came off at the side of the line beside a place called St Paul. We attacked the enemy right away at the line side. We asked some stragglers where the Germans were, and they said they were at the sawmill.

Colonel Anderson asked me how many men I had and I replied, '30 Sir!' He said, 'That will have to do. Get your men to fix bayonets!'

Then Colonel Anderson led us on a charge of the German position and fell immediately with a shot through the head.

When we reached the woodyard the Germans up and ran from us. We never got near them except the machine gunners, whom we did in.

We stayed there until a major came along next morning and he took charge. He took us back and reformed all available men in front of the village of Bray, where he held off the German attacks for a day.

We were then retired to Boulers. The Germans were finally held there: they got no further!

…

There were some of our lads went missing during the Great Spring German attack of 1918 and were found later down at base camp trying to get home. Of course it was such a shambles then.

George Bryan MM, 12th Highland Light Infantry

We were attacked on 21st o March 1918. We were catched doon the dugoot and bombed oot ot. I wis captured wi a lot mair.

I will niver forget fit the guard said fin oor train wis gan by this big toon at nicht on wir wy to East Prussia. This place wis a lichted up like daylicht. He got aa excited and aye kept shoutin, 'Berleen! Berlee...n!' and pintin wi his finger.

John Rennie, 5th Gordon Highlanders

We were all broken up when the Germans came over in 1918. A lot of men were taken prisoner in the dugouts.

Then we lost a lot during the general engagements afterwards during the retiral.

Donald MacLeod, 4th Black Watch

We hid to pull oot bliddy fest fin the Gerry brak throwe. We saa the Jocks first, comin bootin it back in twas an threes.

Fin we retired a bit we lay doon in comfort among the girse in a gran moonlicht nicht. Nae dubs there – it wis gran!

Bert Gow, Royal Field Artillery

girse gorse

Fin the German Push started on 21st March '18, I wis at the cookhoose seein ti the rations. It wis midday and the cook – he cam fae Buckie, said that the denner wid be ready in an ither half oor or so.

So I started awa back – I hid left Corporal Duncan in charge fin the barrage started and by God it wis bad. I jist couldn't get forrit to my company as lang as the shellin gid on. Fin it slackened a bit I managed to reach oor trenches – fit wis left o them – to see they war deserted: oor men must hae pulled back fin the barrage started. This left me on my ain, so I cam richt back and lost my wy in the hellish shellin and laaned up wi the French that hid been on wir flank. I focht and retreated wi them for a feoy days, and then cam on an English battalion. I speired at an officer if he kent faar the 51st wis. He said he did and if I cared to wite twa days, I wid get back wi a wagon that wis gan doon their wy.

Do ye ken I got back to them and discovered that I hid been posted 'Missing, believed killed' and my folk hid gotten word to that effect tee. Bit then ye see – I wis ower coorse to kill!

Fin a new trench was dug, ilkey man got a measured bittie to dig, this wis to ensure that there wis nae shirkers: it wis only fair.

Alec MacHardy MM, 7th Gordon Highlanders

Fin the Gerry broke through I was sent back fae iss country marked fit, efter convalescing and got there in time to help repel their attacks. I jined a bunch that were composed o onybody they could get. At Merville we were preparing for an attack and saa a swarm o fit we thocht were Germans comin rinnin ats. It wis a misty kine o morning and we opened fire and they were bein knocket doon away, we were ordered to cease fire cis they were Portuguese fleeing their trenches. Their uniforms were like the Gerry eens.
Albert Connon, 5th Gordon Highlanders

On 21st March we were lying on Passchendaele Ridge – a mortuary if ever there was. The dead were lying everywhere on the ground. Conditions were so bad that we were only in the line 48 hours at a time – that's all we could stand.

The Germans started bombarding our front early that morning with a more than usual heavy dose of shellfire. Then we heard away on our right, the sound of a terrible and sustained drumfire. This was towards the Loos-Bethune area.

We heard later on that this was the Portuguese that got it; and when the German assault troops went in, they broke through there at once. At midday we were ordered to move and we came off Passchendaele and entrained for Bethune. We travelled all night and when we formed up in the streets of Bethune next morning, the Germans were already at the outskirts.

Along with the rest of the brigade and various other units we advanced to meet them and took up defensive positions to the northern edge of the town. When they attacked we were waiting for them and stopped them with all the fire power that we could muster.
Frank MacFarlane MM and Medal Militaire, 1st Black Watch

I took a patrol out at night before the German Push of 21st March 1918 and we listened to all the sounds of them preparing for battle. We knew fine what was going on out there and what to expect. We were back in the dugout when their shelling commenced and it was terrible.
Alec Robertson, 5th Gordon Highlanders

In the German Push of 1918 we were badly hit when they came over but we stopped them. That's because we were waiting for them. There were so many of them that we couldn't miss them. Eventually we had to retire in the end.

I remember coming back we found an abandoned champagne factory which we broke into. What we found was strong stuff and did not last long.
Robert More MM, 4th Seaforth Highlanders

In the retreat of March 1918, we were lying in a hollow when a German scout airplane came over. It was awful slow – hardly moving. I took pot shots at it with incendiary bullets. This got the petrol tank and it burst into flames and crashed

near us, killing the pilot. I got a severe reprimand from our headquarters people and told never to do that sort of thing again as it might give away our position.
A. Smeaton MM, 5th Black Watch

I only eence seen a Fyvie loon fin I wis oot there. This wis Jimmy Gerrie. Some o us wis detailed to scout oot in front. We were retirin afore the big German Push in the spring o 1918. Onwy we cam on a battery o Artillery that wis trying to extricate their guns fae a richt clorty hole. We jined in to help them and that's fin I met wi Jimmy. There wisna much time bit we hid a news a filie. I dinna think Jimmy cam through the War.

I wis richt sorry for the horses. I saw them lyin wounded at the side o the road. They look'ed at me richt pitify like wi their een; that wis terrible.
Jimmy Scott, Royal Engineers

We went back a little every day firing when we could. Then I remember coming back to a place where I could see 18-pounders dug in as far as the eye could see, all blasting away. They were making no attempt at camouflage. That stopped them: the Germans got no further.
Albert Napier MM, Royal Field Artillery ('Taggart's Own')

We were puttin back an afa wy fin the Germans cam ower in 1918. Then we started gan forrit again and niver stoppet tull the War wis feenished.

I got shrapnel in my leg – slight compared to a lot o them.
Andrew Finnie, 7th Black Watch

When the Gerries cam ower on the 21st o March 1918, oor adjutant wis killed – shot through the stammock.
Jimmy Reid, 6th Gordon Highlanders

I wise er fin the Gerry strack in March 1918. They cam ower in thoosans in the early mornin. We war expectin em and hid the grun a mined ready, an fin we saa them comin we blew up the mines. That didna stop them though an they kepit comin in hordes.

They overran a lot o wir trenches an come time we war forced oot an aa. My certie they widna haen easy catchin me – I ran back loupin throue the barbit weer like a hun dog. I wis left wi half a kilt haen lost the rest in the weer.
Peter Barrie, Cameron Highlanders, later Black Watch

In June we gid doon to the Marne for a rest and train reinforcements fae hame. We stopped aff a day at Paris and hid a great day in the city. We hidna lang settled doon and were gettin the new recruits inveigled in wir wys – fin the Germans broke through. They warna expectin them doon there to try onything o that kine.

That's the wy we were sent doon there for a rest. That wis in 1918.

We were rushed into action and crossed the river Aisne and got dug in wir guns on the ither side.

Fin we gid ower in the morning aathing wis quait and aa that day tee. Fin nicht cam a patrol wis sent oot to tak a prisoner. They cam back wi a Gerry sergeant major and he telt aathing fin they threatened to sheet him. He said that the attack wid commence neist morning preceded by gas.

We didna ken iss at the time and some os were comin back ower the river Aisne for supplies at 3am fin we ran inti gas. The Gerry attack started and we were ordered back to get oor ammunition with our wagons fae oor dump up the line. We however met the trench mortar lads comin doon. They speired far we wis gan. We telt them. They said that we neent bother as the Gerry was comin close behind them.

Noo that meant that the guns o oor division that were up front – 48 hid been aa captured – oh no! there wis een awa at ordnance!

The rest o oor guns that werena across the river were aa richt. We retreated throwe the vineyards; bit the grapes werna ready yet. At length we stopped where the French had batteries of 75s dug in. They were firing aff the shells as quick as they were comin up in larries and coupin them aff. That wis the lads that stoppit them! They were great guns the 75s. You could pit a peel o water on their wheel and it wid niver shift. This gun fired a 13-pounder!

John Russel, Royal Field Artillery

On July 1918, the 51st gid doon by train awa to the sooth o Rheims to help the French. Man the countryside looked gran. They had niver seen kilties doon there. The folk were aa cheerin and cairyin on. The grapes were hardly ready though.

Jimmy Reid, 6th Gordon Highlanders

That battle of the tanks was on November 1917 at Cambrai. We held the line there until the Gerry broke through on 21st March 1918. We got an awful cutting up. I was woken by a Gerry barrage at two o'clock in the morning. We were out of the line at the time sleeping in huts at a place called Le-Bougery. That was some shelling and they started hitting the huts and causing casualties: our sergeant was hit by shrapnel about the head.

We were assembled and rushed into the front line in full battle order. When only newly established in the line – orders came through: 'Every man for himself.' With that Sergeant Gardiner came to me and asked me how many bombs I had. I replied that I had two bags full.

He told me that he was going to pick two or three men to accompany the two of us while we went over to bomb the Gerry who were advancing on us. The sergeant organised the retiral of our platoon while the two of us threw bombs at the Gerries in the communication trench. Three men protected our rear and we retreated a bit at a time, repeating this operation till we reached the 3rd reserve line. We suffered all the same: only a handful of the company were left to answer roll call the next day.

Dave Pitkethly, 4th Seaforth Highlanders

Ninth of April 1918, was when we lost the most of our men. We were attacked at dusk. We didn't see them coming and they were on us like a flash. That's when we lost the most of the local Black Isle lads. The Gerry had a lot of boys in their ranks, but then so had we. I mean I was only a boy myself.

Robert More MM, 4th Seaforth Highlanders

Fin we cam inti Monchy wi the Germans ahins – the French shops war aa left wi aathing in em. I pickit oot the best o tools an took wees, bit fin I wis wounded of coorse I niver saa em again.

Peter Baigrie, 7th Cameron Highlanders/6th Black Watch

ahins behind us

When the Gerries came over in 1918, I was out in charge of a machine gun crew. We tried to withdraw but were too late. There was a platoon left to cover me. When the Gerry came, these fellows took to their heels and ran. If it had been the original men in the battalion – they wouldn't have ran.

I stayed put a while because I thought an officer would take them back up again. I heard later that their officer had got up to lead them on a bayonet charge but he was then blown to pieces – this was when they had took to their bloody heels.

Previously a battalion that was holding the line in front of us had came back through us that morning chased by the Gerry. It was terribly foggy.

This was the Lewis gun I was in charge of at the time. It was a dangerous job but it had its compensations – like being left alone and out of fatigues; but there was no cushy job in the Front. My crew could not get out although we did try and sadly, out of my crew, I was the only survivor. A fellow was going to stick me with the bayonet when his NCO stopped him. I then offered this NCO my fags but he refused and pointed the way back to his rear area.

When a lot of us were being taken back on the march to the rear that day – I noticed two Gerries cutting up a dead horse for meat.

Jock Murray, 1st King's Own Scottish Borderers

At first when our side started using the Machine Gun Corps, the Gerry didn't like it a bit getting a dose of their own medicine – they were very good at that sort of thing.

We had five guns to each section firing over crossed lines and we had the measure of them most times they came over. We sometimes set them up far into No Man's Land to avoid their shells.

Now and then we set them up below the barbed wire; one time when our barrage lifted, up popped the Gerries to fire at our men and we copped them right away. That time we didn't have half the casualties.

In 1918 in March, Gerry struck our line and went through a bit of it. We eventually fell back and we got orders to destroy all papers and letters in case it fell into their hands.

Albert Edwards, 5th Black Watch/Machine Gun Corps

Fin the Gerry chased us back in the spring o '18, it wis oor job to blaa up the bridges ower the rivers as we were the bridging company. On the canals as weel o coorse, bit fin we were chasin them back the ither wy in the simmer, it wis oor job to mak the pontoon eens to replace the brigs the Gerries hid destroyed. We aye had plenty o pontoon sections cis we make a big reserve of them in wir spare time, as weel as duckboards and fire steps and the like, although we didna hae a lot o fancy equipment to lay the pontoons wi – jist sheer manual labour and simple tools.

We got ae lad to sweem ower wi a tow to measure the width o the river or canal – I couldna sweem, an then we kent fu mony sections we rought to jine thegidder to span it.

Jimmy Scott, Royal Engineers

thegidder together

The Germans had broken throwe awa ti the sooth. We were teen doon on trains on a hale day's journey an got oot ower jist at the side o the railway line an gan stracht into action.

George Stewart, 5th Gordon Highlanders

The peer horses war jist tied up in the horse lines simmer an winter an suffered fort in the cald winters. The jist got their hay in a net bag an files some corn tee. The only time I saa the craters enjoying themsels wis the time we war sent doon ti help the French at the Marne in 1918 – fin they war atein grapes as we meeved up – the bree wis rinnin oot o their moos wi them. Some days it wis hard getting watter an it wis aye waar on em. Maistly it wis aye caad up in watter bowies on horse cairts ye ken. I've telt ye aboot gan awa doon er wi railway horse vans an jist sleepit wi the horse on the harness an passed Paris on the sooth side an got a gran view o the place on the wy.

At last we cam till a stop at a place Bunch-er-Seine or something like at an aff loaded wir beasts an yokit then inti wir gun limbers am meeved up the vineyards park efter park inti the finest country we'd seen for a lang time. Oh fut a change fi the dubs and weet o Flanders. We war pleased an the horses – man it wis great ti see them wi aa that luch mait. It wisna lang though afore we hid ti louse aff an fire aff wir guns in action.

A fine bit o country aa richt – the Gerry hid broken throwe there an it wis the

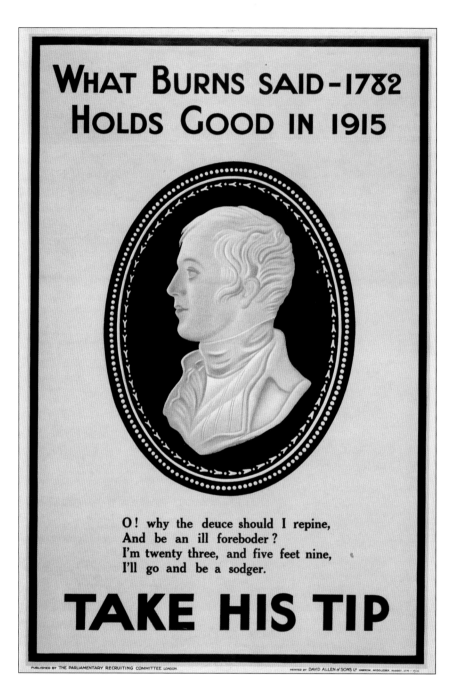

Recruitment poster entitled 'What Burns Said – 1782, Holds Good in 1915'.

Image © National Museums Scotland

Alec Barlow, at the time of the Great War, and in later years.

Courtesy of Calum Beaton

The Marquis of Tullibardine pays tribute to his forebear, Lord George Murray, in the presence of the colours of the Atholl Highlanders, at La Ferté-sous-Jouarre on the Marne, 2018. The sword being used in salute is Lord George's own.

Courtesy of Graham Jack

The Black Watch Soldier Memorial, Ypres, Belgium.

Courtesy of Graham Jack

King George V decorating Private George McIntosh of the 1/6 Battalion, Gordon Highlanders with the Victoria Cross at Ibrox Park, Glasgow, 18 September 1917.

Imperial War Museum

Grave of an Unknown Soldier, Western Front.

Gravestone of A Soldier of the Great War in Tyne Cot War Cemetery, Passchendaele, Belgium.

Courtesy of Graham Jack

Memorial scroll (right), to
accompany the memorial plaque
(below), commemorating
Corporal George Buchanan of
the 8th Seaforth Highlanders,
killed in action at the Battle of
Loos on 25 September 1915.

Images © National Museums
Scotland

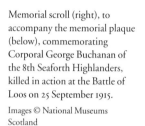

In my last mail I received a letter from my mother telling my brother Geordie was missing at High
Wood. He was 19 and this was the first time in action with the 1st Black Watch. She was also
worried about my other brother Jim, as she had not heard from him for some time. She told me
later that when they got the telegram about Geordie, 'Your Father was gie dowie'. When later I
went out to the washing house the words of the 61st Psalm came to me:

> What time my heart is overwhelmed,
> And in perplexity do thou lead
> Unto the rock that higher is than I.

I then got strength and comfort to carry on!'
William Mowat, 1st Scottish Horse and Lovat Scouts[23]
dowie sad

French colonials, bag mannies like Turks ye ken that oor division took ower fae an oor lads waar sent in ti the attack an a gie lot o them war killed er at Bois de Courton includin Jimmy Barrack.

We hid been on the Arras Front afore this, an fi we cleared at place an Chaumuzy beyond it we war pulled back an sent richt back ti Arras again in the north o the country. This wis the first Heelanmen they hid seen at the Marne doon er – aye the kilties fair took a trick wi the folk doon in the villages as we cam throwe.

Bert Gow, Royal Field Artillery
bree juice, *bowies* barrels, *luch maet* lush food

I remember we were sent into the attack on a wood held by the Germans and came upon row upon row of Senegalese – black ebony big men, slaughtered by machine guns. They were in the French division we had relieved. We didn't manage to take the wood either (at the Marne July 1918).

A. MacEwan, 6th Gordon Highlanders

Last 100 days

We were rushed up the line through Arras and Ypres and laand at Bullecourt, an underground village. Efter a file we went on to Havrincourt, and then went on to Messines. There, we jined the remnants o the 1st Gordon Highlanders.

There I met wi Sunny Lorimer fae the village o Byth here. He hid been in a gweed filie.

Noo fin we were there, anither batch jined us that hid been trained in Edinburgh. They hid amang them Jocky Fordyce, the grieve fae the Castles o Auchry, and the grieve fae Hilton o Banff. Then I kent a Pittendreich fae Boyndlie; twa fae Foggieloan; a lad Topp and a lad Dundas fae Turra wy.

We aa advance fae there and laand at Hellfire Corner and saa the Virgin Mary hingin fae the steeple at Albert.

Oor rations were nae keepin up wi us and we were daared nae to ate mait off the tables that the Germans left, for fear o pooshon. We cam on a park o carrots and we jist cleaned the lot. I didna think we even took time to clean aff the dirt: jist gid them a dicht and man they were richt fine!

Advancin to Rumilly, we cam on a park o tatties and did the same to them as we did to the carrots – jist like a flock o sheep.

pooshon poison, *dicht* wipe

…

We gid in to a sunken road; we war in reserve for the attack. A sergeant cam up to me and speired, 'Are ee twa brithers?' I says, 'Aye are we!'

'Weel,' he says, 'I'll hae to shift een o ye!' So my brither hid to gang inti a different company fae me. Ye see, we were baith in the same machine gun team and they didna like it if brithers were the gether.

Robert MacRobbie, 1st Gordon Highlanders

When I got better in hospital, I got leave and then back to Cromarty camp. From there I was posted back to France, getting back into the line on the 6th September 1918. This was at Arras. From there we moved to Cambrai where we were reserve to the Canadians who were to attack Cambrai.

I remember reading the placards the Gerry set up on the walls of the town this said: 'Cambrai is yours Canada – take it.'

Well, in front of Cambrai was a canal with a railway embankment running alongside.

The Canadians attacked and crossed the bridges over the canal. Once they were over, the Germans blew the bridges up leaving the Canadians trapped. They were just slaughtered – I have never seen so many dead men lying in one place.

The Canadians did take Cambrai in the end.

We finally relieved them at a place called Iway.

I was in the line from that time to the 6th November – that was my birthday. Coming out of the line that day, we experienced a barrage of shelling from the Gerry and it was so bad that I didn't think I would get through it, but I did.

We were due to go in again on the 13th but of course the War finished on the 11th.

Dave Pitkethly, 4th Seaforth Highlanders

The Canadians hid been thrown oot o Cambrai three times afore us. They attacked again and we were sent in ahin them.

As we advanced I saa fit I thocht wis the bonniest place I hid iver seen. Oh my! I thocht I wid like to bide there. Awa doon this bonny valley we gid, fin we laand smack in the middle o a barrage. I wis knocket ower fin something strack ma face and I lay there. Fin the barrage stoppet I saa that my gun team hid aa got it: a lad Forsyth fae Aberdour; a lad Cheyne and Peter Angus fae the Garmond. I raise up and spak to Cheyne, but na, na! He niver spak at aa: he wis killed!

The rest os managed to traivel, so we made for awa back and met in wi Sergeant Ewan fae oor section. He said, 'Pack up and ging back to the dressin station!' Peter's chick hid been blaan aff; Forsyth's hip wis hingin doon and I was struck aneth the ee here.

Robert MacRobbie, 1st Gordon Highlanders

My section were ordered to take a factory that was held by the Germans; without a barrage. We reached the stairs and went up three flights without anybody being seen inside the first two floors. Bursting open the third door the place was full of Gerries. Most surrendered on the spot except one fellow who lifted his rifle. I

29. Men of the Seaforth Highlanders helping French peasants to gather potatoes,
Amiens-Albert Road, October 1916.

Imperial War Museum

promptly shot him. This just wounded him and I saw later that my shot had been
stopped by his pocket book otherwise he was dead.
Dave Pitkethly, 4th Seaforth Highlanders

At Solesmes my platoon got the job of entering and clearing the village of the
Germans. On entering the outskirts we were fired on from house windows and we
hurriedly retired to shelter behind a wall. An officer appeared and asked why we
had stopped. I told him we were under fire. He refused to believe me and asked if
anybody would accompany him into the village. I volunteered and we set off
creeping up to and entering a house I had seen the enemy firing from. This was
empty – nobody to be seen. The officer than ordered me to carry on, so I went
outside into the street and beckoned my platoon forward to join me, when a shot
rang out and I felt my arm give way. I fell down and rolled over to the safety of the
gable of a house. I lay there for a long time till I was attended to by medical staff.
They bound my arm and as they had other people to attend to, I walked back to
the dressing station a mile to the rear.

I was wounded in the early morning but wasn't attended to till 9pm. The
doctor took off my arm, probably fearing mortification setting in.
J. Fowlie, 7th Gordon Highlanders

In October 1918 we advanced 10–15 miles each day after Gerry. It was like a route march. I remember one time seeing them rising up away to the front of us and before moving off they threw down some leaflets which when we picked them up, read: 'We are leaving here of our own free will and when we do stop we shall give you hell!' I mind on our planes dropping some to them, leaflets, which showed a fierce figure of a lion with a line of Gerries walking past shoving their own leaflets into its open mouth.

Albert Edwards, 5th Black Watch/Machine Gun Corps

Fin the Gerry retreated in 1918 we war telt strictly to leave aa drink and food alene as it could hae been poosaned and that meant leavin the waals watter tee. Aa it we iver used wis watter oot o rinnin burns, ye wis aa richt er.

Fin Péronne wis cleared, oor officers sent me an an idder lad in to look oot decent digs. Ye see the Gerry hid cleared oot an left the place intact, although there wis a feoy o civilians aboot, the maist o the hooses war teem.

We wiled oot this undertaker's premises wi the hoose attached which wis fu o fine furniture an furnishings an put a cross o fite paint on the door as a sign that the place wis bookit for digs.

Ah weel, weel, we gid awa an fin we cam back wi the officers we fun the place fu o British Infantry and the place wis aa in ruin wi aa the fine piano an furniture lying in bits. Fut a rage wir officers war bit they jist hid to look for anither place.

I mean the Gerry hid left the place in gweed order and this lads hid geen in to loot an destroy the lot.

Jimmy Scott, Royal Engineers
fite while

At the ine o the War they war takkin in a lot o young loons, bit I wis ony 17 masel.

I wis inti the 6th Black Watch, 15th Scottish Division and ae time fin we attacket the Gerry, we sent em back siven mile. Then oor Company wis fired at fae the flank wi shells an I got hit. This wis up near Belgium.

Peter Baigrie, 7th Cameron Highlanders/6th Black Watch

The snipers sat camouflaged up trees at Mons. I mind we fired at the tress wi a machine gun and een cam tumbling doon: that wis the hinnerine o him.

That wis at the ine o the War, after the Canadians hid teen Cambrai. We were reserve to them when they attacked Mons. On the 10th November I was sent on leave and wisna far doon the line fin the War feenished neist day.

John Will, 5th Gordon Highlanders

16

Wounded and Sick

I was wounded at the fighting beside the chalk cliffs in front of Vimy Ridge.
Alec Meldrum MM, 1st/8th Gordon Highlanders

I wis lucky I only got a bittie o shrapnel in my airm; that wis at the Somme.
Jimmy Scott, Royal Engineers

I wis wounded in the back o the heed wi shrapnel ae morning fin we were attackin at Ypres and that wis the end o me in the War. I hid been a hale eer oot fin this happened.
J. Burnett, 8th Gordon Highlanders

I got wounded ae time wi a thing like a big ball bearin that gid in to my shooder. Noo fin I wis doon at the hospital in France; me and a lot mair were sent back afore we were richt better. We kent this wis a sign that there wis something happenin and we werena far wrang – na, my God, na!
Alec MacHardy MM, 7th Gordon Highlanders

I took bad wi fever an dysentery at Mesopotamia an wis teen back an shipped ower ti India lannin up at Bangalore. My – I liket India an wid hae biddin er a lang time – it was that fine. I got plenty of drink an mait there although the beef maybe wisna first class, I was richt gled ot. Fin I wis fit again I wis then sent back to the Front. Noo by coincidence I wis in hospital last eer an wis treated by an Indian doctor. When I speired him far he came fae he replied, 'Oh a place you've never heard of'. Fin I again speired far it wis, he telt ma he wis born at Bangalore and wis richt surprised fin I telt him I wis convalescing there eence. Still I hid a lot o turns wi malaria ower the eers.
Harry Nicoll, Royal Engineers

I was not long in the line when I went down bad with malaria. I was so ill that I was strapped on to a mule's back and taken down from the positions in the mountains by the muleteer who was Maltese. He kept telling me he was taking me to hospital which he eventually did although I was too ill to remember much

30. Extracting a wounded soldier, Western Front. Soldiers are trying to manoeuvre the stretcher out of the main trench into a deeper trench at right angles to it.

Reproduced by permission of the National Library of Scotland

by then. I was in hospital three weeks before I was fit enough to go back up.
Jim Burgess, 2nd Cameron Highlanders

On the way to the hospital the Turks sent over a few shells to help our party on the way. We came on a ration cart abandoned with some Welshmen sitting round it drinking rum and eating cheese.

In hospital I lay down as I was all in and was later wakened by an orderly with a cup of rice and lay down on a stretcher again. When dusk fell, a doctor came round and cried, 'Now all you men will parade and go back up with the ration party!' He looked at me lying there and asked if I could manage to which I replied that I wasn't sure. He said that I looked all right anyway, and told me to parade with the rest.

I managed to rise but must have been pretty helpless looking because the orderly sent for the doctor again, who again looked at me and asked me if I thought I could manage along the beach to the embarkation station and get on the hospital ship. Of course I said I would manage.

I managed to reach there with a struggle with many rests on the way. Each time a lighter came in there was a rush of people to fill it and I was left stranded each time. It was near dawn before I got finally picked up and taken aboard the hospital ship. I was given a cup of coffee and a slice of bread and this was a great treat, we hadn't seen bread for weeks.

A friend from the Fife and Forfar Yeomanry and I shared a stretcher to sleep on all the way across the sea to Egypt and there seemed to be plenty room – we were that thin.

On the way across, the weather got warm again and I remember some of the troops singing *Keep The Home Fires Burning*.

I threw my overcoat overboard – it was just like a board of clay. At Alexandria Hospital I discarded the rest of [my clothes] and was given my first hot bath since before I landed at Suvla. When I was seen by a doctor, he asked why I was so emaciated. I told him about having dysentery and reporting sick only to be sent back up the line again. However, this doctor thought I had maybe contracted TB and sounded me thoroughly but finally came to the conclusion that I was just suffering from malnutrition – a state that rest and food would soon put right.

I had recurring bouts of dysentery however, and one day a doctor asked if I would like a trip back home. I was delighted to accept and was transported from the hospital to ship for Mudros. There transferring to the *Britannic*. This had been her maiden voyage – to Gallipoli, to receive the many casualties from the evacuation that was being planned. We sailed for England.

The evacuation was finished by the time I got there without the fearful carnage expected. The Scottish Horse were now back in Egypt.

After hospital in Bristol with good food and rest I was pronounced fit and cured of dysentery and got ten days' leave.

After enjoying my mother's home comforts I reported to base at Dunkeld where the doctor sent me home for another month, I was still a bit puffed up like.
William Mowat, 1st Scottish Horse and Lovat Scouts

I got wounded when my first leave was due. There were so many wounded that time when I arrived at Reading that the place was blocked by stretchers.

When I got to the dressing station in France, they were going to take off my leg but I wouldn't let them, but the wound was bad. An Aberdeen doctor came to see me and said, 'Let me have a look at it Sandy and I'll see what I can do. If I have to take it off – will you let me?'

I agreed and he did a good job and three days later I landed back on the boat to this country. At Reading the doctor opened up the wound again and cleaned it up because it was all swollen up. From then on it got better although I had a bit of bother with the matron when I decided to go to the toilet alone – a thing I was strictly forbidden. You see I had about 20 stitches in my backside but I didn't want to bother anyone. Anyway I got off the bed and started creeping with crutches across the polished floor when I skidded and fell on my back. Of course I couldn't rise and when she came on me there was a terrible rumpus. She was right though – this didn't do my injury any good and from then on I behaved myself.

I was sent to a convalescent home and there I was treated like a lord by volunteer nurses, some toffs among them.

After a month the doctor sent me home for a week and suggested I go and see my home doctor if I didn't feel all right. That was Dr Fuller at Aberdeen, Castlegate who was in the Terriers at Ellon before the War but he was too old for active service.

I didn't need to see him however and reported back to Rippon Camp. My wound was now dry but I thought I would be sent back on leave again but instead they wanted me to go back to the Front and if I didn't feel well, to just report sick. They explained that they were very short of men out there. I left next day and sailed from Folkstone. We had a hellava time getting across, stopping now and then due to enemy ships being on the go, but after much delay we got safely across the Channel to France.

Alec Robertson, 5th Gordon Highlanders

I wis wounded fin I wis beeried wi a shell blast. They hid ti dig ma oot. I couldna spik ava. This was up at Arras in the trenches. I hid nae recollection ot at the time. De ye ken I couldna spik again for aboot sax months. It wis concussion it did it. Weel I wis sent back fae hospital efter they thocht I was better, though I wisna feelin weel ata and I jined the lads at Cambrai fin I got back. It wis jist a case o – if ye could waak – if ye ken fit I mean.

Tom Rearie, 5th Gordon Highlanders

spik ava speak at all

The first time I got hurt I landed up in hospital at Eastbourne. The second time was spent at Newcastle. During the train journey there among the wounded in our carriage was a man who had lost both his arms and legs – a terrible fate!

A. MacEwan, 6th Gordon Highlanders

If they had to send away all the men who were sick at Gallipoli, there would have been no one left. When you reported sick with dysentery or malaria, unless you were near dead you were just sent back up again. The malaria got you in the right hand side. Dysentery was bad and not much wonder for the bully tins – you could shake them and when they were opened – the flies were on them right away. They firmed up again though with the chill of the night.

William MacGregor, Lovat Scouts

I took a dose o diarrhoea New Eer's Day 1918. I wis sent to hospital. Fin I got back to the line, there wis a feoy kent faces missin fae my company. They telt me there hid been twa bombin raids on the Gerry lines.

J. Fowlie, 7th Gordon Highlanders

I was wounded three times. Also one time a bullet struck my pay book and then into the copy of the New Testament passing through King George's head and partly through the New Testament itself. As I always had them both in the left hand pocket – this prevented the bullet killing me: this saved me!

Robert More MM, 4th Seaforth Highlanders

Lord Lovat was a big man and was well liked – I mind him being sent out of Gallipoli with dysentery and malaria. It all got to us to a certain extent, but one had to be really bad before they took you out. I had a hole in a boot which let in water when the great storm broke and with the extreme cold which succeeded it, I got frost bite in a foot – losing all feeling in it and in fact nearly losing my foot on account of it. I went sick and the Fife and Forfar Yeomanry's Dr Stevens had a look – it was all black and blue by this time and he told me I was going to work hard if I didn't want to lose it. He gave me olive oil to rub my feet with, which I did vigorously for hours, after which my bad foot recovered – but it was touch and go.

William MacGregor, Lovat Scouts

When the wounded were left out in No Man's Land after a battle, we took note of where they lay and crept out at night to drag them in. We could not carry them on our backs.

A. MacEwan, 6th Gordon Highlanders

I was wounded in November 1914 and landed back in Dundee Royal Infirmary for treatment. Then I was sent to Glamis Castle to convalescence. I met Elizabeth, then 14 years old and her brother James too. She was an awful bonny girl. I was at the Xmas party at Glamis when Elizabeth presented us all with a card and a cracker. In the cracker was a small Scottie dog. Years later I wanted a jeweller to put in a pin so that I could pin it to my tie as a memento. On examination of it he stated that it was made of gold. I have it among my things there – I'll let you see it!

Nurse Anderson – a sea captain's widow – always took my arm and escorted me around and called me 'My Highland boy!' She offered me her late husband's rings and things but I would not accept them. 'Oh I see,' she said, 'Highland superstition!'

...

The second time I was wounded I was buried by a shell burst. The trench had collapsed and when I came round I felt congealed blood on my body, so I had been unconscious a long time. I felt very sore although my legs felt all right. I felt somebody digging and when I was eventually pulled out, I looked up at a sergeant of the Argyll and Sutherlands. His face was all pock marked by the explosion as though somebody had blown dust in his face.

My head and kilt were all saturated and I felt very weak but I couldn't have got a nicer man than that sergeant. He put on field bandages on me and said, 'This will get you home my friend!' Yes he was a fine chap; very kind!

Donald MacVicar, 1st/2nd The Queen's Own Cameron Highlanders

They gid us whale ile to pit on oor feet. This wis to stop trench feet.
Alec Wilson, 7th Cameron Highlanders

I was wounded the second time before I was 18 years old. This time I did not get to Glamis. When I was recuperating, I took measles and went on leave to Grimsay (Uist). I took the malady with me and caused terrible devastation on the island. One or two died – one of them the missionary's wife, May Hughes.
Donald MacVicar, 1st/2nd The Queen's Own Cameron Highlanders

I near got blaan up when a half-daft bugger drapped a grenade in the trench. It exploded and killed a lad Cruikshank and blaaded aa the side of my head.
Wull Dryden, Gordon Highlanders
blaaded bled

I wis stannin aside Sir Arthur (Grant of Monymusk) when he had his airm blaan aff. A shell burst abeen wir heed and that wis him oot o the War. He wis wi us e gweed file in France and wis afa weel liket.
John Rennie, 5th Gordon Highlanders

Fin I wis wounded I wis sent hame to a hospital. I dinna think I wid hae gotten, if it wisna for the fact that the Canadians were gassed at Hill 60. They were needin beds and a lot o us were shifted and put on boats. We laand up in Cambridge in little mair than a shed.

I wis there a gweed file, and fin I wis better, I got hame leave. To croon aa, I took measles. Efter getting clear o that, I hid to report to heedquarters at Keith.
Jimmy Reid, 6th Gordon Highlanders
to croon aa to crown it all

I got Blighty aa richt nae lang efter an it wis at Murrial – it hid been flattened wi shells an we wis jist witen to gang in neist morning. The nicht afore I wis sent doon for rations wi the horse cairt and I wis sitting on ae beast jist ready ti caa awa back up the line fin a shell exploded hine awa faes an man, I felt something strick the side o the heed an I felt the bleed poorin doon the side o ma face. The horses wisna touched – that wis the peculiar thing.

I cam off the beast an cried doon a dugout an the lads cam oot an put a dressin ont. I wis teen doon ti the dressing station wi the stretcher-bearers. The doctor that attended me took oot a bittie o shrapnel oot o ma heed an telt me that it wis lodged a half inch fae ma jugular vein.

I wis presented wi the bit o shrapnel a it wis a wee bittie the size o ma thoomb nail an it hid deen a gweed bit o damage apparently. This wis a Blight ean this time.

I wis sent doon to a hospital ship at Calais an wis laid inti a bed ont an I mind the date fine – it wis 10th April 1917. Noo a sailor twa beds awa telt us that his ship hid been torpedoed the nicht afore an he'd been wounded in the blast an his ship hid sunk. We sailed that mornin early an waar weel oot fin a German torpedo strack us at ten meenits past eicht and this terrible explosion caased the boords and beds ti shift an the noise wis something infernal. Folk war baalin an shoutin and the boat started ti coup. I got oot o bed and I loused aff a lad neist ti ma – his feet war tied ti the fit o the bed. I couldna help him though, I hid eneuch helpin masel up the stair wi a crowdie tryin ti dee the same an a lot o folk cryin for assistance an I managed ti get on ti the deck.

I got to ae lifeboat bit a sailor in charge telt me ti keep back. It wis apparently loaded ti the gunnels wi Gerry prisoners o war. This sailor cut the ropes wi an axe an sent the boat heelstergowdie and the Gerries weet inti the sea.

I wis pittin on tae anidder boat an lowered inti the water safely an it wis jist clear o the hospital ship, an it wisna afore time edder cis the ship jist raise inti the air and gid a shudder an gid stracht doon an disappeared aneth the waves.

I dinna think there wis time ti save mony o the wounded; I niver saa a lot o wounded survivors. I didna see the lad I loused aff an I couldna trace a lad McGillvary fae Peterheed either that wis in the Gordon Highlanders wi me – oh na, they hidna a chance. The ship was caad *Landfranc*.[24] We were landed at Poole an I wis sent ti hospital.

John Brown, 5th Gordon Highlanders

heelstergowdie head over heels

I wis oot a gie file efter bein wounded at Third Ypres and wis fine please to get back to the same company. A lot hid happened– this wis efter the German Push and my company were aa strangers.

Albert Connon, 5th Gordon Highlanders

I was wounded on the 23rd of March 1918 as I rase out of a shell hole. This was by a burst of machine gun fire which caught me in both arms only. That was lucky I can tell you! I got them bandaged up and walked back to an ambulance which took me to Du-Lens. It was bombed and I got shifted farther down and then over to this country.

Dave Pitkethly, 4th Seaforth Highlanders

I waakit back for miles in the dark – jist masel and collapsed wi loss o bleed. Efter a file I heard folk comin newsin by an I spak oot ma an by christ they very near shot ma – they thocht I wis a Gerry. This wis twa lads comin by wi German prisoners an they seen bun up ma wounds an got the Gerries ti gee me a han doon ti the dressin post. I wis en attended tull an fell asleep. Fin morning cam I wis as wike as a bairn an couldna rise ata. A doctor cam ti see ma an atten ma wounds, he telt me that I hidna an inch o bleed left in ma body. He said it was a miracle I wis still livin.

I wis teen ti a Belgium hospital an ma folk got wird, I wis 'Missing Presumed Killed' fin I wise er.

Then I laand at hospital at Boulogne, far I looket ower the sea at the fite cliffs o Dover, jist lying in bed er jist fair mangin ti get hame – so far yet so near bi wy! Fit made it waar wis a doctor aye callin oot the names o the eens that war gan hame. It aye laand up wi me speirin if I wis gan neist – an saying ti the rest 'Jesus – I'll niver get oot o iss!' Tull ae efterneen he cam ti see ma and said he wid like ti sen ma hame bit only if I wis fit ti waak a bittie. I telt him I wid manage aa richt and rase aff the bed an tummeled doon on the fleer wi a rummel.

They were richt gweed and the nurses got ma claes on an put on a stretcher an teen doon ti the boat an inti the gunnels o the ship, inti a bed wi fancy swivels at baith ines. This keepit the bed on an even keel aa the time ye see – nae maiter fit the wider did. I hid a hellava job wi ma han: it wis scoobed iss wy look, and at the hospital I wis in, the doctor got on ti a matron for nae deein awa wi the scoob. He said ma han wid be clenched aa ma life if it wisna teen aff.

Fin they took it aff, they hid a hell o a time ot tryin ti strachen ma fingers – they cam aa richt, bit wi a tyav.

Fin I got better I laand up in Edinburgh Castle. There, Glesga recruits jined us an caased a lot o trouble. They war put up ti Fort George oot o the road.

We hid neen o that trouble up the line – at kine o folk war aa quait eneuch oot er.

Peter Baigrie, 7th Cameron Highlanders/6th Black Watch
seen bun up soon bandaged up, *wike* weak, *mangin* desperate, *rummel* crash, *tyav* struggle, *quait eneuch* quiet enough

There wis a lad Davie Burnett wi me. He was in the War fae the start and hid been fe-et roon the Turra wy afore the War. Do ye ken, that lad hid nae nerves ataa, aye he hid nae fear and wis a gie wild lad at the best o times.

Weel, he wis wounded five times. Dave telt me, fin it wis the fourth time, the doctor jist shewed him up and he wis teen doon to a place they caaed the Knackery. This wis because there wis nae hope o them getting better and were teen doon to dee. He wis telt they could get onything they wintit – they only had to speir: so he asked for Scotch and they gid him it.

Noo to croon aa, he pulled through and got back inti the scrap again and got wounded a fifth time fin he wis wi me. This time his leg hid to come aff and that wis him feenished weet.

He mairriet and gid awa sooth and did weel; bit fin he cam hame to Turra he aye looked me up for a news and a lach.

Alec Barlow, 1st Gordon Highlanders

I went down with flu and was very ill in hospital from December 1917 right through to March 1918. Then I was sent home on leave for 14 days. When I was there the Germans had came over on the offensive on 21st March. I expected to get called back from leave but never did.

When I got back, I was kept at base as they didn't know where to put me at first, as there was not many left of my battalion – the 6th. Eventually I was sent up to Arras to join the 1st Gordon Highlanders.
A. MacEwan, 6th Gordon Highlanders

Fin we cam oot o the line we bade at a place caa-ed Mailly-Mailly.[25] Then it wis back to Beaumont-Hamel and Y-Ravine to spen the hale winter tull Mairch 1917. Great dugoots, that wid hae held a hale battalion at a time, bit then we were oot in the trenches the maist o the time. There I took frostbite, and lost aa the feelin in ma feet. Twa stretcher-bearers telt ma to tak aff ma beets. I did, and couldna get them on again.

That nicht I traivelled wi a feoy mair for twa miles on tap o the hard frost wi ma stockin feet. Some o the men were on stretchers. I wis in hospital for a fair filie afore ma feet coured up.
Jimmy Milne, 2nd Gordon Highlanders

Once when I was wounded in the leg I went back to a dressing station manned by blackies. They dressed it and I went back up again. Shortly after I got hit in the hand. Again I went back up again after it was attended to.
Robert More MM, 4th Seaforth Highlanders

I landed up in Blighty in a hospital in Manchester for three months. I got home leave and reported back to Rippon. There I saw the new recruits being trained there and they were the scrapings of the barrel – they were only cannon fodder.

A sergeant stuck up a sign – I mind fine, it was a Sunday night – and this read 'Orders for tomorrow. Volunteers wanted for Machine Gun Corps!' We called them the 'Suicide Corps'.

Next day I went up to join but the sergeant wasn't going to put my name down at first but I insisted.

Ten of us were enrolled and were sent off to do our training at Sherwood Forest and I enjoyed it fine.
Albert Edwards, 5th Black Watch/Machine Gun Corps

I was with the 1st Yorks and Lancs when the Germans came over on 21st March 1918. This was near Bethune and I was wounded on the first day quite badly. I was taken down to a French hospital near Boulogne where an American doctor came to see me and I knew him. He had done a while in our battalion, 5th Gordon Highlanders, before the Americans came into the War. He recognised me and said, 'Hello Robbie – you will be all right now!' He newsed a while and gave me a jag in the chest and that put me out.

The next thing I remember is being down at the quay side lying on a stretcher. There I spent a whole night with many more wounded both officers and men mixed all together. During that one night many of them died before we were lifted on to a ship in the morning.

I landed up in a hospital in St Andrews Square in London run by a Russian princess. My next bedmate was Lt Colonel Thom of the 6th Gordon Highlanders, who had been a professional soldier before the War. I knew his brother who was an adjutant in another Gordon battalion.

I went for a convalescence to a hospital in Blackpool. This was a converted hotel.

When I got better, I had to report for PT and map reading. Then I was sent home on seven days' sick leave. Although I went out to France with batches of drafts several times I never got back to the Front again.

When War was finished I was in charge of a musketry school at Sandwich Bay.

Alec Robertson, 5th Gordon Highlanders

This is a poem [below] composed by a friend of mine and it describes one's feelings when ill with malaria.

William Mowat, 1st Scottish Horse and Lovat Scouts

Malaria
by Jimmy Gould

When your body's all ashiver and your brain is all afire,
And your legs become too clever and to antics weird aspire.
When you hate the sight of rooty (bread) and posey makes you sick;
When the very thought of duty makes your every nerve go click.
When your life seems one more blunder and your world is upside down;
You curse the War like thunder and you always wear a frown.
When your mail no more attracts you and you never want to write;
When delirium attacks you and you blether all the night.
When the tent pole seems to fidget and the time will never pass;
When your closest pal's an idiot and the MO seems an ass,
Then you've got it poor old chummy – the dingie dose I mean,
And they'll soak your little tummy with that horrible Quinine.

Struma Front 1916

31. Soldiers at military hospital, Rouen, France, June 1915. The group includes a Lovat Scout, a Gordon Highlander, and an Argyll and Sutherland Highlander.
Image © National Museums Scotland

Killed

The dead were half buried with uniform and kilt. They were disinterred and buried properly later on.
Robert More MM, 4th Seaforth Highlanders

We hid a Captain Mellis and a Sergeant Major Crystal. That Sergeant Crystal wis a staiger in peacetime: he traivelled a stallion. Weel they were stunning wi a gunner oot in the open, fin a shell cam ower and laand atween them and jist blew the three o them to bits. That wis at Cambrai. Captain Mellis was an afa nice man!
Bert Gow, Royal Field Artillery

My brither cairted deed doon fae the Somme for three months.
Alec Wilson, 7th Cameron Highlanders

Man, that Sergeant Crystal traivelled a staig doon in Buchan – I dinna ken farr. He wis killed the nicht afore he wis due to gang hame on leave.
John Russel, Royal Field Artillery

There wis a lad fae Byth here listed in '14; him and his brither, Jimmy and Farquhar Craib. Jimmy wis killed at Loos and his brither wounded. Jimmy wis killed ana fin he gid back. Na he didna lest lang!
Robert MacRobbie, 1st Gordon Highlanders

I got my breether killed the hindmost days o the War.
John Will, 5th Gordon Highlanders

I had a cousin in the Gordon Highlanders blown to pieces. When I was home on leave I went up to see his mother in New Deer and to offer my condolences. She showed me a photograph of his grave. I didn't say anything. This what makes me sad for the mothers. None of the dead were buried in a real grave but just on the battlefield. For instance – when we relieved the Canadians once – they were lying out in front of our trenches three deep.

We went out at night and buried them.

…

I was once talking to a man by the name of Cameron in this front line trench, when he was killed by a shell splinter just in front of my eyes. His father was a gamekeeper away up Inverness way. This lad was a lieutenant and I was then a captain at the time and he had been in the South African Police before volunteering, when War broke out.

…

Major Fowlie[26] was the first man to be killed of the 1st/5th Battalion Gordon Highlanders near Armentiéres in the War. He had a farm outside Oldmeldrum.
Alec Robertson, 5th Gordon Highlanders

There were a lot of corpses of the Yorkshire Yeomanry lying out and not a pretty sight. The Turks had taken their boots. Letters and photos lay scattered round them. We did our best to cover the bodies with lime as we couldn't bury them at the time.
William MacGregor, Lovat Scouts

Our dead were buried in their kilts.
A. Smeaton MM, 5th Black Watch

Fin we gid oot first at Mons-St-Éloi in 1914, aside Ancre, there wis only three graves in the kirkyard; they war airmen. Fin we cam back again the nesit year, all sweer there wis sax acre o graves. The maist o them were beeried shallow and I mind ae corps – they hidna even happit his taes!
Jimmy Reid, 6th Gordon Highlanders
happit covered up

Looking around a burial ground behind the Front we noticed a New Zealander had been interred there. Later that week I was going on leave to this country and met a chap newly arrived. He told me his brother had been killed. I asked his name and battalion and by a coincidence this was the same one.
John MacRae, 18th Battalion ANZAC

17

Horses and Mules

Horses and horsemen

One time a Cavalry regiment (King Edward's Horse) was struck by German fire, I think it was during an attack on the German lines but I am not sure. The horses started coming charging back through our lines, some with bad wounds. I managed to catch one fine black beast. This was in peak condition; I held on to it until the CO heard about it, and demanded I give it to him. I told him that would be all right provided I could acquire some bottles of my favourite rum. This was done.

The poor dead horses we disposed of by burying in shell holes; although the Frogs took a chunk out of the rump of a freshly killed beast, they said it was the finest meat of all. Not us – oh no.
A. Smeaton MM, 5th Black Watch

32. Royal Horse Artillery going into action. The field gun is pulled by a team of three pairs of horses, with one rider to each pair. An officer rides in front. The Royal Horse Artillery provided light horse-drawn guns to give the firepower to support a cavalry charge.

Reproduced by permission of the National Library of Scotland

The Frenchies were richt gweed horsemen on the ferms though. They hidna ony haimes I noticed, and jist used ae rine – the idder side of the heed wis tied back. Great horses they war tee – like Belgiums ye ken! Maist o the French Army beasts were gie hard lookin brutes, except their officers.

haimes hames (curved wooden beams attached to the collar), *rine* reins

…

I mind eence the German airplanes cam ower an drappit a shoor o bombs into oor horse transport lines. We were sleepin nae far awa fae them that night and saa fit happened. Michty fut a damage! This bombs jist took the peer beasts feet clean aff, leavin nae ither damage to the craturs.

Jimmy Reid, 6th Gordon Highlanders

It was the Indian troops that came up with the mules with supplies that amused me. When they were frightened, you could literally see the whites of their eyes.

When the mules came up to the Front, they walked very cautiously, but going back they put back their ears and ran like hell.

Alec Meldrum MM, 1st/8th Gordon Highlanders

33. A line of mules carrying ammunition for Field Artillery. Each animal has a pair of panniers, loaded with eight rounds of what appears to be 18-pound shells for a field gun. Mules were better able to cope than many of the horses in the extremely muddy conditions.

Reproduced by permission of the National Library of Scotland

Sandy Fraser in my company, was a little wee mannie – a staiger, and a great character. It was often argued whether he left more family round the countryside than did his staig.

William MacGregor, Lovat Scouts

I hid a beast that flopped on its belly whenever our own guns opened up over our heads or when any shell burst near.

A. Smeaton MM, 5th Black Watch

We hid an ald mule that took up wir rations at Ypres fae Brielen an there wis a fork in the road half wy up and the beast widna meeve farrer – he jist steed up and got richt thrawn. We tried to pull him wi ropes and that, bit at length we cam to ken to leave him be to mak up his ain mind as he finally set aff up some o the twa roads. There wis neen o them safe onywy as they were aye bein shelled.

Jimmy Scott, Royal Engineers

thrawn stubborn

34. An Army mule tied in a wooden crush or stocks to hold it steady while it is shod. Two soldiers are standing chatting nearby. The farrier's bellows can be seen in the foreground. They appear to be foot operated bellows and would have been used to heat the charcoal to soften the iron for the horseshoes.

Reproduced by permission of the National Library of Scotland

35. Hidden dangers to horses. Notice reads, ' Kindness to animals. 500 horses are lamed weekly by nails dropped on roads and horse lines by cookers carrying firewood with nails left in. Please remove nails'.

Reproduced by permission of the National Library of Scotland

The horses mostly came from the South American Pampas and were wild and strong. We had to break them in and that was quite a job I can tell you.

…

I was sorry for the horses, they were tied up without any shelter summer and winter and many died with cold.

Albert Napier MM, Royal Field Artillery ('Taggart's Own')

The winter wider took an afa toll o the peer horses and in the ine we war only left wi eicht still livin an on the day o departure, the craturs got their last task o pulln oor guns doon to the beaches an then they were slaughtered – shot dead – that wis the reward the peer things got for lestin throwe aa their time wi us throwe shellfire an shot at Gallipoli for nine month.

James Smith, Royal Field Artillery

I hid a name for aa the horse – een I caad Dick wis strack on the Somme wi a bittie shrapnel that gid inti his mane at ae side and cam oot at the idder. Bit he cam aa richt ye ken. Bit oh, we lost an afa horse.

Bert Gow, Royal Field Artillery

36. Horses on the front line. Showing the difficulty of transportation of gun limbers in muddy terrain.

Reproduced by permission of the National Library of Scotland

Some o oor lads war nae eese amang horses, they hid niver seen them afore they jined, that wis the wy folk like masel got aa the handling o them to dee.

They got corn and hie to ate bit the hie wis afa coorse stuff.

William Shearer, Royal Field Artillery

A poor horse had got entangled with the barbed wire. It was helpless and too sorely damaged that it had to be destroyed.

A. Smeaton MM, 5th Black Watch

I heard this horse comin gallopin doon the road. It wis pullin a wagon wi a Lewis gun mounted. I stopped the beast and it wis split aboot the nose and a wheel wis a bittie broken. I kent it wis een o oor ain so I took it back to wir lines. The driver said that shellin hid started and he hid jumped aff and lat the beast go.

Alec Nicol, 7th Gordon Highlanders

An auld donkey wis oor mascot for a lang time. It aye eenced to gang in front o us fin we were on the march. Man it wis richt cute: it kent fin the shells wis comin close or nae. He steed up and listened and his lugs shook back and fore. If he steed his grun, sae did we; bit if he made a breenge aff the road then we did anaa. Aa

149

weel, in the end he made a mistak and got killed peer breet. We missed him cis we hid him a lang time ye ken. Oh aye!

Alec MacHardy MM, 7th Gordon Highlanders

breenge jump/plunge

When the mules came up at night with supplies their ears were forward and they were very thrawn to move – they were feart at the noise and shelling and that. When we unloaded them their ears went back and they took off at the gallop down the line to safety. It was like a derby with their drivers jumping on to their backs. It gave us a good laugh.

Albert Edwards, 5th Black Watch/Machine Gun Corps

I wis aye richt sorry for the horses: they were big targets fin the shells were fleein aboot.

Bert Gow, Royal Field Artillery

I was in the guard of honour to Lord Roberts' funeral ceremony and by God! the French had the finest horses I iver saa. They were like fit ye see on the White Horse whisky bottles: sma heedies, sma leggies and lang neckies – jist the royalty o shalts.

Jimmy Reid, 6th Gordon Highlanders

I spent fower winters oot there, eence at a place caad Brail we bigg'ed stables. Aye, bit jist the reefs ye ken! Civvies cut the trees for us and we made shelters o twa staas at a time. A lot o the peer horses de-et wi the cauld and this wis aye a reef to the peer breets to shelter them fae the cauld.

    They got hie to ate. This hid to cam fae England. Although we did eence cut a park o girse awaa back a bit and caa-ed this stuff to them in aa. We got a ration o corn for them as weel.

John Russel, Royal Field Artillery

girse grass

I niver seen sae gran horses that belonged to the Indian Cavalry – Arab shults – aa toppers.

Harry Nicoll, Royal Engineers

This is something might interest you. There was an outbreak of strangles[27] in our horses in England. It is like flu in people and only certain folk were delegated the job of looking after them. A lad Noble did it for our troop and had to disinfect his boots and gear. Anyway they got over it. Strange thing there was no cases of grass sickness – that I think was never much seen till later years and was a terrible killer amongst mostly working farm horses. There was no cure.

William MacGregor, Lovat Scouts

Some o the horses got accustomed to the shelling if it wis nae ower close. I mind seein a horse team comin gallopin doon a road in daytime – this wisna far fae Ypres. There wis some sna on the grun an it wis a Sunday, bit a fine morning as we war sittin aboot oot in the open weel back fae the front line.

Suddenly salvos o shells began explodin ahin them bit they kept gallopin up this lang road wi us expecting them to be blaan to bits at ony meenit – bit na na, they made it aa richt but it wis a close thing.

Jimmy Scott, Royal Engineers

The poor horses were lying dead everywhere and some still alive but couldn't rise. That was a terrible sight.

Robert More MM, 4th Seaforth Highlanders

I wis glad I wisna among horses oot er as I first winted, cis the craters hid an afa time ot.

Peter Baigrie, 7th Cameron Highlanders/6th Black Watch

Commandeering horses

The Army cam roon the ferms and commandeered ony horses that they fancied. I aye mind fin they cam to Fyvie Kirk on Sunday service and took aa the good shalts that wis there aat day. Of coorse there wis plenty o shalts and gigs, that's aa there wis at that time ye ken.

George Carroll, Machine Gun Corps

I got a letter fae hame sayin that ma gweed pair o horses I vrocht afore I gid awa, hid been commandeered by the Army. I jist could near hae grutten fin I read that. In the letter, my mother speired if I wid look oot for them – but there wis nae much chance o that.

John Rennie, 5th Gordon Highlanders

grutten wept, *vrocht* worked, *speired* asked

Fin the War started the Army cam oot to Dallachy Ferm and commandeered gweed horses. They were peyed for them of coorse bit then some o the richt horse dealers got involved wi buying horses here and er for the Army and they fairly swickit them I'll tell you – there wis nae doot aboot that.

William Shearer, Royal Field Artillery

swickit swindled

I mind the Waar hid jist started and this Sunday I took ald Meg doon to the kirk at Fyvie fae the jiners at Monkshill wi the shult an gig. Onywy I likit to deet an she aye gid me a saxpence. Aye a sixpence wis a lot o siller to a young apprentice ye ken at that time. Weel the Army cam an lifted five shults fin we were in the kirk an at wis the five best eens an there wis plenty o shults and gigs an dog cairts there. Weel fit do ye think – ald Meg's een wis een o the shults teen.

It wis an afa thing to dee, leevin naething bit a teem gig and folk left stranded to waak hame. Weel ald Meg couldna waak far, so I traivelled richt back fower mile and got her neeper's shult – aye, Coburn the sooters een, it wis a sam beast, an took it richt back to the kirk to bring Meg and the gig hame.

They did leave the harness though. Oh na, they didna tak it.

Jimmy Scott, Royal Engineers
neeper's shult neighbour's pony

18

Behind the Lines

We war billeted in a French barn eence fin we were oot o the line foe a rist.

I wis playin aboot wi a stick an chappit it into the clay waa. A wifie cam rinnin roon and shouts, 'Ici! Ici!' She was in an afa rage, so I gid awa roon wi her an fun ma stick hid cam oot in her kitchen abeen the churn.

...

The dogs hid to work – awite they hid! They caad the churn, penned into a criv affair wi a wheel wi paddles ont. The craturs traivelled on this paddle and this caaed the churn.

Files they used ae dog, bit I've seen them haein twa, my god I thocht it wis great!
Jimmy Reid, 6th Gordon Highlanders
criv enclosure

The French thought the War would be lost if the Virgin Mary fell off that cathedral in Albert, so they wired her to the wall and she never did [see note 20].
Albert Napier MM, Royal Field Artillery ('Taggart's Own')

It wis the reliefs I didna like. Mony a lad got the works comin in or oot o the line.
A. Smart, 5th Gordon Highlanders

I wis an afa smoker oot there. I drove oor major aboot in a motor bike and sidecar. His fadder was a director of Craven A company. He presented me wi a tin o 50 every day. I've seen ma tongue hingin oot fair kepperd. I've seen me smoke twa at a time!
Jimmy Scott, Royal Engineers
kepperd kippered

I mind fin we were oot o the line, I sat on the binder on a French ferm. Some o the other lads helpet oot tee. We like't to de-et.
John Rennie, 5th Gordon Highlanders

There wis ae wild mannie – he was aye in trouble – got drunk ae time we were oot the line. Fin comin back he got afa impudent wi the duty sergeant and startet fechtin wi him. The lads on guard collared him and the sergeant put him on a charge. He widna waak to the guard room and said, 'Ah weel if am arrestet, then am nae gan to traivel – you'll hae to cairry me!'

They carried him aa richt, bit they wuppit him up in barbit weer first. Fin the roster officer saa him later on, he ordered the weer to be teen aff. He said, 'Who the hell did this? There's no prisoner should be tied up like this!'

That lad wis teen awa faes aa thegither in the end.

Alec Sim, 7th Gordon Highlanders

wuppit wrapped

Spies

At Bethune yonner a mannie hid a fite horse. He wis a Gerry spy that vrocht as a farm servant. Fin oor folk were on the march he wis aye seen oot on the parks wi the horse: then doon cam a barrage on the road. The French finally jaloused he wis a spy and took him awa.

Norrie Cruikshank, 6th Gordon Highlanders

I think the Gerries hid a lot o spies ahin the line. I mind ae time it wis getting rale dark an a puckle os war sittin outside hain a blether fin twa officers cam doon by. Een o oor lads thocht there wis something nae aa thigidder richt aboot them efter they hid gone oot o sicht. So we decided to investigate and follow them to see far they had geen, and a feoy os includin masel gid aff to trail them. Weel, we niver fun them, they hid skedaddled aff back to their ain lines in the dark maybe jalousin we war onto them. Oh aye they tried aa the tricks o the day ye ken.

Jimmy Scott, Royal Engineers

19

On Leave

I cam hame on leave fae the Front efter a lang time oot. I gid to a dance in the Howe. There I saa Corporal Knox – a great worthy, hame wounded fae the 1st Gordon Highlanders. He wis showin an ald bullet wound to some young ferm loons an they were geein him nips. George fair likit a dram an I thoct, 'By God George, yer fair in clover the nicht!'

Bert Gow, Royal Field Artillery

nips measures of whisky

I didna like leave, although the leaves I got wis fin I got wounded and that wis fower times: eence at Ypres, eence on the Somme, then oot a bittie fae Arras, and at Rheims.

Onywy fin I wis on leave folk said, 'Oh yer hame are ye? Ye surely didna bide lang awa ... !' They didna realise fit wis goin on oot er. Na, na, I aye liket to be back amang the lads.

…

I winted back a German rifle: it wis really a great gun. Bit then ye see we werena allowed to tak back a thing, so I thocht up an idea. I put on bricks instead o a kilt and put the gun doon ae leg at the leave boat. Of coorse this gid me a stracht leg. A Red Cap (RMP) wis houndin aabody aboard and een paid particular attention to me and shouted for me to get a move on and nae hinder aabody, so I fell oot on him and telt him that if he he'd a leg like mine he widna be fit to gang about and mak sic a soon like he wis deein.

Weel do you ken, he apologised and efter aat they couldna dee eneuch for me: they even escorted me aff the boat at the ither side and on to the train. That's fit a hard neck dis for yet.

Alec MacHardy MM, 7th Gordon Highlanders

bricks trousers (breeks), *soon* sound/noise

I got leave after a year in the front line and got two weeks at home.

A. MacEwan, 6th Gordon Highlanders

I got hame leave wi anither lad fae Fyvie, efter a hale eer in France. We only hid siven days, so we planned to bide another wick.

We gid back to the Front thegither.

To get by the Military Police at the stations, fa war aa lookin at passes at the railway gates, we jist hade till the trains war near pullin oot an then rushed by them shoutin we were late an flashin oor passes in their faces. They aye hurried us on withoot lookin. Weel we got richt back to wir units an they niver jaloosed a thing.

John Webster, Royal Field Artillery

hade held on, *jaloosed* suspected

I cam hame on leave an flung aff ma claes in the shed afore I gid into the hoose. They were jist meevin wi lice.

Alec Pratt MM, Royal Horse Artillery

I came home on leave for the first time after a long time out there. Going back I had to stop off at a camp at Rippon. I walked into the place and pulled out a fag and lit it. Immediately I heard a shout from the guard room, 'Put that man under arrest'. The guard turned out and grabbed me and took me to the guard room where I was charged with smoking before 10am. I later got dinner and was asked by a regimental sergeant major if I wanted a court martial or sent on my way to my train. I replied, 'No no, just let me out of here!' So I was taken down to the train and there I saw a draft of men – over 100 for France. With a wad of papers as thick as this, an officer asked me to take charge of them. I said, 'No Sir, I won't touch them – I am on open arrest'.

The officer then came all the way over with me with the draft and handed them over to me on the other side. Then he took the boat back. I knew as soon as I got to the other side I was clear of the charge then.

There was nothing they could have done about it anyway. Don Sutherland and another lad had got done at Rippon for the same thing. They had made a hellava noise about it apparently and got free – but not me, oh no! My medal was handed over in the open one rainy day after waiting with a lot of others for hours. After this terrible wait a high ranking officer handed it over.

Robert More MM, 4th Seaforth Highlanders

By this time I had served five years in the Scouts and was now due discharge. There was many other time-expired men there and we were asked to sign on again and go home for a month's leave and I had no hesitation in doing so. I think the boat I sailed home on was the *Transylvania* from Mississippi and we reached Devonport and took the train for Edinburgh and stopped all night with a lad Finlayson – a piper who came from Plockton. He took me along to see this lassie he knew at Leith by the name of Campbell. We went along to catch a tram for

Leith when the power for the trams went out and we walked all the way. There had been a big fore in Edinburgh that night and rumours were about that it had been caused by a German airship and the next rumour we heard was that a German spy caused it.

Anyway we walked out to Miss Campbell's house and I remember she welcomed us into the house and I met her parents and sat in front of a roaring fire and listened to records – a far cry from Gallipoli. We walked back and slept in Waverley Station and headed up north next day.

I stayed with my brother Eddie where he was keeper on the Findhorn on Brodie Estate. I enjoyed my stay helping him and fishing for salmon in the Findhorn every day. I went to a local dance one night and I had a devil of a time getting a partner – they were all booked up – I had never seen the like, although I did get a look in now and again – I saw to that all right. I also had a lot of good evenings with my mates who were home on leave like me.

Time came for me to go back on the long road to Egypt, where I rejoined my brigade at Kharga Oasis and remained there till October 1916.

William MacGregor, Lovat Scouts

Fin we got hame leave we hid to tak wir rifles bit wi nae ammunition. Weel fin I wis gan on to the boat I fun some ammunition still in my belt. Well michty me, if the MPs hid gotten ma wi that on me – I wid hae been puttin stracht back to my company withoot leave. Weel I managed to hide them in time. At hame I made sure they were aa fired aff, afore I got on the road back, in the Howe o Tifty.

…

I managed to smuggle back a richt gweed Stanley plane – a thing I aye hiv yet min. I used it aa my days.

Jimmy Scott, Royal Engineers

Ae day fin we were oot o the line, some os gid doon to this placie to hear wir pipe band playin. I spoke to Piper Jake Gow fae Strichen a gie filie. I later saa oor quartermaster caa-ed Sim and spiered aboot my leave – I hid been oot for 14 months. He said that my leave wis noo due and that he wid lat ma ken onytime. Sim wis a big Glesga bobby bit a richt fine chiel. Twa nichts later, I wis jist beddin doon and I heard him giein me a cry and I loups oot o ma bunk. He said, 'Come on Milne youll hae to be on your wy!' Weel I swear I shifted mysel then and got awa doon the road. There wis a big doo on fin I wis awa and oor battalion got an afa smashin. This wis on the end October 1917. There wis jist een o my machine gun crew left. This wis the Battle for Gheluvelt.

Jimmy Milne, 2nd Gordon Highlanders

There wis ae lad fae aside Macduff invited me hame wi him fin we were trainin in Aiberdeen. This wis a wickend pass. Noo his fadder hid a ferm and my pal telt me to watch fit I wis sayin cis his fadder wis afa religious. He warned me nae to start atein at the table tull grace hid been said. Onywy I got on great and didna blot my copybook.

That same pal hid to ging hame to Blighty wi a maist peculiar injury, up in the trenches at Arras in the winter o '16–'17. That wis a clay hole if iver there wis and a dashed cald een: the frost wis terrible. Onywy a bittie o clay hid frozen hard tull his knee so he'd raxed doon and pulled it aff and man! didn't he nae tak skin and flesh and aa. This wis jist afore the Battle o Arras.

He wis oot o action a lang time and I never saa him again becis he wis killed fin he gid back. I jist missed him at Aiberdeen station. He wis gan on to a train and I wis comin aff anither een. I ran in tull his sister in the station; she hid been seein him awa. She telt me, 'Willie his jist geen awa wi that train the noo – you've jist missed him!' Ah weel! That wis the feeenish o him: he wis killed shortly efter. His folk had a place at the Langmanhill.

Alec Barlow, 1st Gordon Highlanders

The second leave I got I stopped at a place in London – I had been advised what to do by some chaps that were in the know. I said to this chap at the counter that I had missed my train for the north. He gave me £2 and went back to the pub. We got free food there into the bargain. I did this a few days till they began to know me, even though I changed my tickets with the Gordon Highlanders. Then I went off home on leave. By that time our leave had to be seven days at home.

Robert More MM, 4th Seaforth Highlanders

Commandeering rails

Then I mind fine fin they cam an commandeered railins roon the hooses for scrap metal an if ye look at a lot o big hooses' dykes at the present day – you'll see naething but the stumps o the steel railins. That wis niver renewed. Apparently there wis nae compensation for the rails – weel at least that's fit I heard.

Jimmy Scott, Royal Engineers

20

Medals

Oor company wis ristin jist witein to gang into action at High Wood so I wis half asleep kine, fin I got a bit kick to waken up. This wis to alert me to the adjutant comin up. He telt me that I had been recommended for the MM. I wis ass tired I could hardly tak in fit he wis sayin.

A feoy wicks on I wis lyin in a hospital in Manchester. There wis twa o us Scots thegither. Ae day I spotted twa MPs approachin wir beds. I says, 'Michty me fit hiv I deen wrang noo?'

Weel they cam up to ma and een o them speired if I was MacHardy and I says I wis. 'Oh well,' he says, 'I beg to inform you that you have won the Military Medal and you are being asked if you would like to be presented with it in hospital, or would you rather wait to be presented with it in front of your regiment!' Well I kent the hale battalion would have to be paraded for an affair o that kind and I didna care for that ava. I said to the Red Cap, 'Na na that's ower muckle bother – come awa weet! Geese huds ot!'

'Oh no,' he says 'You will have to wait a week: we'll get up a high ranking officer and do it in style!' Well the matron wis richt guid tull me and got up a 'doo' for me and I got presented withoot much bother and ceremony. She even laid on a cake for me.

Alec MacHardy MM, 7th Gordon Highlanders
geese huds ot give me a hold of it, i.e. just give it to me now

Three Ypres. Steenbeck for us was a bad battle – we had a lot of casualties. Private McIntosh[28] was in my company there and when we advanced we came to a stream and while crossing it we came under fire from a Gerry machine gun post which pinned us down. McIntosh went off through the stream alone and charged the post killing two

37. Private George McIntosh.
Gordon Highlanders Museum

159

men and injuring another. He then carried back two machine guns with him completely oblivious to enemy fire. That was bravery although I cannot tell you what bravery is. He got the VC (see art section) and was just a loon.
A. MacEwan, 6th Gordon Highlanders

I remember going up the line and Sergeant Gardiner said to me, 'I have you in for a medal Dave'. I replied, 'Look Jock, if I come out of this with my life – that's all I need.'
Dave Pitkethly, 4th Seaforth Highlanders

21

Vermin

_____

The lice were an awful job: we were always glad of a change of clothing.
George Bryan MM, 12th Highland Light Infantry

We hid an afa nesty officer: naebody hid a guid word on him. He aye sure wark he
got deloused every fortnicht, bit wisna neen concerned aboot us – eence the twa
month wis aa that we got deen. It wis decided to play a trick on him: we started to
collect lice in a spunk box fae ae body and aabody a wick afore. So fin the officer
cam back fae bein deloused there wis a fine hungry set o lice aa witin for him in his
bunk. Man, he wis nearly atein alive. Fut a lach we aa got, and do ye ken iss, that
did the trick: he took the hint and we got doon mair aften.
…
I mind ae chiel driven frantic wi the lice, took aff his sark, hung it up on a post and
fired a shot at it. Man, I'll niver forget that!
Jimmy Scott, Royal Engineers
spunk box matchbox, *sark* shirt

The lice wis afa – we niver got clear o em. We changed claes bit of coorse didna
weer muckle in the heat onywy. The sandstorms fin the win rase wis terrible. It
wis an afa place o thunner and lightnin tee.
Harry Nicoll, Royal Engineers

The first lice we got were aff the Algerians, fin we moved into their billets efter
they left. Great big black lice they war.
Alec Pratt MM, Royal Horse Artillery

We usually tried to get a regular bath in the sea at Gallipoli. We were no distance
from it. We tried to burn the lice out of the seams of our clothes and even cut out
the seams altogether and sewed them up again but that hanked them too narrow
for comfort. I've seen us when away on our own like when at the Balkans – we
were never troubled with lice but as soon as we went into positions vacated by
other troops down we went with a big bloody dose again right away.
William MacGregor, Lovat Scouts

We eenced to be sittin roon a fire wi wir sarks aff pickin lice, an then we ran a candle up the seams. We thocht neething aboot it!
Bert Gow, Royal Field Artillery

'Jesus! We niver got clear o the lice. Ae trick wis to rub wir claes wi creosote – bit aat burned like hell.
Alec Nichol, 7th Gordon Highlanders

You couldn't avoid the lice because we just lay down where other troops had lain. When we got our clothes washed – the ones we put on were worse than the ones we took off. We all got scabies as well. The ointment we got for that was strong.
…
There was an issue of a blanket apiece but it wasn't long before it could walk faster than you could with the lice on it you see. We mostly didn't bother with them but just huddled down with our coats round us.

We washed our kilts with strong disinfectant but this rotted them.
Dave Pitkethly, 4th Seaforth Highlanders

We wis aa richt lousy tull the last day o the War. You couldna weer seemits nor drawers – ye wid hae been aten alive. I mind ma midder makkin twa flannen sarks an I wore een fin I wis on leave an took the idder een back to France wees. Fin I got oot er I had a files lookin for my battery. I fun em ristin in a barn doon at Valenciennes. Noo at place hid been in Gerry hands for eers an fin I settled doon in the strae I wis jist as lousy a hell in nae time.
Bert Gow, Royal Field Artillery

I mind eense gan doon to Armentiéres to the landry wi a puckle mair, fin we were oot o the line to get a delouse. We gid in to a shed and steed aside a canvas door and stripped aff aa wir claes and haand them in through a hole in the canvas to some giggling quines to steam and iron. They warna lang aboot it though.
John Rennie, 5th Gordon Highlanders

We aye keepit tyavin and fidgetin aboot wi the lice. I think this helpit keep ye warm, aye ye ken – fae freezing in the cald nichts.
Alec MacHardy MM, 7th Gordon Highlanders

The first time I met in wi the lice wis fin I gid oot the first time – at Boulogne. There wis sax os spent the nicht in a bell tent on the sands. Fin I lookit oot in the morning – I saa twa lads jist across faes wi their sarks aff pickin aff lice. I shouts oot ti the ither lads ti come an see iss. Then in a feoy minutes we war aa scrattin wirsels – the sands war fu o em.

In a fortnicht wis claes and kilts war aa rotten wi em. I eenced ti tac a cannle up the seams and ye could hear em crackin again. We eenced to get a steam bath noo ni an; aa bare nyaakit an ye could see the dirt comin [rystin?] aff yer skin an ging rinnin doon. Wir claes war aa deen inaa – aa steamed an ironed, bit in the space o aa nicht we wis a loosey again.

Peter Baigrie, 7th Cameron Highlanders/6th Black Watch

Simmer wis afa het an we noo in an gid doon ti the sea, bit nae ower mony at a time – an dookit in the water. That helpit relieve ye o some lice, for wir claes an the sma o the back wis jist hatchin wi them aa the time, an de ye ken, fin the lice mixed and bred wi the Turkish eens, they took on a new lease of life – oh aye! there wis hell to pay.

At the bathing party – the quartermaster sergeant issued ye wi a new washed sark an ye gid him your een, bit by the neist day it wis jist heesin wi lice again.

I fell heir ti a lot o blankets fin I got on for the quartermaster sergeant there masel, for then I made sure that I acquired the personal blankets o aa the deed, an all tell ye they cam in right handy fin the terrible cauld winter cam.

James Smith, Royal Field Artillery

The lice were terrible and ass thicks we couldna pick them aff. The first eens I saa wis, fin we did a trainin spell efter we laand in France at the Bull Ring. The lice were crawlin aa ower the place. It wis hard bloody trainin though.

John Will, 5th Gordon Highlanders

38. Soldier having his hair cut, probably at Ypres, 1915. With the problems of lice in the trenches, short hair was less likely to harbour infestations of insect life.

Image © National Museums Scotland

The lice were on everyone from the CO down. We never defeated them.
Alec Meldrum MM, 1st/8th Gordon Highlanders

I was on guard fae midnicht to twa in the morning. There wis sna on the grun. Weel, I niver saa sae mony rats. The sna wis jest meevin wi them: they were rinnin aa ower ma beets ana. They couldna get mait and were scavenging for it in the streets and aa way.

…

Ae deed lad – I kent him fine – hid to be guarded till sic time as we could get him beeried. I did iss in a cellar itherwise the rats wid hae atein him.

…

Fin we was at ae place, there cam on a fite shooer. This wis a ruined village. We war gan in tull a timmer hut to bide in that nicht. This wis on tap o a brae. Noo the village wis meevin wi rats and we aa thocht it wis better to gang up there to get clear of them.
John Russel, Royal Field Artillery
fite shooer white shower

The bloomin rats were afa. Eence oor detachment were sleepin in shelters made o corrugated iron. At nicht they eence to scrape their wy up ae side and efter a file ging slidin doon the ither. Een o them must have been gassed; he wheeshed oot something infernal aa night and ivery night. We tried to get him bit never did. This was at Brielen nae far fae Ypres.
Jimmy Scott, Royal Engineers

They were terrible: like dogs, and livin on deed bodies. Eence fin we were livin in the deep German dugoots, I wakened up and fun a big rotten lyin deed atween my feet. I had squeezed it to death fin I wis sleepin.

Some o oor game lads acquired ferrets – gweed kens far fae – and they turned the craturs lowse. Man they fairly killed the rats and they in turn bred like hell tee. Oh, you've nae idea fit gid on!
Alec MacHardy MM, 7th Gordon Highlanders
rotten rat, *gweed kens far fae* goodness knows where from

The rats were the size of cats. I used to feed them food and got great sport shooting them – my pastime out there.
A. MacEwan, 6th Gordon Highlanders

At Arras we lived in cellars. Rats were everywhere. Some lads baited them with bread and sniped at them when they showed.
J. Fowlie, 7th Gordon Highlanders

Wild abandoned dogs were everywhere on the Struma Front and were shot on sight, but I remember when out with a patrol one night getting a right good fright when we disturbed a herd of pigs when we were creeping through a field of corn. They were frightened too I suppose and came schweeling out and charging right through is. We were only out in the first place because folk had been seen there that day. We didn't fire though. Snakes abounded there and I once woke up with one up my trouser leg and was glad to kill it before it did any damage.
William MacGregor, Lovat Scouts

The rats were all over the place as big as that dog there. When you fired a bullet at them, it had to be a shot in the head that would kill.
Robert More MM, 4th Seaforth Highlanders

Aye wis niver sae pleased ti get oot o Passchendaele. Duckboards were the only means o gettin aboot; I niver saa grun sae weet, an at nicht ye could hear the rats plapperin aboot on em. We tried wir best ti kill em bit they near aye got awa. They war livin on deed bodies an war big an fat an multiplied like hell.
John Brown, 5th Gordon Highlanders
plapperin splashing

We war infested wi rats an wild dogs anaa, aa feastin on the deed bodies – oh yiv nae idea!
Peter Baigrie, 7th Cameron Highlanders/6th Black Watch

Malaria became a problem [at the Salonica Front]. We heard that some parts were uninhabited during the summer due to infestment of mosquitoes and we eventually occupied the high parts to escape them. Almost three quarters of our force were infected.
William Mowat, 1st Scottish Horse and Lovat Scouts

22

In the Line

I widna blame naebody for rinnin awa. They barket at ye aa the time and treated ye like a dog.

…

It wis a case o getting rale wilie fin we war oot a filie. I eenced to aye look afore I jumpet.

We jist bedded doon in the winter ootside wi wir cwites on and a blanket roons. We jist sat doon and smok'et and fell asleep.

Norrie Cruikshank, 6th Gordon Highlanders

wilie cunning, *cwites* coats

Sentry-go wis a sleepy job an ye hid tae hae yer wits aboot ye tee an hae a gweed look oot aa the time. I mind stunnin on the firestep fin I hears this soon like folk creepin aboot, awa oot in No Man's Land. Then I hears feet plouterin aboot so I cried, 'Who goes there!' an naebody replied; an I cried a second time and there wis nae answer. I got a Mills bomb ready an got ready ti pull the pin and throw it. Then I cried a third time an got an answer fae Jim MacArdle fae Boddam – him that had the larries. I telt them to advance an be recognised. I eenced to chew the fat efter the War wi Jim aboot at. I drove a larry for him wi cattle and sheep an that to marts for a gweed file.

John Brown, 5th Gordon Highlanders

plouterin splashing, *larries* lorries

I didna smoke ataa, and eased to gamble aa my Red Bazaar fags that I got.

Alec Nicol, 7th Gordon Highlanders

In the early days the Germans used dum-dum bullets which left terrible wounds. We blamed the Prussian Guard.

Robert More MM, 4th Seaforth Highlanders

The langest time I wis in the front line wis a month.

Jimmy Reid, 6th Gordon Highlanders

There hid been an attack on the German lines. Twa days later we were there and aa the deed were still lyin. We saa oot in front os the bodies o the Highlanders lying on their faces with their kilts aa flung forrit wi their backsides aa bare. There wis ae lad and a Gerry held up by barbet weer and their bayonets still stickin in een and ither.

John Webster, Royal Field Artillery

The boldest lads that war blain fit they war gan to dee to the Gerry, were nae aye the best, fin it cam to the real thing – na faith ye!

George Stewart, 5th Gordon Highlanders

blain blowing (off), i.e. boasting

The Australian sentries fell asleep ae nicht. The Germans cam ower, got the hale lot sleepin and bayoneted aabody. Well, that's fit I heard!

Norrie Cruikshank, 6th Gordon Highlanders

The sentries went up and lay on the parapet every 30 yards apart with their eyes firmly fixed to the front. They were later relieved by another who had been stood down in the trench. They took it in turn. A sergeant or corporal had to keep in touch with them every now and then.

If a sentry was caught asleep – the NCOs were supposed to report him but they didn't unless they were accompanied by an officer. Of course the NCO didn't let him off but warned him as sternly as they could of the consequences.

Alec Robertson, 5th Gordon Highlanders

There wis ae pairt o the line it the Gerry an wirsels eence ti news ti een an ither. We were that close. I mine they files socht bully beef and we wid fling a tin ower ti them and they wid hae geens something back. They werna bad ata – we didna wint ti upset een an ither. In fact there wis gweed drinkin watter atween the line an there wis an unerstannin ti baith ging fort thegither.

…

I mine we were lyin in the lyth o an ald hoose an the Gerry hid been shellin awa ats for days. We ran oot o tobacco, so I peeled broon waapaper aff a waa an rolled aat and smokit it, bit oh it was coorse!

Peter Baigrie, 7th Cameron Highlanders/6th Black Watch

lyth lee/shelter

The 1st and 2nd Gordon Highlanders hid nae time for us at a start. Oh no – we warna trained sogers by their wy. Bit then they were seen aa killed aff by the time o the Somme so they war ready to accept us then as equals.

Alec MacHardy, 7th Gordon Highlanders

39. Soldiers crossing the river Ancre, France. This photograph depicts four British soldiers using a fallen tree trunk as a temporary bridge over the river Ancre.

Reproduced by permission of the National Library of Scotland

The man on sentry [at Salonica] that night was very nervous – he kept seeing movement and getting excited. I told him there was nothing there but that didn't placate him. I could hear ducks in the water but that was all. Eventually Wattie's nerves got the better of him and he lay down and moaned an carried on – I expect his baptism of fire they day before had been too much for him. I got him taken back and in fact I never saw or heard of him again.

William Mowat, 1st Scottish Horse and Lovat Scouts

Glasgow lads were sent to us as reinforcements and they were very wild lads and caused a lot of fights for a start, but after a while up the line they soon quietened down. This was towards the end of the War and a lot of them were killed at Cambrai.

Up at Arras was the nearest we were to the Gerry trenches.

Dave Pitkethly, 4th Seaforth Highlanders

There wis nae clear nichts in the trenches; there wis aye something gan on; aye somebody gettin it in the neck.

We sleepit stunnin up. There wis dugoots we made at the boddom o the trenches bit they werna worth a damn – jist clay holes far we sat doon in atweem guards. It wis jist a case o sleepin stunning up. There wis sentry duties to dee on the fire step. To fa asleep fin there wis punishable by death. I eence fell asleep – I couldna help it – bit I wakened up afore the duty officer cam roon, itherwise I wid hiv got the works.

…

In daylicht it wisna safe to pit as much as a finger abeen the parapet: ye wid hae gotten a bullet through it richt awa – oh aye! The Gerry were very good at the snipin. I dinna think we snipit to ony extent – nae like them.
Willie Gavin, 5th Gordon Highlanders

In the early days in 1914 we made horseshoe positions on tap o the grun wi sandbags cis the trenches were fu o dubs an watter.
Jimmy Reid, 6th Gordon Highlanders

When going into the trenches, we sometimes had miles to walk on duckboards if conditions were bad; this caused a lot of casualties from sporadic shellfire.
Jock Murray, 1st King's Own Scottish Borderers

I've seen us jist deein for a drink o watter and takkin it oot o a shell hole that later revealed dead bodies in int. We het up the watter in dixies wi twa cannles aneth them. The cannles we got, fin back at the Sally Annes.
Alec MacHardy MM, 7th Gordon Highlanders
cannles candles

We did a little bayonet fighting – I got nicked here look. But didn't report sick. I just wrapped it up.
Alec Robertson, 5th Gordon Highlanders

There was a very strange occurrence happened when a sergeant took me along while we paid an inspection of our machine gun crews out in No Man's Land. This was in the dark of course. Off we went carefully over to where the first machine gun crew was set up but the sergeant seemed to miss it and deviate towards the German Front. I was amazed to see him suddenly stand straight upright and hold up his hands and set off to the German line crying, 'Kamerad … Kamerad … .' It was quite dark but I could see that much. The Germans threw some grenades and one of them silenced him – I had gone to ground by this time. When things quieted down I crept forward and found him lying badly hurt. He was able however to get back to our own line supported by me when the commotion died down completely and was sent down to the field hospital on a stretcher. I heard that he died of his wounds. His intention had been to surrender there was no doubt. His nerves must have been bad and had been unable to take any more.

I didn't report what he did though there would have been too much bother. He came from Glasgow way.

…

I was promoted to corporal which made me responsible for ten men but I refused to be a sergeant when they offered it to me.
A. MacEwan, 6th Gordon Highlanders

Oor job wis to rig up observation points. So we made an imitation metal tree. First we made a measurement ot in the dark. Then we made it and a ledder to gang up the inside ot, wi slits for lookin oot at the enemy. Then we shew the tree doon in the dark and installed the metal een in its place.

The warst scare I got at that caper wis fin we were riggin up a tree hine back fae the Front. In spite o using camouflage mesh the enemy spotted us. I wis up on the tap and I think I meeved the mesh wi ma back. Onywy they sent ower a salvo o shells and doon aabody gid except me; I wis stuck hard and fast wi twa hooks on my tunic on this mesh. Man the Gerry kept hauddin them ower and aye the rest of the lads were shoutin in atween 'Are you all right Jock!' Thank God it stoppit, otherwise I widna be here the day.
Jimmy Scott, Royal Engineers

Coming out at Hill 60, the 2nd Cameron Highlanders lost a lot of men. It was a silly blooming officer that put them the wrong way. We usually came down the way and out at a railway line but he put them the other way, where they were exposed on a ridge.

I was on a reserve line at the time and I saw the whole thing. It was a terrible scene when the whole barrage came down on top of them. Of the Somme, Arras and Ypres Fronts, I think Hill 60 was the worst.
Donald MacVicar, 1st/2nd The Queen's Own Cameron Highlanders

Bombing was a tricky job. I was the bomber for a while and had to lead the advance and throw grenades to make room for the rest of them coming.
Robert More MM, 4th Seaforth Highlanders

23

Over the Top

You didn't linger long when you were going over the top of the trench – that's when you were the target. You had to first scale the ladder and if you dachled at the top, then you were as good as dead. You had to be pretty smart about getting down the other side. Gerry had all their rifles and machine guns trained on the lip of the trench all the time; some on fixed tripods.

The favourite saying at that time or one of them was, 'I'll see you in Cairds restaurant next Saturday!' They got their Cairds restaurant all right and that was zip-zip of the bullets laying them low.

Albert Edwards, 5th Black Watch/Machine Gun Corps

dachled lingered/hesitated

Witen at nicht afore a big push wisna afa great. I jist filled ma pipe an pulled ma cwite roon aboot ma. I wis in a lot o them tee an maybe I didna aa thegidder like them, I gid awa that I didna care a docken – ye got eesed tult I suppose.

…

Files we got rum afore a doo an it aye started wi a barrage oot in front an wis aye lifted a bit aa the time as we gid forrit. Aa the same it wisna lang afore the Gerry machine guns war playin on ye.

John Brown, 5th Gordon Highlanders

Ae night I gid doon the line to visit some o my ald pals I jined wi in the 7th Gordon Highlanders. This wis at Arras an I hid a gran news o the lads onywy we were jist aside een an ither in the same brigade o the 51st. Weel they gid ower the top neist morning wi wirsels – the 4th in support and they got a terrible dustin up – an afa casualties, an the lad I jined up wi that I been newsin till the nicht afore, wis killed ana.

Charles Smith, 7th and 4th Gordon Highlanders

The first time we went over the top – we got rum. Later on we only got it when we got back – but more of it.

Alec Robertson, 5th Gordon Highlanders

Some men followed tanks when going into action. The first ones were slow but the Whippets later on were fast. Many of the tanks were useless when they went in to shell holes: they couldn't get out. We hated the shelling when we were in a wood because the shrapnel ricocheted off the trees.

Robert More MM, 4th Seaforth Highlanders

We were foolish lads in the early days; we attacked the enemy in a bunch and their machine guns had a field day, but later on we stopped doing that and spread out thinly and got on better. Then another silly order was to just walk and not rush fast over No Man's Land which was idiotic – no sense at all. This was at High Wood on the Somme. The corn was still standing but the trees were all blasted with no leaves at all.

I experienced a few COs in my time and many changes of the NCOs too.

A. Smeaton MM, 5th Black Watch

At Schwaben Redoubt on the 13th October 1915 we were going over the top to attack this heavily defended fortress. This was a Saturday afternoon assisted with a barrage from Canadian Artillery. Two English regiments had tried before us and failed. When the time came to go over we all remarked on the unlucky 13th when the order was cancelled. It was only postponed and on next day Sunday 14th we attacked. Going over that afternoon I mind on the Gerries standing up head and shoulders over the top of their forts firing at us.

I was a bomb thrower that day carrying 14 Mills bombs and two smoke bombs. I got right up to the Gerry Front within range and started throwing my bombs when I was wounded in the leg.

The battalion suffered terrible number of casualties that day.

Albert Edwards, 5th Black Watch/Machine Gun Corps

Our pipers played us over the top all the time.

Donald MacVicar, 1st/2nd The Queen's Own Cameron Highlanders

24

Conditions at the Front

Gas

I went up the line and took over D Company because their platoon sergeant had been killed by a sniper. I had been without sleep for days and once I saw all was in order, I lay down to sleep.

I was awakened by shelling with gas shells so we donned masks.

It stopped, and later when I thought the air was clear, I took off mine. I had forgotten, however, that gas lingers deep down in the bottom of a trench. I fell victim right away.

I was led down the line by a man that had been shot in the arm – I was completely blind.

Later I landed up at Sunderland Hospital. I couldn't speak; I lost my head of hair and eyebrows. I was speaking again in three months but it was touch and go whether I would see again, but I did!

Later on I was transferred to a hospital in Richmond where I got special treatment. Doctors came from far and wide to see me. They knew about mustard gas but they didn't know so much about this other gas I had apparently been afflicted with!

George Bryan MM, 12th Highland Light Infantry

We near aye hid time to get on wir masks fin we heard the shells ging 'plop' and heard the gas comin fissin oot.

Aa the same I hiv seen some lads that hid been gassed lyin deed and aa swalled up.

Jimmy Scott, Royal Engineers

I got gassed at Denain outside Cambrai. The gas masks were supposed to be proof against all gasses, but this time the Gerry sent over tear gas which penetrated right through the masks. This caused us to cough and sneeze and so take them off thereby leaving us prey to more deadly gasses.

That's what happened to me and although I was really ill, I never reported sick because I was afraid I would be charged with 'self inflicted wound'.

40. A Gordon Highlander in a gas mask.
Gordon Highlanders Museum

I was in a bad state though when we were relieved by the Black Watch. The gas was terrible. Small shells they used. When the Germans broke through at the west of Ypres it was gas that preceded the attack.
John MacRae, 18th Battalion ANZAC

I met in with Jim Imlach of the Arygylls later that day, he asked me if I had seen Wull MacDonald from the village among the Black Watch. I said that I didn't.

The next day I met Jim again and he told me that Wull had came down the line gassed. I told him I wasn't surprised at that, as I wasn't feeling too good myself.

I suffered from my chest for years after. I never complained to a doctor though; maybe I should have.
Dave Pitkethly, 4th Seaforth Highlanders

I got gassed at the La Bassée Canal on a very foggy day. The canal seemed to attract the fog and the gas; at least I thought so. Anyhow the gas was in the air and we started vomiting and coughing. While others were taken out of the line, I stuck her out.

I found that panic was the worst thing about being gassed: keep your head and you were all right. Keep clear of the bottom of the trench for it tended to go down. With mustard gas – if you got a bit on the kilt, then wash it in water to disperse it.
Frank MacFarlane MM and Medal Militaire, 1st Black Watch

I got tear gas and wis blin for three days. All I got fort wis draps.
Alec Wilson, 7th Cameron Highlanders

The whiff of gas I got, knocked me oot for six months. It happened fin we were gan back efter bein relieved. It must have been lyin aboot in the boddom o a trench.
George Stewart, 5th Gordon Highlanders

Some o wir men hid their very een burned oot wi gas.

In 1917 up at Ypres I got a touch o gas. I wis carried oot. I couldna get breath – my throat and moo wis aa brunt and I wisna able to spik. In hospital I turned ass wike that I couldna pit ae leg by the ither.

Fin I got better I wis discharged. I got a job at Rumanach as horseman there wis aye plenty o wark aboot a ferm toon: there wis nae scarcity o that.
Norrie Cruikshank, 6th Gordon Highlanders
wike weak

41. Gas mask drill for Artillery horses. Horses were a vital resource at the Front both for cavalry and transport roles.

Reproduced by permission of the National Library of Scotland

42. Cleaning of a Lewis gun with a foghorn in the foreground to warn of gas attacks. By 1917, every Infantry section of between eight and ten men had a Lewis gunner and assistant. The gun, which could fire up to 500 rounds per minute, was of far greater tactical importance than the rifles of the other Infantrymen.

Reproduced by permission of the National Library of Scotland

I was scared of gas. The first time we were exposed to it we had no masks at all. These shells came over and dropped with a slight 'plop', and we thought, 'My Goodness – they are sending over a lot of dud shells …', but then we smelt the tear gas which made you retch and rub your eyes. We later got masks which protected us against most gasses and I never had any trouble again. That tear gas was bad enough because you couldn't open your eyes to see your rifle or anything – oh no!
A. MacEwan, 6th Gordon Highlanders

Mines and tunnels

I remember the blowing up of Hill 60. This was the most tunnelled place there was in the War. It was blown up before the Third Battle of Ypres to prevent the Germans seeing our lines of communication.
John MacRae, 18th Battalion ANZAC

Fin a mine gid up at Givenchy a pal o mine caa-ed Raxton got sic a fricht he gid fite heeded in a feoy days. He hid got some o the blast. His broon heed o hair wis na mair. It wis a hell o a blast aa the same. The Germans hid come in and occupied the cratur.
Norrie Cruikshank, 6th Gordon Highlanders

During mining operations, they picked men who had particularly good hearing. I once went down a tunnel when they were mining. I was a sergeant at the time. A mine once went up below the trenches of the 5th Gordon Highlanders – I think A Company got caught. There were twins and their two uncles killed by it. They were all from Fraserburgh. The explosion didn't kill many either as we dug the most out alive although a few were never found. After that tragedy – the Gordon Highlanders didn't allow close relations to be in the same company.

Lieutenant Vincent Bruce, Inverquhomery House, missing never found.[29]
Alec Robertson, 5th Gordon Highlanders

Sergeant Major Wullie Watt wis blaan up bit wis dug up and cam hame wounded in the heed. He hid the ferm o Allathan ye ken. My brither Eddie wis in that same lot ana. He wis oot in front o me fin the Germans exploded the mines in the dark aneth the trenches o the 5th Gordon Highlanders. Michty I mine it fine. 'Weel weel,' I thocht, 'that's my brither Eddie got it!' Bit no! it wis on baith sides only – the middle escaped. This wis at Arras on a pitch black Sunday nicht. There wis a lot o fireworks gid on becis the Germans hid rushed the line. I'll tell ye fa wis collared that nicht – Freddie Kindness: he wis teen a prisoner there fin they cam ower (March 1916).
Bert Gow, Royal Field Artillery

That wis a hell o a caper, that tunnelin. I've seen us lissenin to the Germans diggin close by. Mony a een got blaan up wi them ye ken.
…
Oor company helpit dig some o the tunnels at Hill 60 an they warna afa big – jist enuch to waak bent doon. Ye aye heard ither tunnelling goin on hine awa fae ye an it aye gid ye a hellava feelin fin ye kent it wis Gerry eens. I mean they dug a tunnel richt aneth een o oors.

The tunnel spoil wis cairried oot in bags wi lines o folk jist hannin the bags fae een to the ither. Coal miners supervised the wark an they could spot if a reef wis gan to cave in or no.

We wis shiftet fae there afore the Hill was blaan up though an didna see it.
Jimmy Scott, Royal Engineers

A puckle os wis eence detailed to help the Sappers and I dina like at cairry on ata. I wis into this mine and could hear the Gerry pick-pickin somewy awa in the gunnels o the earth asides an My God I didna like at ata. Oh no gie me the open air ivery time!

Alec MacHardy MM, 7th Gordon Highlanders

Shelling

We were fire at nae lang efter as we advanced to meet the enemy [at the Marne, July 1918]. Advancin on a wid we cam inti the warst shellin I hid iver experienced. There wis nae cover naewy. They were crashin doon aa roons, an een laand close by – we were aa flappit ye ken – an my pal Jimmy said he wid ging inti the shell hole for shelter, an in he gings – I bade far I wis. Some lads thocht that a shell niver laand in the same hole twice.

Weel a shell did laan in the same hole an he wis blaan to bits. I missed him a lot cis we'd been thegither a lang time.

George Stewart, 5th Gordon Highlanders

Twa os were stunning guard in the dark oot in the open. There wis shells comin ower no in an. We thocht we could tell if they were gan to be landin near han or no – at least I thocht I did.

I heard een comin wi a fair fustle, bit I thocht we wid be aa richt an I said to the idder lad – we were newsin thegither at the time – 'Lat's stick her oot!'

The neist thing I kent wis bein flung throwe tha air an laanin on tap o a pillbox richt on ma tin hat. I lay there a filie steen deaf, an took some time to get ma wits aboot ma again. I cralled aff the pillbox an lookit for ma mate. It wis rainin makin the grun an awa sotter.

I heard him cry oot an fun him lyin in the dubs wi a wound in his lower belly. It wis a gie hole an I stappit a dressin intil it.

I then pickit him up ower ma back and tyaved doon wi him to a dressin station aboot a mile back, sometimes wi dubs up to ma kweets.

I left him there and bade a file wi him an he newsed awa nae sa bad, bit apparently he deed na lang efter I left him.

…

This shellin wis the warst we iver experienced. The Great German Push hid started an we hid gotten word o Haig's order to 'Stand Fast'. The trench wis bein demolished on aa sides.

Twa lads hid gotten hud o a sheet o corrugated iron an were sittin in the boddom o the trench wi it ower their heeds. They were lachin an jokin fin I hid seen them. Fin I cam roon the traverse again they were baith gone.

It wis a funny thing, bit a little cover like that sheet o iron, did gie ye a feelin o safety.

…

I mind eence comin oot for a rest in the dark. We were halted in front o a battery o heavies which were firin on aa the time ower wir heeds, is they hid been deein for wicks.

We lay doon at eence as we were aa dog tired an fell asleep.

Something woke me up. The rain wis poorin, an I wis weet to the skin, bit it wisna that, that waakened me. Na na, it wis the silence. The heavy guns hid stoppit firin. This waakend aabody else tee.

…

Ae day we'd been dug in nae far fae a road. By cam a hale battalion o English troops. They war jist anents fin a heavy shell cam ower an exploded richt in their midst.

We helpit gidder up aboot 30 deed and a lot mair wounded.

…

There wis ae village we raked aboot in to see fit we could scrounge. Some lads hid fun a cellar wi wine in it. They were aa drunk.

I didna bide lang bit took aff rakin roon the idder hooses.

Fi I cam back again that wy I saa that a shell had laand and killed them aa.

John Webster, Royal Field Artillery

We war on the march fin a shell knockit aff the heed o a lad in front os. It wis uncanny – he waakit on a feoy paces afore he fell ower.

A. Chapman

Oor battery gid into a sunken road. Gerry began shellin wi 5.9s. We were ordered to wheel in line. That means that ye turn ilkey team richt roon an proceeded back the wy ye came. It was C team. A and B war in front o me. Afore we'd even started to turn, a shell laand richt on C team o sax black shults, blain them to smiddereens. A great chunk o horsemeat laand on my knees still twitchin.

Funnily eneuch, the driver wisna muckle touched.

…

We were stunnin at a cross roads – three os, fin a shell burst and a bit shrapnel gid richt throwe Jock Wilkins steel helmet an into his heed. His fadder keepit the cemetery at New Deer. There wis neen o the lave os touched. We aa thocht he widna live, bit he did. They apparently put in a steel plate in his heed.

…

Our supply wagons brocht up 72 shells at a time.

Bert Gow, Royal Field Artillery

Bit bein a cauld nicht we thocht we'd rig a brazier wi sticks we'd fun. We didna ken that we were under observation by the Gerry bit we war: they hid seen oor fire and a shell cam ower wir heeds and laand at the back o the hut. The neist demolished it. There wis 20 os in there bit we aa struggled oot and took aff inti the nicht amid this afa shellfire. A lad Anderson shouts, 'Iss wy! Iss wy!' So I followed him up a sunken road and flappit in a gun pit. The rest aa gid doon to the village and looked for us, thinkin that we must hae been killed.

John Russel, Royal Field Artillery

fun found

The first time we came under shellfire was during the retreat from Mons and it was shrapnel shells that they were using. We were that ignorant of their nature, we just stood like stookies looking at them exploding. They weren't too near otherwise we would have all been killed. There was not much shelling for a start but it was a different matter later in the War when we had to endure some terrible bombardments which caused a tremendous amount of head and shoulder wounds with shrapnel as well as folk being killed.

Frank MacFarlane MM and Medal Militaire, 1st Black Watch

Two of us were detailed to accompany a young officer to another position. We had to travel over a line of duckboards over the mud as it was particularly bad in that section. It was dark and we were feeling our way along, when the Gerry started to bombard. A shell landed among us and my mate and I flopped down instinctively. The officer didn't – perhaps he thought it was 'below his dignity' to do so. He caught the blast of the shell and lost an arm. He shouted for me to bind it up, but as it was dark, I said to him to make a run for it till we got to safety and then I would do the necessary. We made it before he fainted and got him attended to. The shells were still coming over so the first dugout I saw, I dived into. I was covered in blood off the wounded officer so the occupants thought I was hit. The officer was given aid and I never saw him again but I suppose he was all right.

When I got back to my unit I was rather tipsy having acquired some rum from well-wishers along the way who thought I was wounded.

…

They said a shell never lands in the same place twice, but that's only a fallacy.

In Arras we filled a large gymnasium with ammunition. When we finished stockpiling the shells I went away to my billet close by. A little later I heard this shell coming and thought, 'My God that's coming close!' It struck the dump dead on with a terrible noise and destruction all around. Many of our fellows were buried but I think we got them out all right.

…

The shells that landed at the front of the parapet, I didn't mind; it was the ones that landed on the wrong side that I didn't like because we didn't have so much protection there. One time we were being shelled heavily and I dug a shelter into the side of the trench. It was wonderful what a little shelter did to restore your morale. When a shell burst just over the side it was so near that I could have reached over and touched it. I remember the colonel came along and said to me 'If that German gunner would just raise his elevation a few millimetres, that shell would have landed right on top of you and blown you to pieces.' I replied 'That wouldn't have been a bad idea Sir'.

…

The colonel said to me that the Germans had moved their Artillery over from the Eastern Front and they now had the biggest concentration against us since Waterloo.

…

I was acting runner at the time when I heard this scream of a shell coming. This landed about two feet way and never exploded, otherwise I would have been blown to kingdom come. I looked at it and saw it was of a device that exploded before it went to ground.

…

At the Somme there were two exposed places: one was called 'Hellfire Corner' and the other 'Ironcross Corner'. I once had to go through Hellfire one night. I was that scared I don't think my feet touched the ground all the way.

Albert Napier MM, Royal Field Artillery ('Taggart's Own')

There was a big naval gun at Dickiebusch we called Dickiebusch Liz.

John MacRae, 18th Battalion ANZAC

We aye hid a hellava time wi whizz bangs fin we opened up wi machine guns.

I mind a chiel Roy – fae Dufftown, wis playin the melodeon. I wis at the back o him and a lot mair were listenin, fin a whizzbang laand richt in the middle o us and killed Roy and a puckle mair. It blew him and the melodeon clean oot o the trench.

Norrie Cruikshank, 6th Gordon Highlanders

Shellin wis richt demoralising. 'It peys ti be little,' I eenced to say ti the idders. Mony a een wis drivin mad weet.

Tom Rearie, 5th Gordon Highlanders

I was two days once driving up ammunition to an English battalion. I came on a crowd of them killed stone dead, some still sitting up. When I examined them there was not a mark of injury to be seen. This was concussion from a high explosive burst that had done it.

Robert More MM, 4th Seaforth Highlanders

We usually got peace to come up with ammunitions at night. The fact was, Gerry liked peace as well to do likewise; if they sent over a barrage they got the same back. That was not always the case though, shelling went on all the time during a big battle.

A. Smeaton MM, 5th Black Watch

I mine eence gan up and helpin set up a Lewis gun in a shell hole, fin a shell laaned me smack on the twa os. Ma mate wis thrown hine awa and killed bit I wisna touched although I wis flung a bittie ana. It jist gangs to see fit luck dis ye ken.

Mortars gid us the warst trouble. We heard then ging 'powk' and they wid come ower and stop deed abeen oor heeds; then they wid come stracht doon.
Alec Nicol, 7th Gordon Highlanders

We caaed the Gerry grenades 'Donald Dinnies'.[30] Fin they threw iss things they cam swinging through the air ats like a games hammer and lay afile afore explodin. I aye mind ae lad gid ower to een and wis gan to pick her up to throw her back like we eesed to dee, bit oh man! Up she went and him we-et.
Jimmy Reid, 6th Gordon Highlanders

When you heard the swish of a shell you knew it was past and you were safe, although one was inclined to get careless and not bother taking shelter.
J. Fowlie, 7th Gordon Highlanders

We eased to get an afa pounding fae the Gerry shells. The tin hat saved us a lot fae the shrapnel but I wis nae eese against the bullets like the sniper fire. Aye, mony a lad got shot through the tin hat.
John Will, 5th Gordon Highlanders

In the early days of the War, the Gerry had all the guns and we got all the shellfire but in 1916 we had plenty too. On the Somme it was formidable – nothing but a mass of fire day and night on their front line just like a town on fire. I remember one prisoner saying to me, 'You don't know what real shelling is!'

We knew what real shelling was all right – the Gerry had plenty all through the War; when we were in the line near Theipval at a place called Death Valley, the Gerry gunners caught a column of our Artillery coming through in the night and blew the lot to smithereens. When we came through the next day – what a scene of carnage we saw of men, horses and guns lying everywhere in bits.
Albert Edwards, 5th Black Watch/Machine Gun Corps

The minewerefers were afa damned things – weren't they what! They fired them ower and they eensed to hing abeen yer heed and then doon they cam to create havoc. Oh aye they were domino!
Wullie Gavin, 5th Gordon Highlanders

The French 75s had a special device in them – the secret of which they jealously guarded. This was a fine gun that fired 23 rounds to 15 from our 18-pounders.
Albert Napier MM, Royal Field Artillery ('Taggart's Own')

We eence hid a battery o Australians at the back os firin 15-inch shells ower wir heed and I can tell ye, that wis some soon and some weicht gan ower's.
Jimmy Reid, 6th Gordon Highlanders

Every time I came under shellfire I shook like a leaf. I remember being in a corner trench with another twelve in this traverse when a shell exploded beside us. I could feel my body ready to burst with the terrible concussion. Some of the chaps beside me were killed. I never met the Lovat Scouts or the Scottish Horse when I was at Gallipoli; nor did I, the 4th KOSB who were in the 52nd Division.
Jock Murray, 1st King's Own Scottish Borderers

'Toot sweet' is what we called the Gerry short range shells. We heard them leaving the gun and simultaneously bursting over our heads.
Dave Pitkethly, 4th Seaforth Highlanders

We affen hid to dive inti wir dugoots fin the Gerry high explosives got on tulls.
William Shearer, Royal Field Artillery

Machine guns

I jined a machine gun crew an we sat oot in front in a shell hole witen ti catch Gerry if he cam ower. Ae nicht they hid a patrol oot an we didna hear them comin bit they hid kent we wis er. Maybe the'd spotted us throue the day. Onywy they started throwin tattie chapper grenades ats an een cam gie near an this explosion caused a bit shrapnel ti pierce ma cwite an jist draa bleed on ma airm here. I said wi a lach ti the idder lads, 'Nae eneuch for Blighty here!'
Alec Nicol, 7th Gordon Highlander

The Gordon Highlanders had their own machine guns at first but this was stopped in favour of machine gun battalions although we still had Lewis guns. A tailor from Ellon – our Sergeant Major Crosier – was on them. The machine guns were away back and fired over our heads but the Lewis guns were in the line or in front of you and Maxims too.
Alec Meldrum MM, 1st/8th Gordon Highlanders

The Gerry airplanes used to fire at us with machine guns. We replied with rifle fire but I have never seen one hit.
Dave Pitkethly, 4th Seaforth Highlanders

Snipers

There was two brothers MacLean from about Strichen who were snipers in our battalion. They were well over six feet in height. I knew the Sandy one best who was a policeman in Glasgow before the War. They didn't take part in battle but were kept in reserve for that work, which I for one didn't approve. I mean, I was once observing a German get out into the open to pee – when down he went. Oh no, I didn't believe in that sort of thing.

The MacLeans mostly went out at night to do their job: just picked a suitable place behind our lines – a bush or a bit tree which commanded a view of the enemy fortifications – when daylight came.

The last I saw of Sandy MacLean was when I met him on a train going back to France. I was away from the Gordon Highlanders by that time. I am not sure if they survived the War either.

We had a lot killed by snipers too. I had a fellow – Jimmy Barclay in my company who was a farm servant round about Ellon – he was at school with me. We were in this sunken road with just sandbags for a parapet at the time. I roared at him, 'Barclay – get your head down!' but I was too late – a sniper had got him. Next morning a chap Ewan showed his head at the same place – I shouted but I was too late – the same thing happened.

Alec Robertson, 5th Gordon Highlanders

We had a VC in our company – our sergeant major. He had just cam back off leave and we were occupying a new line which had previously belonged to the Gerry – in fact the dugouts still held some of their dead. Now he went out to get some of their buttons off their tunics as souvenirs to send home to his wife when he was killed by a sniper. We didn't really know if he was dead but when a stretcher-bearer came along, said he would go out and see if he could save him. Well this chap went out and got shot dead by the sniper also. We recovered their bodies and the stretcher-bearer who belonged to our platoon, was just buried beside the trench. The sergeant major VC's body was taken back, so the regiment could hold a big funeral service at Poperinge – a valley near Ypres.

We were all ordered to attend this funeral but resented going as the fellow that got killed trying to rescue him deserved the same. The platoon refused to go to the funeral – this was a sort of mutiny and we didn't care; we never budged. All the others went though.

Jock Murray, 1st King's Own Scottish Borderers

Snipers were a terrible nuisance: they killed a lot of men. Anybody that was a good shot could be a sniper. I was a marksman myself and used to do a bit. There were certain delegated points for sniping from.

George Bryan MM, 12th Highland Light Infantry

The first thing we did when we were sent up to the Front was to eliminate a sniper called 'Percy' by an English regiment. Percy had caused a lot of casualties at Suvla and apparently could see right into the river bed where our well lay. Lord Lovat gave orders to finish Percy off once and for all. We had a large percent of stalkers in our ranks and most of us were crack shots and we carried our own telescopes which in the hands of experts were ideal for enemy observation.

It wasn't long before we found his hide and a party were sent out to deal with him in the dark. I and my mate were sent over with our machine gun to deal with the Turks if they came over at us. We heard bombs going off and a few shots but we didn't see any sign of anything in the dark till we were hailed by the lads coming back dragging the corpse of Percy between them. We had a good look at him back in our lines and we were greatly taken with him – a big heavy lad, and apart from the shrapnel wounds that killed him, he had an old festering bullet wound in one wrist, so he must have decided to stay at his post despite the pain. We respected what he'd done. He had a bag of some kind of seeds on him, to chew on I suppose. Piper Angus MacKay got the credit for dispatching him. He came from Strathnaver.

William MacGregor, Lovat Scouts

I was sent to the 2nd Cameron Highlanders when I returned to the Front. This was at Ypres and a few days later a few men fell dead in my bit of the trench: killed by a sniper. The lad next to me in the trench said, 'I see him about 50 yards out there'; indicating with his hand the general direction. As I was filling the chamber of my rifle I replied, 'Why don't you fire at him then?'

This he did and immediately fell back dead – a bit of his skull landed on me. Feeling really angry I jumped right out of the trench and felt the bullets plucking at my clothes. I saw the Gerry sniper turn and crawl away so I took aim and shot him; then I jumped back into the safety of the trench. With that over the Gerry started to send over whizz bangs. One came straight down and burst in the next traverse, my insides felt as though they were bursting. I went round there and came on three men killed stone dead and not a mark on them.

Donald MacVicar, 1st/2nd The Queen's Own Cameron Highlanders

I eense fun a pig o rum and a puckle os teemed aat. This wis in the front line trench at the time. I hid a fair shot in and picked up a tin of bully beef – we were gettin ready to ate at the time. I huds up the tin in the air and shouts, 'Cam on Gerry and get yer denner!' The tin wis shot oot o my han at eence wi a sniper. Although my han wisna touched, it fairly dirled.

John Will, 5th Gordon Highlanders

puckle os teemed aat a few of us emptied it

Their snipers were good; when we held up a tin hat it was not long afore it was full of holes – they were not much good at stopping bullets: but we did not have them at the start.

Robert More MM, 4th Seaforth Highlanders

A young officer had joined us. We kent fine niver to look oot ower the parapet far we wis. He did and wis killed by a sniper atween the een. Weel, we did warn him!

John Webster, Royal Field Artillery

The devils eense to clim trees and pirk at us.

The Gurkhas were great lads: fin they were fired at by snipers they eensed to hud their twa hans up iss wy and peer throw them. They could aye spot a sniper that wy hine awa.

Alec Nicol, 7th Gordon Highlanders

Two brothers were in different companies. One was in mine and he was shot dead by a sniper one day. There he was lying in the trench covered with his greatcoat when along came his brother to see him and have a news. As he approached he said to me, 'I see some poor fellow has got the works!' Well, I couldn't tell him and just turned and moved away in the trench.

…

A sniper once shot a man sitting beside me while we were having a cup of tea. He was shot clean through the head and his brains went all over me and into my cup of tea.

A. MacEwan, 6th Gordon Highlanders

Snipers were aa first class shots. The Gerries war ana. I mind ae lad settin up a periscope abeen the trench sos we could see fit Gerry wis deein in his lines. This wis the early morning. He said, 'Jesus Christ – look at this' as the bleed gid fleein. The bullet hid geen ping throwe his wrist. I picked the periscope up aff the grun and held it in the air but there wis nae mair shots. I suppose the sniper hid jist seen the flash o the mirror and biffed aff.

Peter Baigrie, 7th Cameron Highlanders/6th Black Watch

I was nearly made a sniper there because I was a crack shot. The sergeant came to me and told me so. An older soldier beside me who was about 40 years old said to the sergeant, 'He's not going – I am!' He was a good shot and knew I was under age – only 17, just a boy. He shouldn't have been there either at his age. Anyway he went on to be a sniper and I think survived the War.

The sniper went out at night and came back in the morning; they weren't out the whole day. If it was moonlight you could see nearly everything – all movement. At night for instance – that was when we were working at our

defences and the Turks were doing the same; that's when folk got killed by snipers.
Jock Murray, 1st King's Own Scottish Borderers

We had some good glass men – it was their job back home at the stalking and especially a little wee mannie called Carver from Cragganmore. He was so good that Colonel Grant of Rothiemurchus, he took him everywhere and even made up a rhyme about him.
William MacGregor, Lovat Scouts

Word was it that the sniper Percy owned a bit of land at Suvla that he operated from.
William Mowat, 1st Scottish Horse and Lovat Scouts

Winter, mud and the kilt

I hid a nerra squeak fin I fell into a shell hole that wis fu o dubs an watter – this wis up at Ypres. We war gan forrit at the time an I suddenly laand up ti ma oxters and couldna get oot.

Twa lads stoppit an ruggit ma oot huddin on to ma rifle, itherwise I wis a goner.
Jimmy Reid, 6th Gordon Highlanders
oxters armpits, *ruggit* pulled

Passchendaele was worse than the Somme because the battlefield was at sea level. Those heavy shells when they landed made a crater anything up to 15-feet deep and by the same time next day, they were filled to the brim with water; so you can imagine what it was like for the wounded that went into a shell hole for shelter and found themselves being submerged. Many lads drowned when they couldn't get out; the edge just crumpled away in their hands.

Even the unwounded had a job getting out: I went in once in the dark and if I hadn't had a good mate with me I would have succumbed.
Albert Napier MM, Royal Field Artillery ('Taggart's Own')

The mud at Ypres was terrible; up at Houlers Forest we had to go on to duck-boards up to the front line. We noticed some dead men that had wandered off the duckboards in the dark – with just their heads showing above the mud: completely sunk to their necks.
George Bryan MM, 12th Highland Light Infantry

The kilt wis hellish in the winter and peeled aa the back o yer leg.
Alec Nicol, 7th Gordon Highlanders

In the winter our kilts froze solid with a mixture of chalky grey mud and water and were terrible on the legs. Kilts were impossible to clean.

Winter was hard. The first one we stood often up to our bellies in water.
A. Smeaton MM, 5th Black Watch

Passchendaele wis afa bad, we war up er a gie filie. The conditions were terrible wi dubs an watter awa. I eence fell into a shell hole, an ye ken I wid hae drooned if I hidna been pulled oot.
William Angus, 2nd Gordon Highlanders

Beaumont-Hamel wis hell in aa. Dubs did ye say! Some folk war deed bit aye held up by glaur, they war ass far in.

Files it wis misty an it poored aa day.
Jimmy Reid, 6th Gordon Highlanders

Mud and more mud, hail, sleet and snow were my memories of the trenches in the winter. A bucketful of snow made a cupful of water.
Alec Meldrum MM, 1st/8th Gordon Highlanders

We couldna pit in guns at Courcelette:[31] it wis jist widin wi dubs. We jist took ower the guns fae the Canadians and they did the same to us. Do ye ken – Courcelette wis the warst place for dubs that iver I saa!

It wis a case o swappin aa the time. I mind we eence tried to tak oot twa guns that had been struck and oot o action. Sergeant Major Crystal says, 'We'll tak oot the guns!'

Well I wis the first een to try wi my ten-horse team and I got on nae sae bad. This caper hid to be in the dark ye see cis Gerry could observe aathing far we wis. Onywy I jist wiled my wy through the clorty mess and by the side o the shell holes. It wisna easy na, weel-a-wite! bit I managed. Bit the ither team got stuck: laired guns, horses and aa, richt to their bellies in glaur. Try as they micht they were fair foundered. I took doon my ten-horse team and yoket them as weel and that wis 20 beasts; bit it wis nae eese; the horses breenged aboot and plitered farrer in. We hid to louse aff and tak oot the horses as it wis comin in daylicht. Neist nicht, we tried again and were successful.
John Russel, Royal Field Artillery
weel-a-wite I must say, *laired* sunk

In the winter time we eence to tie sandbags roon wir knees to hud the kilt on rubbin. The tail ot got frozen and kept rub-rubbin roon the knees: it wis an afa job! I've seen us come oot o the line dog tired and faain asleep at the side o a ditch or a dyke and wakenen wi naething bit the fite frost roon aboots in the mornin.
Alec MacHardy MM, 7th Gordon Highlanders

The trenches oot in France war just a cloort o weet an dubs the maist o the time an minded me on sheep atein neeps in a weetie time. Bit of coorse it was waar in the winter an mony a time we hid ti stan amon water up ti wir kweets. A lot o men hid ti gang oot sick on accoont ot. Passchendaele wis the warst place for stunnin amon watter wi us. Ye niver sleepit richt, ye jist kine o dozed an in fact it wis aboot twa eer afore I sleepit richt efter the War.

John Brown, 5th Gordon Highlanders

weetie wet

There wis na change o claes for 14 days at a time and we were oot in gey weet and cauld at times.

Alec Nicol, 7th Gordon Highlanders

The winter of 1917 was a terrible cold one. We only had boots and puttees and the puttees became wet and hard with the frost.

We got an issue of rum every day. I liked the job of handing it out. There was a small can for dishing it out and if anybody said, 'Oh no, I don't want it – oh well!' it just went down right away.

George Bryan MM, 12th Highland Light Infantry

We were oot in front o Beaumont-Hamel in trenches that terrible weet and cauld winter at the end o 1916. It aye seemed to be weet through the day and wis frost aa nicht. We were rigged oot wi wellingtons and that made the frost cut us waar far they rubbed the back o wir legs.

Jimmy Milne, 2nd Gordon Highlanders

It wis only dry files, maist o the eer it wis naething but dubs and watter aa the time. Oh aye, a hell o a life.

Norrie Cruikshank, 6th Gordon Highlanders

files sometimes

That '15–'16 winter wis terrible: I mind the back o wir legs aa crack'et wi the frost wi rubbin wi wir kilts and ae thing or anither. Wir knees aa chippet anaa. Do ye ken, the grun wis ass hard, ye couldna mark it wi a pick axe. We hid a hellava job makin lavatories or dein ony digging ataa.

Wullie Gavin, 5th Gordon Highlanders

I don't think I could describe the conditions at the Front adequately to anyone unless they were there to see it.

…

The kilt was dreadful in the winter and skinned all our legs.

Donald MacLeod, 4th Black Watch

The winter of '16–'17 was the worst we experienced out there. The frost was in the ground feet-deep. When it started to thaw in March the horse-drawn vehicles fell though and got laired up to their axles and couldn't move.
Frank MacFarlane MM and Medal Militaire, 1st Black Watch

We wore the kilt – but in the terrible cold winter of 1916–17 we got the chance of wearing trousers but nobody wanted to then. That was a terrible winter though.
Alec Robertson, 5th Gordon Highlanders

Fin oor division occupied Beaumont-Hamel efter the 51st hid teen it, we were in trenches awa oot to the front ot. There wis naething bit dubs and watter cis it hid been poorin and rainin for wicks. The shell holes wereaa reemin fu.

We were relieved ae nicht and as we were trauchlin back in the dark twa os fell in tull a shell hole. The dubs and watter took us up to wir oxters richt awa and the cauld jist froze me to the been – it blakit aa. Onyway I took a hud o the ither lad and pushed him oot, but wi a tyav. Noo didn't he nae set aff an leave me lyin there stranded for some reason or ither. There wis naebody left naewy near; I jist kept shoutin for help and tryin to get oot, bit nae makkin muckle ot; the clay crumpled awa in my hand.

I wis richt gled to see anither lot gan by. An officer answered my cry and said he would sen somebody back to rescue me.

Twa stretcher-bearers cam by and said they wid come richt back to me eence they hid teen in a casualty they were cairryin.

True to their word, they appeared, bit that wis half an oor efter and by the time I hid nae feelin left. They seen hauled me oot and michty what a clort I wis in!
Jimmy Milne, 2nd Gordon Highlanders
trauchlin walking wearily, *tyav* struggle

Arras was dubby bit Courcelette wis waar in 1916. There wis harly ony trenches, there wis ower muckle watter for aat. Abbeville wis bad ana.

Ae nicht up at Arras, I wis in a workin party takkin up mait ti the front line troops wi containers. The trenches were aat bad wi dubs and watter that we gid ower the open grun ti get roon aabody. We hid lang wellington beets up ti wir hips bit it wis a hellava tyav getting roon aabody and be that time it wis comin in daylicht. Wir beets gid sookin in and oot o the glaur bit at the same time nearly leavin them ahin – if ye ken fit I mean.

No it wis breakin daylicht and we hid ti mak a breenge fort. My God it wis a hell o a tyav loupin and sprachlin back ower the open, noo beginning ti be in view o the enemy. They started firin sma shells ats. We could hear them bein fired aff – so we coored doon. Fut a job! Bit we gat back aa richt.
Peter Baigrie, 7th Cameron Highlanders/6th Black Watch
loupin leaping, *sprachlin* scrambling, *coored doon* crouched down

25

Entertainment

Music and song

Scott Skinner was a great player. I heard him once in Forres: 1912. His manager had a devil of a time getting him going what with the booze that night. But he could play! He was asked to play his composition, *The Laird of Drumblair*, which he did magnificently and intimated to the audience – packed out, that *Glenlivet* was his personal favourite. 'Its not a tune like Glenlivet!' he said.

He was a cute little mannie was Scottie. He came to various places like Keith and Broadrashes and picked up a lot of tunes off local folk like MacKerron – a friend of mine, and he just scribbled them out like a flash. There was not so many triplet notes at that time and when he played them again he had finished them off nicely with plenty of triplets.

…

Colonel Grant was a great piping enthusiast and encouraged the pipe band of whom Pipe Major Angus MacMillan was in charge. But they wouldn't keep out of the front line – Angus MacKay killed Percy the sniper [see p.185] and another was out on patrol in the Balkans and shot dead two of a Bulgar patrol they ran into. Another old man as grey as a sheep was in the band – he belonged to the far west.

He was a great lad Colonel Grant and he use to tell us to 'Put the fear of God in them boys!' when we were going out in front.

He was the same Grants that were at Rothiemurchus for 400 years or more. Great on pipe music and fiddles too. I mind we captured a Bulgarian fiddle, aye a right good one but the strings were set for a left-handed fiddler. Colonel Grant said to me, 'Give us a tune MacGregor!' I had to reset the strings before I could play it and I tried my best with a tune or two but I was out of practice.
William MacGregor, Lovat Scouts

There wis a lot o gweed fun awa back, wi some great sports among us. Some played the melodeons and mooth organs. Some lads made instruments themsels. Een made a mandolin fae a petrol tin.
John Will, 5th Gordon Highlanders

There was always a comedian among us to keep the fun going.
J. Fowlie, 7th Gordon Highlanders

I wis in the Army wi Jimmy Bolton, a lad fae the sooth – Fife or somewy. Noo oot in Mesopotamia a lad made a fiddle tull ma oot o a biscuit box. This lad wis a cabinet maker in civvy life an man, he made a gran job ot. I played awa at this fiddle nae bad – oh aye it sooned aa richt, bit fin I left Mesopotamia, I said to Jimmy Bolton, 'De yi see this fiddle here – weel tak it, an fin yer throue weet, tak it an throw it inti a trench an get red ot an dinna tak it back!' Noo Jimmy hid been coortin this deem fae Millbrex, Fyvie – she wis in service doon in Edinburgh. I of coorse lost touch wi him an it wisna til a lot o eers later that I met in wi him fin I hid the hotel at Rothienorman. So we hid a great news and he telt me that he cam back an settled doon and got mairried an wis noo bidin nae far awa at Millbrex. Then he telt me that he took hame the fiddle and in nae time at aa, he presented it back tull ma. Come awa ben the hoose an all lat ye see an hear it – oh ay, it fizzles awa nae bad ye ken.

I kent Scott Skinner fin I hid the garage business in Tarland. He wis playin at a concert in Tarland Hall an I gid ti hear him an I fair liket him. Noo neist morning, he cam awa doon ti see ma and I said 'Come awa in ti the hoose!'

43. Ruined La Bassée. Parts of the houses are still standing and the road in the middle of the rubble is still visible.

I wisna lang mairried at the time an in he cam onywy an fin he settled doon I speired at him if he wid ge us a tune. 'Not at all,' he said, 'but get out your own fiddle, and we'll have a tune together … !' Noo thats fit we did and wi my wife in the piano. A richt gweed man an a richt gweed player aye an mind ye that wis first thing in the morning too.

Harry Nicoll (founder member of Kennethmont Loons & Quines[32])

Armentiéres wis the quaitest bit o the line I wis iver in. We liked to listen to the German bands huddin concerts. Ye ken it aa depenned faa wis facin ye in the line.

Alec MacHardy, 7th Gordon Highlanders

I played the melodeon oot there, and I eenced to fizzle awa we-et bad, bit I wisna muckle o a player, na na!

Wullie Gavin, 5th Gordon Highlanders

> Heres to the gay old Gordon Highlanders.
> The gallant Seaforth too.
> The RFA give a grand display;
> The gallant Black Watch too.
> The brave Argylls and Royal Scots
> Went forward in that Push.
> Side by side we fought and fell;
> Each man beside a pal;
> Serving King and Country
> On the La Bassée Canal

Some of the song only, as sung by Dave Pitkethly, 4th Seaforth Highlanders

We pit on concerts. I composed sangs. I can sing them yet nae bather. Jock Russell, Macduff wis anither os.

…

This wis a sangie that I made up fin we wis ristin ahin the lines and hid a bit concert. Jock Russell will mind on iss fine. I caad it 'Dr Crippen'. It gid something like iss – if I can mind the words:

> I am not Dr Crippen nor a monkey from a zoo.
> I'm not a fighting relic from the field of Waterloo.
> I am just a common fighter, I know it serves me right;
> I have not been run over – no; I have just come for a fight.
>
> *Chorus*
> Where all the girls began to cry – try, try, try and just close his eye.
> I did my best but he just let fly. I could see all the stars in the sky.

He kept on hopping round me; he struck me once or twice.
I bit the dust and spat it out because it wasn't nice.
He claimed first blood and got it too as I was there to tell.
I felt quite sure that he would get a second blood as well.

Chorus
For kin, kind and gentle was he; of me he was wary.
He struck me one as big as three, right on my mary.

Between the rounds my seconds said: just try and stop his blows.
I said all right, I know I did – I stopped him with my nose.
He struck me – I struck the ground and how my poor nose bled.
As I lay there exhausted, to my seconds then I said:
I wonder if you'll miss me sometimes; he struck me every time he tried.
I wonder friends if you'll remember how I died.
Don't tell the wife I died loosing; she expected all the winnings when I'd gone.
Just give her my insurance and she'll think that I have won.

Man, it's a lot of rubbish ye ken bit it gid aabody a gweed lach at the time.

Do ye ken I eenced to sing a lot efter I got hame and act the goat tee. I started at Maud Hospital and feenished at Peeterheed prison. Fus aat noo? Nae bad eh?
Bert Gow, Royal Field Artillery

Pipes

Oor pipers were up the line wi us maist o the time. I hiv seen een mony a time playin us into the attack. They volunteered to gang you see.
John Will, 5th Gordon Highlanders

I also knew Pipe Major Willie MacLean[33] of the Cameron Highlanders and Pipe Major John MacColl.[34] I also met Willie Center[35] and John MacDonald of Inverness[36] after the War. I judged the piping at Auchterarder Highland Gathering with John MacColl.
Donald MacLeod, 4th Black Watch

The maist o the 2nd Gordon Highlanders' pipers were killed at Loos, my brither Robin among them. Colonel Stansfield and him were hit by the same shell. Robin was a regular ye ken an wis sergeant at the time.[37]
Davie Stewart, 4th Gordon Highlanders

Our company pipers piped us over to the attack many a time.
Albert Edwards, 5th Black Watch/Machine Gun Corps

Our pipe band piped us out of the Somme into billets away back for a rest.
Alec Robertson, 5th Gordon Highlanders

Our pipe major was Geordie MacLennan,[38] a great player and character.

I started lessons with him in the Army on the chanter.

When he came to compete at Banff Games I used to meet him off the train, and march with him to the Games!
Alec Meldrum MM, 1st/8th Gordon Highlanders

In September 1917 at the Third Battle of Ypres we piped our companies into battle but we didn't get very far. There, the mud became an enemy when the rains came.

Among the pipers I met some great characters in the various regiments. One of the greatest was Pipe Major Willie Lawrie[39] of the Argyll and Sutherland Highlanders. He was a fantastic player and composer. Sadly he took that terrible killing flu just when the War ended and died. A sad loss to piping. He and my father were great friends.
Donald MacLeod, 4th Black Watch

We eence hid a gran concert at Arras fin oot the line – aa wi wir ain folk.

We hid a gran pipe band tee. I mind the pipers playin fin we gid in at High Wood.
Tom Rearie, 5th Gordon Highlanders

Wir pipers played us on the march and even oot o the line fin we gid back a bit. On a lang march, wir heeds wis up and we were swingin awa fine, bit fin they stoppit playin we jist slouched doon richt awa fair tired oot. The pipes brocht ye ti life – Aye christ it helpit!
Peter Baigrie, 7th Cameron Highlanders/6th Black Watch

The finest display of pipe bands I ever saw was in the square at Arras and the Germans were still shelling it at the time. This was the combined pipe bands of the 51st, 15th and the Canadian Highlanders. What a great show they put up. This square was named by us 'The barbed wire square!' Their fine music sounded above all the shellfire.

The town was empty of population and the cellars were full of drink left there. The troops were mad about it and got to it although the MPs tried to stop them.
A. MacEwan, 6th Gordon Highlanders

26

Officers

An officer cam by fin we were stannin wi a big Australian. We aa saluted him bit the Australian didna. The officer stopped and got on to him for nae salutin.

The Australian jist lookit at him and said, 'Make way for a real soldier sonny!'
Bill Minty, 4th Gordon Highlanders

I mind when we dug a trench at night. Immediately it filled with water about two -feet deep. None of us wanted to go in until an officer came along and said in braid Doric, 'Michty lads, you'll hae tae ging in!' The officers out there were different from those we met in this country – more like ourselves. Anyway we went in and got a good soaking; there was nothing else for it as it was coming in daylight.
J. Fowlie, 7th Gordon Highlanders

We hid an officer fa eence to stan on tap o the trench an show nae fear. He won a lot o medals an een fae the French.
Bill Minty, 4th Gordon Highlanders

Captain Oldfield was a big man of six feet six inches and had a snake tattooed round his body.
William MacGregor, Lovat Scouts

There was always bother from British officers when we didn't salute. Our major was just like one of the boys and ate with us as well.
John MacRae, 18th Battalion ANZAC

We hid a great fellow for CO. He wis afa popular as he wis aye up in the line wi us. He wis a Lord or an MP or something.

He made an attack on the German lines in daylicht ae morning. He telt us afore we gid in that the Germans' bullets wouldn't touch us. They would go in at our mouths and out at our arse.

We gid ower to them withoot a barrage and fun them aa doon their dugoots.

We bombed them to smithereens and took some prisoners, then comin back to wir ain lines withoot hardly ony casualties.

The CO got in to hat for that affair: he hid niver telt them at heedquarters. At least that's fit we heard.

He wis teen awa faes efter that and we niver saa him again.

A. Smart, 5th Gordon Highlanders

Lord Dudley Gordon once came past when I was doing sentry duty – he was CO of the 5th at the time. He asked me, 'What have we in front of us boy?' To which I answered, 'That's No Man's Land Sir!'

'Oh no it isn't,' he said. 'That's the Gordon Highlanders' parade ground!'

A. MacEwan, 6th Gordon Highlanders

I was never pulled up for any misdemeanour except once and that was for not bringing my men to attention when saluting the Prince of Wales. I was out with a platoon at the time scraping mud off a road. I saluted myself but I didn't stop the men working. After the Prince – whom I didn't recognise, passed, a captain came over and reprimanded me for not properly saluting the Prince of Wales. Later I was taken in front of our own Captain Lyall from Turra. He told Sergeant Major Hay to send in Sergeant Robertson saying he didn't want to make a big doo of this.

Captain Lyall asked why I didn't salute. I told him that I did but didn't stop the men, adding that I thought the work came before the Prince of Wales whom I didn't recognise – he just looked like another officer to me.

I was then sent in front of the CO Major MacDonald, who was acting colonel at the time, later full colonel. When I told him what happened he said, 'I know – we'll just have to forget about it. We won't put anything against you in print or anything'.

Sergeant Major George Hay from Turra came round later and chewed the fat about it, saying that the Prince of Wales said he didn't mind in the least me not saluting him.

It was a silly carry on all the same. We weren't far from brigade headquarters so I think that has something to do with it.

That same captain who pulled me up for it – I met later in the War when I was then a captain myself and I told him straight what I thought of that episode and his part in it.

I was at that time scouting officer but only on a temporary basis.

Alec Robertson, 5th Gordon Highlanders

We were eence on parade as a guard o honour to some o the hich ups. There wis wir ain an the French officers, an as they cam slowly doon wir line inspecting, michty me! Fut a stink o scent the French hid. They mush ae been laripint aa ae the time.

Jimmy Reid, 6th Gordon Highlanders

At Arras, a young officer who had no experience of men – joined us. I had a boy who was a Jew in the company; he was on sentry. I accompanied this officer – as he wanted to make an inspection – to help him learn the ropes. When we passed this sentry, the officer said loudly to me, 'Oh here is my Jew friend!' He then asked the soldier, 'Have you anything to report?'

The soldier replied, 'Yes Sir!'

So the officer enquired, 'Well what is it?'

The lad then said, 'I saw a Very light[40] going up over there!'

Officer: 'Oh did you, and did you see anything else?'

Soldier: 'Yes Sir I did!'

Officer: 'Well out with it – what else did you see?'

Soldier: 'I saw it coming down again Sir!'

The officer told me to put him on a charge of insubordination but I didn't do it. When I saw the lad again, he said, 'I'll teach him to call me his Jew friend – he's no friend of mine!'

George Bryan MM, 12th Highland Light Infantry

We hid Dudley Gordon a file, an he eence to speir fit land that wis oot in front o wir trenches an if we said 'No Man's Land' he wid hiv telt us: 'Nonsense, that is the Gordon's parade ground!'

I mind we hid Lt Buchanan-Smith as oor company commander a filie.

John Brown, 5th Gordon Highlanders

I beeried an officer at Ypres. He jined us at fower in the efterneen, and wis killed at siven. He wis killed by a shell. I niver kent his name an I hid niver spoken tull him. Jist a young boy! I saa him comin up wi some new recruits and he volunteered to tak up some rations to some dugout – jist to get acquainted. He wis killed wi a shell and I helped beery him that nicht at nine.

John Russel, Royal Field Artillery

I wis pulled oot alang wi ither twa lads fae the 7th and sent as guards at General Plumer's headquarters. This wis in wy o a rist. They did iss wi lang term sodjers ye ken!

Well he wis a gran lad. He cam oot ae morning and speired at me, 'How old are you?' [Alec joined at 16.] Well I didna like to tell him the truth bit jist replied, 'Oh, I'm a fair age Sir!' So he tried anither tack. 'Then when were you born?' So I just telt him and he lached and said, 'I know now, you scamp!' He then keepit me wi him for the rest o the War.

…

Oor company commander was Billy Riddel; he wis heedmaister at Stonehaven Academy.

Alec Nicol, 7th Gordon Highlanders

I mind bein in a working perty layin barbit weer in the dark. A young Black Watch officer hid newly jined us as replacement for een o wir ain that got knocke't oot and he hid been sittin away oot in front far we were layin the wire. Me and anither lad were getting on gran bit cam up against a lad sittin in wir wy, I shouts, 'Get in your erse ye muckle bugger!' I got a fair bigake fin this officer rase up and gid awa haein a gweed lach. This was my first introduction tull him.

We come to like him afa weel; he eence to come roon us aa and news to us at nicht. I mind he organised a concert fin we were oot o the line and I played a moothie alang wi three ithers.

Jimmy Milne, 2nd Gordon Highlanders

At Cambrai we lost Captain Beveridge. His father was headmaster at Whitehills school. Our CO was Lt Colonel Fraser of Saltoun.

Alec Meldrum MM, 1st/8th Gordon Highlanders

An officer's life was about two and a half month at the Front. I myself didn't like to show any sign of rank when going over the top. I wore a private's jacket and many other officers did the same. I did this mainly to cover my identity from the enemy and also to save my uniform getting dirty. This I had to pay for myself. I think I was the first officer to do this but they all started to emulate me in our division.

Alec Robertson, 5th Gordon Highlanders

Colonel Grant was terribly thin – in fact we thought if he stood sidewise, then the snipers would have a hellava job catching him. One of his ancestors had once pursued the cattle reivers off his land and caught up with them beside a wee loch near Aviemore and in the ensuing fight, got killed. Now that loch is called in Gaelic 'The Loch of the Thin Fellow' to this day. Isn't that a coincidence? We called him 'Bones', nothing on him, but he had courage!

William MacGregor, Lovat Scouts

A Turkish sniper shot dead a sentry by the name of MacLennan and Sergeant Fitzpatrick wakened me that night and asked my help to bury him. I and a companion carried the corpse in a blanket down a communication trench to a hollow behind our line and while doing so my trousers were soaked with blood.

I had a terrible job digging, I was so weak. I had always prided myself on my fitness and it was a shock to me to discover how bad I was. So was the other chap and we required many rests before the grave was deep enough.

Lieutenant MacLean arrived and he asked us to sit on either side with a blanket round us with our backs to the enemy while he conducted a burial service, which he did by reading from his bible and saying a prayer. All done in a dignified and reverent manner, using a candle. I always had a great respect for the officer after that simple service which he carried out in spite of the fact that the sound of machine gun and rifle fire could be heard all along the Front. Another officer whom we didn't think very much of – a major, came along the trench just when we were crouching low on the firestep during a particularly savage burst of rifle fire from the Turks. He stopped and asked my friend Geordie Fraser what he would do if the Turks came across. Geordie replied that he would just keep firing at them. This didn't seem to please him for his instruction was to go out there and meet them which seemed silly. This major must have been thinking of a Cavalry charge as he had formerly been in a crack Cavalry regiment. He was given to temperamental outburst of rage but this incident with Geordie he showed how stupid and unsuitable he was for trench warfare.

Another officer we had no time for, used to creep up on our sentries while they were doing duty to catch them asleep.

…

Some of our officers were very good but there were some not so good. There were some that had been regular cavalry men that had been retired and volunteered when War came. They tended to look down on us as being below the standard of the great cavalry regiments they had been used to.

William Mowat, 1st Scottish Horse and Lovat Scouts

Lt Colonel Grant was struck with a shell burst on a Sunday morning in the front line. I remember standing back to let him pass in this trench when it happened.

Colonel MacTaggart came after Grant. He was a wee man who came from the Lancers. When we came out of the Somme, he addressed us and said that it was an honour to die for our country, but I don't think we appreciated that.

…

When I was sent back to this country to train to be an officer, I went to military school at Berkhamsted. After I passed, I was asked what regiment I preferred. I said the Gordon Highlanders first, the Cameron Highlanders next, then the Black Watch. I got neither – I was sent to the Yorks and Lancs 1st Battalion. Their CO was Lt Colonel Blunt. I served under him for nine months.

Sergeant Gavin was a sergeant in the 5th Gordon Highlanders at the same time as myself. He was the schoolmaster's son from Drumwhindle where I attended and also was later commissioned in the Gordon Highlanders. Our two names were later displayed on a plaque at the school as having been commissioned as officers in the Great War.

I remember the schoolmaster of neighbouring Savock – Mr Ferguson, a big man, became a major in the Gordon Highlanders. Then there was a Major Law from Strichen as well.

Alec Robertson, 5th Gordon Highlanders

A man Archibald fae Huntly wis een o wir officers at Loos.

Jimmy Reid, 6th Gordon Highlanders

27

Sixth Sense

Once I was sitting on the ground when we were back a bit. I had on my greatcoat and was cleaning my rifle. All of a sudden I made a dive out of there. A shell then burst above my head and shrapnel smashed into my coat and rifle. I found the nose cap of the shell still stuck in my coat and my rifle was ruined. I wasn't touched.

This was on a lovely sunny day in the reserve lines. This was sixth sense that saved me.

Donald MacVicar, 1st/2nd The Queen's Own Cameron Highlanders

My platoon sergeant wis an ald regular; he had an afa bad fit and aye fell ahin on the march in spite o the fact that we cairried his equipment. He wis weel like'd and wid hae got a hurl wi the baggage cairt bit he jist winted to be wi the boys. He wid niver gie in though and we were richt sorry for him. Weel weel! He wis puttin awa on a course and the corporal wis put in charge. He wis nae ease and tried to chase us aboot a bit tull he got damned richt unpopular. During an attack on the German lines, the Gerry started huddin in the shells so I flappit in a shell hole to hide wi anither five men and the corporal. Then some urge telt me to gang oot and I wis nae seener oot o there than a shell laand and blew them aa to kingdom come.

Jimmy Milne, 2nd Gordon Highlanders

Some lads kent fine they war gan to be killed; on the ither han some like masel eence to say tull themsels, 'Na na, ma number's nae on this boord yet!'

Alec Nicol, 7th Gordon Highlanders

They came into our trench and an old soldier who was hit badly was cursing and swearing at everything in particular. I heard he had died later, which brought to mind what my friend Andrew Shaw had told me about this old soldier – Joe Barton, had remarked as their lighter had approached the beach at Suvla Bay. 'Well, I'll not come out of this!' I noticed many others had this presentiment of death.

William Mowat, 1st Scottish Horse and Lovat Scouts

I dinna ken fit wy I survived. I hid the funny idea that if I charged sideways I widna be shot.

Jimmy Reid, 6th Gordon Highlanders

We were advancing at the time and there were five of us taking shelter in a shell hole from the enemy fire: suddenly an urge or instinct told me to get out of there at once. As I was in charge I shouted to the rest to move, 'Get to hell out of here!' One of the lads said that they were fine sheltered there, but when I dived over into another hole they all followed. Then a shell came crashing down and blew up in the one we had abandoned. I don't know what it was that made me do it but it was pretty strong urge I can tell you.

A. MacEwan, 6th Gordon Highlanders

28

Prisoners

I met iss wee Jock comin by wi siven big Gerries. I says till him, 'Faar are ye gan wi at Jock?'

He replied, 'Oh the deil gan very far if I had ma wy!'
Alec Pratt MM, Royal Horse Artillery

We took a lot of prisoners in the trench that we took. Our sergeant made them teem their pooches and ae Gerry hid a lot o Gordon badges. Noo the sergeant gid fair wild and I thocht he wid sheet him for that. The Gerry thocht the same and got oot a photo o his wife and bairns and lat him see them.
Donald Petrie, 5th Gordon Highlanders

44. A soldier helping a wounded German prisoner, Western Front.

Reproduced by permission of the National Library of Scotland

We were never sent to a prisoner of war camp, but we were used to work for them ahin the lines aa the time as slave labour.

We didna get muckle mait and some os de-et. I gid doon to sax steen.

I mind gan to a doctor fin I got ass wikes I couldna walk. I hid to parade in front of him and fin I got till him he speired fit wis wrang wi me. I said, 'Weak knees!' Wi that he got aa turket and raise up and baaled oot o him, 'Weak knees? Weak knees? … Nix! Weak knees! Rouse … Rouse … !'

Alec Wilson, 7th Cameron Highlanders

ass wikes so weak, *turket* fierce

I was sent to a POW camp in Germany to work in a quarry. They couldn't feed us. You got a loaf of bread to last five days and a bowl of soup made with veg for lunch. We went down to six and seven stones.

In the big hut there were only four Scots fellows; the rest English. Two of the chaps got in touch with the cook who left them the tattie peelings that they made the soup with, but they were green and they took poisoning and died.

After we were there four months we started getting Red Cross parcels and they were marvellous with tinned fruit, herring, pilchards and sardines and so on. We were now better off than the Germans.

The Germans I worked with were too old for the fighting – told me that they just got one bit of butcher meat once a fortnight.

At this village I got on fine with them. We were shown no hatred and they were clean, tidy, just like our ain folk.

In the huts, we lay on the bare boards, but on our sides as our bare backbones were too sore otherwise. The Scots started the favourite saying, 'I could do with a jelly piece!' Oh the starvation was terrible!

Jock Murray, 1st King's Own Scottish Borderers

45. Massed German prisoners, France
Reproduced by permission of the National Library of Scotland

29

Enemies and Allies

The enemy

The Prussian Guard put the fear in me. They cam on shooder to shooder. Huge lads wi helmets gleaming. I pirkit at them wi ma heed below the parapet – bit of coorse I wisna lang oot at the time.
Bill Minty, 4th Gordon Highlanders

Dinna lat the Gerry come ower close, bit use the bullet instead. We were afa determined an didna like the Gerry to get the better o us. I mind we eence took a pill-box in the dark.
George Stewart, 5th Gordon Highlanders

Maist o the Germans wid pit up a bit o a skirmish wi us, bit nae for lang: they didna like the bayonet; except the Prussian Guard, my God na! they didna run awa. They were a teuch lot. Aa the same they didna like up agaist us, na fegs!
Alec MacHardy MM, 7th Gordon Highlanders

I remember helping a Prussian Guardsman I found lying wounded in a dugout. Well he actually rose up and walked outside to a stretcher and lay down and died.
A. MacEwan, 6th Gordon Highlanders

Allies

The Americans didna hack awa at the same bit o line like we did, but if they warna coming oot o the bit – they jist gid smack I at anither bit.
Jimmy Reid, 6th Gordon Highlanders

The Americans weren't much good that came up to relieve us at Aveluy Wood. We went back supposed to get a month's rest but were sent back up again after a fortnight. They couldn't hold the line; yet when we met them the first time they were shouting, 'It won't be long now Jock! It won't be long now!' They were quiet lads when we saw them the second time; they were just a fortnight in the line; that finished them! There were no trenches there – just shell holes you see.

…

We liked the Algerians – they were beside us at Aveluy Wood. We got on fine with them.

George Bryan MM, 12th Highland Light Infantry

I aye mind; there wis a German machine gun awa oot in front o Beaumont-Hamel that pinned us doon aa the time. Five Bengal Lancers cam up and gid richt up in front and stopped in the back o a wid. Ae lad held the five horses and the tither fower disappeared inti the wid. Efter an oor or so they cam oot and collected their horses and cam back through wir lines again. Noo we war niver annoyed wi that machine gun again. They fairy settled that!

Jimmy Milne, 2nd Gordon Highlanders

We liked the Australians and they liked us: we got on great thegither. Aa the same we hidna the siller that they hid.

Lea Birnie, 1st Gordon Highlanders

The Irish I liked fine – they were gie hardy billies like wirsels, bit I aye thocht that the English war a bittie mammy dooy kine!

Jimmy Reid, 6th Gordon Highlanders

Before the Americans cam in we were gie sair pushed.

The French were an untidy lot and left their stuff lying about all over the place.

Robert More MM, 4th Seaforth Highlanders

I saa the Americans for the first time fin we war hine awa back risten. That wis efter the German Big Push. The Yanks cam inti oor canteen and started blaain fit they war gan ti dee. There wis some o oor lads hid been eers in the Waar and didni like iss cairry on. Ae Jock says ti een, 'Al that ye see far the War is!' and gid him bowf in the face. Of coorse at caased a bit o ruption bit it wisna muckle winner.

There, we were that short o men that they war amalgamatin the battalions inti een. I masel wis puttin inti the 6th Black Watch. We war aa sair cut up.

Peter Baigrie, 7th Cameron Highlanders/6th Black Watch

The Anzacs wid hae geen onywy wi us – they liked to be asides.

Alec MacHardy MM, 7th Gordon Highlanders

We couldn't stand the Portuguese – they were aye ready to run.

A. Smeaton MM, 5th Black Watch

'Pork and Beans' we called the Portuguese. When going up the line at La Bassée we were alerted that Gerry had broken through. After a while we saw what we thought were the Gerry coming running at us and when they were within range we opened rapid fire causing them heavy casualties. Suddenly we were ordered to cease fire. This was the Portuguese doing what we called 'skinning out of the line'.
Dave Pitkethly, 4th Seaforth Highlanders

30

Laughs

On an exercise near Hawick we had an officer called William Lyon. He came from St Andrews where his father was a church minister. He was a popular officer and was six feet six inches tall.

After the end of an exercise, in which the recruits were firing blank, the officer held a rifle inspection during which the men held their thumb in the breech during which the officer looked through the barrel from the discharge end.

There was one fellow clowning about and not doing it properly. 'Jackson,' the officer called sharply, 'there is a bloody fool in every platoon, and you never know, you might be it!' Lieutenant Lyon was killed in France.

George Dick, Black Watch

I remember a funny incident at Alexandria when a lad Duncan Fraser was on guard. It was a hard job keeping watch on the locals as they would steal anything from our tents if they got in about. Duncan halted a crowdie of them and a big buxom wifie came up and squirted milk to blind him while the rest tried to slip by to the tents.

William MacGregor, Lovat Scouts

Major Cuthbert from Tain was a hellava lad. He was well liked. He was a wee fellow who liked a good dram. One time we were camped out in a French barn and this particular barn had a midden with a cow urine cesspool at the side. Major Cuthbert came in one dark night with a good shot in and looking for his quarters; he wandered the wrong way and fell into the cesspool of cowshit. Extricating himself with difficulty – he cursed and swore his way about in the dark until he drew attention of two alert MPs who grabbed him and hauled him off to the guardroom bawling and shouting, completely immersed in liquid dung. They thought it was just another stupid private that had too much drink. After washing him down they got quite a surprise and quickly let him go. He was a great favourite with the lads and when he got wounded in the leg – he never went to rear, but just bandaged up and came back and went about on horseback. He didn't worry a damn about anything.

Robert More MM, 4th Seaforth Highlanders

There was another Aberdeenshire sergeant with me training recruits and his name was Jimmy Sanderson – I think he later was in the Strathbogie Hotel in Huntly. Well he was the greatest comedian out; he had us all in stitches all the time and all in the pure Aberdeenshire dialect. One I remember is about a dealer who sold a horse to a man. Two days later the man came back to the dealer and asked him to take the horse back. The dealer speirs fit wis wrang weet:

'Oh man, the beast is blin.'

Dealer: 'Oh na, it canna be blin.'

'I tell ye its blin aa richt, it waakit inti a lamp post yesterday.'

Dealer: 'Na na, it canna be – at beast is soon as can be.'

'I'm tellin ye its blin – it traivelled through a plate glass window this mornin'.'

Dealer: 'Ach na, the beasts nae blin – its jist gallus!'

Jimmy was a great horsey man and in fact owned a saddler's business as well as the hotel. He was in charge of all the horse transport and he was in his element then. I mind I once went over my ankle and could hardly walk and Jimmy produced a bottle of horse embrocation and when I rubbed it in it burned like hell a while but helped alleviate the pain, but my my, I smelt like high heaven for a long time after it. What a fellow for telling stories, folk just sat down and laughed themselves to death.

I met him years after the War in Dunfermline after I came out of the bank in Dunfermline and I spotted him right away but he went right past me so I pulled him up short when I hailed him, 'Jimmy Sanderson, you would pass an old Army friend – cut him stone dead in the street too!' Well, we had a great take on – he was just the same as ever and his stories too. He spent the night with me and we caught with the news. He had come down to Dunfermline to see his daughter at the college here. I knew the lassie well for two years but had not connected her with Jimmy. I had nicknamed her 'Huntly'.

Jimmy told me he was now a director of Forbes Simmers of Hatton – the biscuit people.

George Dick, Black Watch

Alec Pratt was my sergeant. He was a great character and a hard man. He knew all the ropes being an old regular. I mind in France he came round inspecting the horse lines and we were on parade standing by our horses in the early morning parade.

Away down the line I heard Sergeant Pratt say, 'What the hell are you grovelling there making such a damned noise?' I heard the poor fellow say, 'The horse kicked me Sergeant!' Sergeant Pratt snaps back, 'Well, get to hell on your feet and kick the bastard back!

Englishman in Scotland looking up Army pals

I wis a while sergeant drilling recruits and there was a sergeant Bob Milne of the Gordon Highlanders doing the same job – just training young laddies to be soldiers. Now Bob had at one time been a farm servant in Aberdeenshire. He wouldn't speak English for anybody. Those laddies, if they didn't know what Bob was saying at the start of the training programme, they certainly knew it by the time it finished. It was a fairly intensive stint of eight weeks' duration consisting of basic PT, musketry, rifle drill, foot drill, bayonet fighting and so on.

Anyway we got a new captain who had been delegated in charge because he had been badly wounded. He was gie red-faced and smoked a pipe. He was English and declared he had a great belief in Scots as fighting soldiers.

Anyway he came up to Bob Milne as he was drilling a squad of 18 year olds and said, 'Sergeant Milne, what have you been doing with your boys today?'

Bob replied, 'Weel Sir, I've jist been doon ti Colchester Baths dookin ma geets!'

The captain was fair flummoxed and came ower to me where I was standing listening. I gave him a fair interpretation that Bob had taken his lads down to the baths for a swim.

George Dick, Black Watch

46. The Gordon Highlanders form a Guard of Honour. Field Marshal Sir Douglas Haig talking to a Sergeant Major of the Gordon Highlanders who formed the Guard of Honour.

Reproduced by permission of the National Library of Scotland

31

The Bull Ring

I hid a turnie at the Bull Ring efter I cam back ti France efter bein wounded. They made ye rin, clim an craal amon dubs fae mornin to nicht. I wis fair gled ti get back amon the lads efter that.

John Brown, 5th Gordon Highlanders

I was doing a course at the Bull Ring at Etaps when a riot took place. There, a corporal of the 4th Gordon Highlanders was shot one Sunday night supposed to be by a Red Cap as he was leaving a cinema.[41] He had been due to go on leave the next day. What the disturbance was about I wasn't sure, but after that things got out of hand. This Red Cap was on the staff at the Bull Ring so apparently the troops involved went down there to Etaps – which incidentally was out of bounds – and created a riot. The Black Watch were predominant in that incident. They were blamed for wrecking the place. We were moved away quickly and sent back to our regiments.

Alec Meldrum MM, 1st/8th Gordon Highlanders

We first git to Etaps to the Bull Ring and hid a hellish time ot. The morning aye started wi a march o three mile wi full marchin order. Michty! We hid an afa cairy on up there and wis gled to be sent up the line.

Jimmy Milne, 2nd Gordon Highlanders

I wis eence up at the Bull Ring at Etabs and they gied us hell up there. Bit there wis a riot efter that and a puckle folk got killed. Efter that they teemed Etabs and put aabody inti the line. Australians and New Zealanders hid deen a hellava damage there apparently. They were aa big stoot chiels.

Norrie Cruikshank, 6th Gordon Highlanders

Fin I recovered fae ma wounds, I wis sent back ti France. There I wis sent up to the Bull Ring, for trainin. De ye ken – it wis waar than the fechtin. They chased us on aa the time. I wis gled to get oot o er an wis puttin in to the 8th Gordon Highlanders. I wid hae preferred back to my ain company in the 5th – bit na, na!

A. Smart, 5th Gordon Highlanders

I gid first to Etabs to the Bull Ring. They were richt thorough at trainin us at nicht fechtin.

Jimmy Milne, 2nd Gordon Highlanders

I was an instructor at the Bull Ring for six weeks. I tried to teach the Yanks our methods but it was no use. I could do nothing with them: they had their hands in their pockets all the time. It was like talking to a stone wall; they just laughed and said, 'That's all right Jock! That's all right!' They were smoking away not worrying a damned hair.

Robert More MM, 4th Seaforth Highlanders

Both times after I was wounded I was sent to the Bull Ring at Etabes before resuming my place at the Front. Up there they gave you intensive training in battle and tactics with a predominance of bayonet practice through the day, and at night we had to get rid of the mud off our uniforms and spruce up and parade for inspections. The instructors bawled us about all the time. I mean it was ridiculous – I saw no good for it at all. I was a veteran like most of the others and knew more about front line fighting than the instructors. All the same I didn't like having to be sent to the 5th Gordon Highlanders after the second time. Oh no, I would have preferred back to my beloved company in the 6th.

A. MacEwan, 6th Gordon Highlanders

Eence at the Bull Ring fin I wis there – the second time – the Americans were gettin bayonet trainin. They were hellava awkward at it and the instructor wis gettin crabbit, so he took the rifle fae ae lad and demonstrated fit to dee, then he haaned it back sayin, 'Now, do as I did there and you may become a soldier!'

Noo aat didna please the Yank; he grabbed the rifle and jist stabbit the instructor richt through, killin him steen deed sayin, 'You can write home to your mother and tell her you'r dead then!'

De ye ken, there wis nae soon aboot it itherwise the Americans wid hae played up. Oh no it wis aa hushed up.

John Will, 5th Gordon Highlanders

I got a while at the Bull Ring at Etabs. By jove – that was some place that: they murdered you up there! They told me that the Canadians, the Australians and the Jocks had mutinied there. When they were all lined up in the early morning none of them moved when ordered to do so by the officers.

Dave Pitkethly, 4th Seaforth Highlanders

My certie! I didna like the Bull Ring – that wis gie teuch!

J. Burnett, 8th Gordon Highlanders

teuch tough

32

Supplies

Food

Some o the young French quines eesed to come richt up ti the front line sellin oofs and ither mait. They got the maist o oor siller, extras like at wis richt welcome.
Bert Gow, Royal Field Artillery

You've seen a horse chaain a neuk o a post – wearied like? Weel at wis us, tryin to ate a hard biscuit. They blaket aa! Of coorse there wis a lot o mait spiled by bad cookin.
Jimmy Reid, 6th Gordon Highlanders

We couldn't chew the hard biscuits. I used to hit them with a trenching tool.
George Bryan MM, 12th Highland Light Infantry

There were Australian rabbits on the menu. They were compressed and dried, heeds and aa. Some lads compleened that theyd gotten the een in their stew. I niver, bit of coorse we war thankful o onything ye ken!
Jimmy Scott, Royal Engineers

The Salvation Army were the finest folk that iver wis. Mony a time we gid in tull em withoot a roost bit aye got something. I'll niver say naething against them; they were gran!
Alec MacHardy MM, 7th Gordon Highlanders

Do ye ken, the Germans aye hid plenty o mait compared to oor boys. We eenced to hear them barkin like dogs – bow wowin!
Norrie Cruikshank, 6th Gordon Highlanders

We were kine o bare maited, and I wis eence on a working party helpin to mak roads. Farrer doon the road wis a German working party; aye, prisoners ye ken!

Weel a horse draan canteen o het soup cam up and gid stracht by us to feed the Gerries. Noo thats fit happened – bit we got naething!

It wis a hellava job the workin parites; making trenches, laying weer or even takin up rations. Maist ot hid to be deen in the dark.

We were supposed to get a rum ration bit I only seen it once, except ae Hogmanay, bit wir rations were afa short – there wis a daily issue o a bittie cheese that wis that sma, it wid hardly feed a moose. There wis a bittie extras on New Eer's Day wi rum and that. The English relieved us for Hogmanay. We did the same for them for Christmas.
Alec Barlow, 1st Gordon Highlanders

I remember one day we received welcome ration of frozen meat which was cooking away in my mess tin. Everyone was doing the same and the Turks had got alarmed with the smoke emitting from our trench and probably thinking it was the prelude to an attack, sent over a long fusillade of rifle fire. After the firing had stopped, I got down off the firestep to attend to my steak and found it full of sand. I tried to wash it clean from the meagre supply of my water bottle but it was fairly gritty steak I devoured with anything but relish.
William Mowat, 1st Scottish Horse and Lovat Scouts

Fin I gid oot fist there wis nae dugoots or damn aal. Neething bit bully beef and hard biscuits.
John Will, 5th Gordon Highlanders

Fin we gid into a café after the War, a gweed meal only cost us three half pennies. Oor money wis worth an afa lot oot there. The Merk wis worth naething.
Alec Barlow, 1st Gordon Highlanders

There were many threshing machines at Salonica. They were all made in Germany with the name of Swartz on them and were driven by steam engines. The grain mostly grown was maize. We had two lads – two brothers by the name of Fraser who were meal millers at Beauly – they got a water mill going and got some of the lads to thresh some of the maize after which they ground it down. We mixed it with oat meal as it was in short supply. We made porridge and it wasn't too bad – we just had to put up with it. I remember some of the Gloucesters passing by when we were at our porridge and one remarked to the others about the Jocks eating poultice. There were no population, they had all fled the fighting.
William MacGregor, Lovat Scouts

They took up the mait on ponies and in guana bags. So there wis hair among the sugar and nae milk. The watter wis in petrol tins and they niver sweeled oot the petrol edder. This aye gid me the hertburn; so I thocht I wid dee something aboot it. I heard that if ye pit a stick among billin watter – then that will clean'ed. So I fited a bit wid to fit my Dixie and tried at, and awite it worked; this took oot the petrol!
Jimmy Reid, 6th Gordon Highlanders

We got a loaf in the morning and had to spin it out. At night we got a hard biscuit supposed to be full of vitamins but they were hard, hard!
Albert Napier MM, Royal Field Artillery ('Taggart's Own')

I mind we got a flour ration a-piece afore a push. This push wis stoppit cis it cam on a blizzard o sna o thon big flocks o snaflakes that blottit oot aathing. The push wis stoppit an we laaned up in a ruined kine o hoose in a village. There wis a lad Thomson an Cattanach fae Auchterless an masel aa pooled wir flour. We fun a big tin an battered it flat ti mak a girdle. It wisna lang afore there wis a fire goin in the fireplace wi sticks an at, an then we mixed the flour wi watter an made bannocks. The smell that cam aff the bakin bannocks wis jist domino – it jist remindeds o hame – oh it wis great. Bit the feenished bannocks wis nae like midder's eens, oh na, they war like elastic – ye could hae raxed them fae here to Auchnagatt. They didna taste bit middlin, bit of coorse they gid doon fine wi the bully beef.
Bert Gow, Royal Field Artillery

The nicht afore gan over the top at ae push, bein up on the firestep o the trench, an I spiers at a mate if he saa fit I saa. This wis a hare an it was ploutering aboot in the half dark fair lost.

I took a shot at it an it fell ower deed. I craaled oot fort fin it got richt dark – it wis only 50 yards or so an took it back. We didna mous ti at beast al tell ye. I skinned it richt awa.

Man, I've seen ma gang oot at nicht an fin the deed bodies for ony mait that they hid on em. Hunger dis terrible things ti ye.
John Brown, 5th Gordon Highlanders

Hard biscuits were hell in aa. Nae eese them it hid false teeth, they wid hae broken them.
John Russel, Royal Field Artillery

My first lesson about food was when I landed in France. We entrained in box-wagons – six horses and 30 men apiece. We were each delved out a few days' food rations and I thought I had received far too much and dumped some. I learned to regret that as I quickly ate my way through what was left and had to do without for quite a while. So that lesson learned, I never did anything so stupid again – food was scarce out there. Oh no, never throw food out, rather dump clothes. Unless it was winter of course, we needed all our clothing then. Keeping warm then was not easy in the trenches and after heavy rain the water came up to our knees.

Speaking about food – I once found a crate of oranges at a village called Douai not far from Arras. Some of us lived on oranges for a few days after.
A. MacEwan, 6th Gordon Highlanders

The English – I didna care for them afa weel – could ate as much as you and me thegither and then plenty mair. Oh my heavens! I widna a liket to be their cook, na michty na!
Norrie Cruikshank, 6th Gordon Highlanders

Food was bully beef and hard biscuits and when one opened a tin the bully had turned to liquid with the heat and swarms of flies attacked it at once.
William Mowat, 1st Scottish Horse and Lovat Scouts

We gid in to iss French café for something to ate and they gid us some fried kine o affairs. We ate iss stuff and like'ed it weel enench. Anither lad speired, 'Fu did ye like the puddocks' legs – gyad sake!' But they werna common puddocks – they war great big legs ye ken. It wis us – the 7th – that shot the cheese. Oor rations were comin up in the dark, fin a cheese hid rolled aff the cairt. Later on the quartermaster saa this fite thing on the grun and bein half can't at the time – shot the kebbik. Somebody made up a rhyme, it gid like iss:

> It is sorry to say the kebbik suffered an untimely disaster
> To be out for king and country's sake and shot by its own quartermaster!
> Ony ither battalion it gid by eence
> To aye torment us by speirin, 'Fa shot the cheese?'

Alec Nicol, 7th Gordon Highlanders
puddocks frogs, *kebbik* a cake of cheese

The hard biscuits I crunched awa at, bit they hidna muckle taste. Still I wis gled o onything ti keep awa the hunger. I mind fin we hid a lang march an laaned up in a barn at nicht being aboot as famished as I hiv iver been. I saa crums on the wa left ower wi the wheat that hid eence been stored there an di ye ken iss min, I scrapet them aff the wa an ate them.

Annider time we wis on the march an fin we stoppit aside a ferm, I grabbet a hennie that wis steerin aboot. I drew its neck and plukket it an cleaned it. I split it wi aa the lads in my section an we got a fire goin and wis sizzling it rale fine in wir dixies fin we got orders ti fall in on the march again. Man we didna waste it – it gid doon fine – raa as it wis.

The CO led the wy on his horse fin on the March.
John Brown, 5th Gordon Highlanders
raa raw

We hid a lot o Gaelic spikkers. My best pal cam fae the Eest. His midder sent him oot parcels o breed and venison and that wis richt fine – aye, we lookit forrit tull aat.
Peter Baigrie, 7th Cameron Highlanders/6th Black Watch

47. Soldiers of the 2nd Battalion, Gordon Highlanders, France.
Reproduced by permission of the National Library of Scotland

I crossed the Jordan twice fin we took Damascus. Drinkin watter wis hell in aa to get and fit we did get wisna gweed. It cam in bags and wis clorinated.

We had a puckle gran officers; some o them hid risen fae the ranks, wi some Boer War men amang them.

The rations were nae great dale: maistly hard tac, and fin we biled them, weevils aa cam to the tap o the watter and were scooped aff. Weel nae them aa maybe!

George Barclay, Royal Field Artillery

Most of the food was stolen by the time it got up to the front line. The rations were a loaf of bread between two men as a rule, but when it came up to the trenches it became a loaf between eight. There was one time my platoon were assisting the transport men and part of our duties was taking up the rations. There I saw them fling a bag of food over a hedge to where their digs were. We had steaks for breakfast that time, so that was not reaching the Front for a start. Oh no, that never reached the trenches. When we were out, we could get a fairly decent meal in the Salvation Army canteen.

Jock Murray, 1st King's Own Scottish Borderers

217

Drink

During our advance in 1918 I was crossing a field and saw a patch of brown dead grass, my suspicions were arouse at once and I stopped and investigated this unusual sight.

I cautiously lifted a square of grass which revealed a trap door. When I realised this I saw that I had uncovered a large stock of Champagne. This must have been a store made by the French farmers to hide it from the Germans. I took a large supply away with me. Later the CO came and demanded some off me as he was going to be entertaining some party of officers.

I said, 'What Champagne?'

He said, 'Come now Smeaton, you know fine!'

He got some in exchange for my favourite rum. I didn't like Champagne; although I have never seen drunker men than the chaps that were that time.

A. Smeaton MM, 5th Black Watch

We wis a filie deein guards at docks efter the Battle o Loos. There wisna mony os left o the battalion then. This wis to gie us a rist an lat us get reinforcements fae hame.

That's fin I got scunnered o reed wine.

Jimmy Reid, 6th Gordon Highlanders

We eence cam on a brewery that wis deserted. A lot o barrels were lyin ootside and some inside, fu o stuff. We broached them and filled oor dixies wi the stuff and man, it wis richt fine and sweet. Well man, we drank wir fill and I think we poukit holes in aa the barrels and it wisna lang afore aabody wis fu. Weel it wis fine kine o wine stuff ye see. Onywy a kine o a mishunter happened to een o the men. He wis fun inside the store. He hid knock'ed the heed aff a barrel and tummeled in. Only his beets war stickin oot. Drooned he wis!

Well neist day we gid in to the front line. Do ye ken iss, we hid to be teen oot ot again wi dysentery. It wis jist fleein faes like watter away. The wine must hiv been immature or something.

Alec MacHardy MM, 7th Gordon Highlanders

I fair liket their tea; nae sugar, nae milk, jist black, and it wis richt gweed.

…

Ye hid to be as strong as a horse oot there, itherwise it wis nae eese. We got a nippie o rum noo and again bit only in the wintertime.

Norrie Cruikshank, 6th Gordon Highlanders

On a route march in England we were aa halted at a pub caad the 'Cat and Whistle'. Fin we left there we had drunk the place dry.

Jimmy Scott, Royal Engineers

We were being shipped to France from Taranto in Italy in a French ship, and many of our boys had got bottles of Cognac earlier in the town. They were all half cant. Major Grant of Rothiemurchas sent for me and asked me to find out where they were getting the drink. I was later able to report to him that I never found out. This was when the War finished. I remember it was horse flesh that was served up.

William MacGregor, Lovat Scouts

We were using a high building for an observation post. Our sergeant stepped down off the roof and said, 'Why don't you fellows go down to the village and get us some booze otherwise the Germans will soon be here and get the lot.' So we went down to the village – three of us. The population had fled; and so we went into this estaminet and took a whole case of Champagne and also filled a sack. We were on our way back when we were stopped by two Australian officers who said, 'Don't you know you buggers are looting?' Well, I replied, 'The Germans are coming along soon; its no use leaving it to them. Would you like a couple of bottles?' With that they departed quite happy. Our officers came to hear about it; no doubt attracted by the noise we were making that night. Some of them swooped down on us in the cellar and demanded to know where the hell we'd gotten all the booze. So I told him and suggested helpfully that we go and get some for the officers. Which we did later that night: loading up the officers' mess wagon.

Albert Napier MM, Royal Field Artillery ('Taggart's Own')

We aye got a nippie o rum to ging ower but nae sae muckles the Germans got. I aye mind fin they cam ower in 1918 – although I wis in hospital at the time, I wis seen put up the line again and it wisna lang afore I heard and saa them – they were singing: boozed ye ken, fu o drink.

John Will, 5th Gordon Highlanders

It wis the winter we hated. I didna mind the War in the simmertime. We hid a character nicknamed Sailor. He stole a pig o rum fae the officers' dugoot. That keepit us gan for some time in the terrible cald.

...

We niver saw rum. The officers got it lang afore it got to us.

George Stewart, 5th Gordon Highlanders

Up there we could get a glass o brandy for twa sou, bit efter the Canadians cam they upped the price tull we were peying through the nose. Afa greed for money they Froggies!

Norrie Cruikshank, 6th Gordon Highlanders

We were told to use rainwater for making tea which was not easy to define. Once I made tea from a shell hole which later dried out slightly and revealed a man's feet sticking out.
Robert More MM, 4th Seaforth Highlanders

There wis a rum ration cam roon an I hid a deal wi some o the lads that didna drink that I would get their rum in exchange for some Craven A fags that I hid plenty o – bein driver to the major who wis a director o Craven A company – he gid me a tin o 50 ilkey day.

The fags issued were caad Red Bazaar and I aye said they were fulled wi horse dried dung. Aye they wir coorse!
Jimmy Scott, Royal Engineers

I niver saa a Rum ration bit I suppose somebody wis gettent.
Peter Baigrie, 7th Cameron Highlanders/6th Black Watch

Kit

As a Highland regiment we wore shoes that were no use and I got issued with a pair of Glasgow boots. Then we got shoemakers attached to us which were a great improvement. So it was boots and putees from then on.
…
We jist hid on the kilts, nae bloody pants or onything, wi a flannan sark and a jersey that wis as lousy as hell!
Jimmy Reid, 6th Gordon Highlanders

The kilt wis nae eese; it froze roon oor legs. The skin at the back o wir knees aa crackit.
George Stewart, 5th Gordon Highlanders

Cattanach fae Auchterless, wis ruggin awa tryin his best ti get aff iss Gerry officer's lang bonny leather beets. He hid been deed for a file an wis aa swelled up.

He says to me, 'Sit on him!' I sat on him to hud him doon and the twa os managed thegidder. Fut a lach aat wis. He wore them a lang time as they were better than ony o oors.
Bert Gow, Royal Field Artillery

They issued a blanket apiece so twa os sleepit thegither and got mair heat. There wis nae billets at that time.
Alec MacHardy MM, 7th Gordon Highlanders

33

Patrols

I wis at Ypres fin HQ detailed me to tak a patrol oot to tak prisoners. I pick'ed fower – I niver took mair than that. We only took a bayonet apiece; there wis nae pint on humphin rifles aboot in the dubs. We managed to tak twa onywy and took them back to headquarters. Gan back to wir lines I decided to hae a rist becis there wis plenty o time fors till mornin. So we gid in to this shelter to sleep and that wis the last thing I mind on, till I wakened up in hospital nesit day. Apparently a shell hid laaned and blown us up. The fower men that wis wi me were killed. Some lads hid come lookin fors fin we didna come back in the mornin and fun the ither men bit nae me. Then they thocht on meeving some beam or ither and there wis I beeried in aneth it.

…

Ae time oot on patrol at nicht we sat doon for a rist ahin a fain tree. We niver made a soon at aat caper and the Gerry were the same. Aa at eence I noticed a Gerry patrol sittin on the ither side deein the same as wirsels. Baith sides pairted company gey quick I can tell ye.

…

I eence gid three days withoot a kilt. We war oot on a raid ae nicht to tak prisoners. Gerry hid kent we wis on the go and opened up on us wi machine guns. I made a breenge for cover and got stuck fest on berbed weer. I hid to get oot o there quick so I loused aff the kilt. Do ye ken, I hid to wite tull een o wir ain lads got killed afore I got anither yin. They hid naething for us at the start: nae uniforms. We hid to train in civvies!

Alec MacHardy MM, 7th Gordon Highlanders

I wis aften on a patrol on the Gerry lines. I've seen us gan richt up against their trenches listenin to them chatterin awa. This hid to be deen in dubs an weet at times. Of coorse the Gerry did this tee, mony a time hiv we met them fin we were comin back bit neen os likett to cause any bother bit jist juket by een anither. That wisna aye the case of course – mony a scrap happened oot there.

Wullie Gavin, 5th Gordon Highlanders

48. Injured German soldier being tended to by German first aid worker.
Reproduced by permission of the National Library of Scotland

A patrol went out one night but came in in a hurry when the Gerry started shelling. One of our chaps had left his bayonet sticking over the parapet and one lad had spiked his leg on it while coming in. It was a bad wound but this lad wouldn't report sick. 'Oh no,' he said, 'they would just say it was a self-inflicted wound!' He got it bandaged up and suffered in silence for a long time and do you know it got better – it healed nicely.
A. MacEwan, 6th Gordon Highlanders

When out on patrol at night, we went out as far as the German wire and listened for movement behind their lines, like the transportation of supplies – ammunition and the like. When we got back, the Intelligence Officer would question us all, and from the combined information, he would assess what was really going on. This officer was quite hard on you and didn't take it for granted that you were telling the truth.

I remember being out with a patrol once, when heavy shelling started. Luckily there was an old Gerry dugout handy to go into for shelter as the shells continued to crunch around us.

The Gerry patrols were out doing the same as us and we sometimes passed them. We didn't interfere with them if we saw them but just let them pass. One time I was lying out there in a pitch black night with an arm stretched out, when I felt the grass disturbed between my fingers then a German crept past – as close as that. This was early in the War when the grass and grain grew between the lines.
Alec Robertson, 5th Gordon Highlanders

I was on sentry duty, when I was jumped on by four Gerries. I bayoneted one in the throat, another in the chest and then the others ran away.
Sergeant, name unknown, Aberdeen, 1st Gordon Highlanders

I lay oot in front on sentry ae nicht jist listenin an lookin.

Aa at eence I heard a soon o scuffling nae far oot. I threw a Mills bomb. It exploded an somebody shouted a password. I telt them to come forrat. The explosion didna hurt onybody, bit the sergeant wis in an afa rage. He said, 'Fit are ye tryin to dee? Kill wir ain men!'
Alec Wilson, 7th Cameron Highlanders

We went out patrolling at night over No Man's Land and tried to creep up on them and grab one. Not so easy in the dark, but when we did succeed, the Gerry came quietly.
Robert More MM, 4th Seaforth Highlanders

We eenced to ging ower and tantalise the Germans at nicht wi Mills bombs. They sent up Very lights; they supplied aa the lights. Fin that happened we aa tried to hide. I mind I stappet ma heed doon a hole bit ma feet wis outside. At length the sergeant said, 'Come oot o that Wilson, its aa ower!'

49. Barbed wire in the trenches.

Reproduced by permission of the National Library of Scotland

We eence gid oot to get some casualties at nicht fin we heard them cryin oot, bit the Germans hid them picked up first.

Alec Wilson, 7th Cameron Highlanders

I wis eence on sentry in the trench wi an English lad that wis afa windy. This wis in a fine meenlichty nicht. Aa at eence he shouts, 'They're coming! They're coming! Stand to! Stand to!' Fin I lookit oot – aa a could see wis a caffie rinnin aboot bumpin inti the barbet weer.

Jimmy Reid, 6th Gordon Highlanders

In front of our trenches we had listening posts about 20 yards out in the dark. I remember one lad was wounded going out to it and we told him to lie there and we would come and get him. Well when we got out there we never found him. It looked as though the Gerry patrols had got him first or that he'd started crawling the wrong way.

Dave Pitkethly, 4th Seaforth Highlanders

A pal o mine by the name of Simpson fae Udny, said, 'Look Alec, if I dinna come back; sen iss photograph to my wife!' This wis o her and his twa bairnies. I says, 'Aye fairly aat!' thinking naethin aboot it. Noo he gid oot on patrol that night and wis never seen again. The Padre sent the photograph aa richt an do ye ken I made up my mind to gang and see her fin I got the chance and do ye ken – I niver did, I niver did! I shid hiv! I wis aye richt aff o maself for nae dee-int; awite I wis!

Alec Nicol, 7th Gordon Highlanders
awite in truth

The German front line was so near that they came at night and stole our wire. We did the same to theirs.

George Bryan MM, 12th Highland Light Infantry

We niver went doon the Gerry dugoots withoot flingin doon a bomb first. They sometimes hid mair than ae openin ye see.

John Will, 5th Gordon Highlanders

We were fired on, my mate and I, as we were wannerin aboot on the ald battle-field. We gid up to this Gerry in the shellhole. He wis in an afa state, his leg hid been blaan aff at the hip an wis fu o maggots. I think he wis needin us ti pit him oot o his misery.

George Stewart, 5th Gordon Highlanders

It was there that we come on some o the bodies o the 51st. They must hae geen throwe the hale German lines and been killed. They were lyin in bits o trenches and shell holes. It wis only possible to tac them oot in the dark. Oor sergeant, if he fun a letter wi an address on then eenced to write and tell their folk the circumstances that they hid been fun.

Jimmy Milne, 2nd Gordon Highlanders

Life was cheap and you were expendable. An example of this was when I was sent out alone to find a crew of a machine gun that had not reported back one morning. Now when you were out with the Lewis guns the teams always came in before dawn and reported so. Anyway the team in question had come back but had not done so and there was I crawling out in front in daylight. I crept through a village and came on bodies of Gerries lying in the street there, although at first I couldn't tell if they were dead or not. After a detour I crept back and thankfully reported into the shelter of our trench. The officer who sent me had gone off but the sergeant major said to me that he didn't expect to see me back alive. Now that's what they thought of you – life meant nothing.

...

Once at Vimy Ridge there was a Highlander and a German slouched over but still standing – stone dead with their bayonets stuck in each other, away out in the barbed wire.

A. MacEwan, 6th Gordon Highlanders

I've been oot on patrol and on bombin raids. I mine I eence gan richt throue the German first line and there wis naebody er ata – it wis teem. So we proceeded ower ti their neist line and there wis only een or twa er – we could hear me spikin. We then craaled ower ti their reserve line an fun them digging like aa at.

We didna caase trouble bit war jist listenin at time. Sometimes we took a prisoner – if we saa a sentry – we wid aa surround um, an they aye cam quiet.

Peter Baigrie, 7th Cameron Highlanders/6th Black Watch

The Germans aye had the advantage o haein the sun at their backs the hale War, an could see us better than we could them.

...

The Gerry sent up Very lichts at night. There is a sang we sung that gid something like iss:

'You can't put the wind up the Very light man …'

Alec Wilson, 7th Cameron Highlanders

34

Unusual Events

You have heard of the 'Red Baron' – I saw him brought down. We had just been relieved in the front line by the Black Watch and were going up to our huts away to the rear for a rest when it happened. It was just dawning in the early morning when we watched the Red Baron's planes coming over. They were painted all the colours of the rainbow and we called them the Flying Circus – they were well known over our front. They first shot down the French observation balloon which took fire. The poor observer jumped but his parachute caught fire off the balloon and he came down like a stone and was killed. Then they spotted us and came at us with their machine guns blazing but we took cover in the ditches and fired back with our rifles without success.

Suddenly we saw two of our planes come at them and one of them got the Red Baron's plane. It came down and crashed beside us. I went over and saw him sitting there as dead as a doornail. The plane didn't go on fire either. I was later mad at myself for not taking away a souvenir off it.

The pilot who shot him down we learned later was a fellow called Ron Brown. Later on the British came over with twelve planes and dropped wreaths of flowers on the spot he was killed.

A. MacEwan, 6th Gordon Highlanders

We saa a lot of airplanes fechtin abeen wir heed an there wis ae pilot we caaed the 'Mad Major'. This lad efter a scrap wi the Gerry planes wid aye fin he wis comin back to wir ain lines, swoop doon ower the Gerries trenches an straich them wi machine guns as he kent they were oot watchin the scrap.

Weel ae plane o wir ain eence crashed near the canal asides at Ypres. This wis a hellava frosty time an the horse wagons were crossing back an fore loaded to the gunnels wi supplies to the Front – the ice wis that thick. We were watchin the scrap as usual an saa this plane o oors comin doon an then the pilot jumpit oot an come sailin doon an landin smack on the ice on the canal an gan clean throwt an wis niver seen again.

Bert Gow, Royal Field Artillery

I made a portrait frame oot o a hard biscuit – aye it wis aboot size fower inches by three – they were ass hard you couldna chaa them onywy. So I jist scrapit oot a square wi a knife and inserted my photo. I fact I posted hame mair than een.

Fin I got my first leave I took maps o the front lines wi ma an devised a code so that ma mither could pinpoint fit place or front I wis in. I wis jist twice hame ye see. This wis detailed maps that I cut to size six inch by five inch o France and Belgium. I numbered them and took back wi me a complete duplicate set o map sheets. This sheets were the same size as wir letters and by pittin a holie wi a preen throwe ma letter and wi the number o the map ont – ma mither hid nae difficulty jalousin far I wis.

Jimmy Scott, Royal Engineers

I mind on that statue o the Virgin Mary hingin upside doon fae the steeple at Albert.

Alec Pratt MM, Royal Horse Artillery

I will never forget the statue of the Virgin Mary hanging there upside down as long as I live.

A. Cheyne, Moose Jaw Battalion, Canada (Greens, New Deer).

In the early days of the War, one of our lads had been spared by a Uhlan who had just touched him on the shoulder with a sword when he could easily have killed him. From then on he made up his mind to do a kind deed to the enemy in return some day. This happened when he came on a German officer lying wounded in No Man's Land. He personally rescued him and took him to his own line and got a safe return to go back to his own. Of course this was in darkness and him working off his own bat.

A. MacEwan, 6th Gordon Highlanders

I got my callin up papers efter I hid been a eer in France

John Will, 5th Gordon Highlanders

35

Comrades

I saw this New Deer loon I was at school with coming down the street sitting with a lot more fellows on this lorry. The lorry stops and I shouts, 'Hello Sachie!'

He rolls our over the lorry and grabbed me. He was as pleased as punch and said, 'Good God Abbie! this is the first time I've been called Sachie since I left New Deer.' Sachie had been in Canada for a number of years and had joined the Canadian Army when War started. We had a great news and he wanted to know if there was any other New Deer lads there at Poperinge so I directed him where to find them.

…

There was another chap called Jock Fraser; an old pal of mine from New Deer. I had been in this staminet in Poperinge [Belgium] and had newly left. Jock then came in and enquired if there was anybody there from New Deer. A voice said, 'You have just missed Abbie Napier.' Well Jock told them he was going up to that crossroads and was going to stop every bugger that came along. So shortly after, I heard this voice shouting after me and I thought, 'Am I in trouble or something?' This was Jock and that was some reunion. He was some character.

Albert Napier MM, Royal Field Artillery ('Taggart's Own')
estaminet a small café, bar, or bistro, esp. a shabby one

There wis een o the Gilberts wis wi me fae the start. A great pal o mine, he wis promoted to sergeant an a richt gweed chiel tee.

Weel I aye mind he hid a richt peculiar sayin fit I didna think muckle aboot, bit fit he aye kept repeatin aa throwe the War: 'He wis a lucky man that wis killed at Mons!' Weel he got killed on the hindmist day!

Jimmy Reid, 6th Gordon Highlanders

Dr Craib, the doctor at New Deer, wis hame on leave at the same time as me, an I gid up ti see him wi ma fadder, he did his horses' feet – aye lookit efter his beasts aa the time. The doctor speired far I wis an – he wis in his captain's uniform ye ken, so I said it wis the La-Bassée Front. 'Strange,' he said, 'I was there too, and had to attend to a great number of casualties the week before I left including 25 amputations.' He speired fu lang leave I hid an I telt him ten days, an that I wis startin back neist day. He newsed awa a file aboot the terrible conditions oot er and telt me that he would be pleased ti sign for me ti get anidder wik's holiday. Weel I thocht aboot it a filie an then telt him I wid raither be back awa amon the lads. This wis fit happened ti ye fin ye got hame – ye missed the comradeship and wantit back, for there wis nae body at hame hid ony idea fit wis happenin oot er. Albert Napier an masel eense ti say efter the War, that it wis comradeship that hid won the Waar.

Bert Gow, Royal Field Artillery

I never wanted to get too acquainted with new lads after a while, after getting all my close friends killed – that was hard on you.

A. MacEwan, 6th Gordon Highlanders

I met Charlie Miller from Cawdor in Cairo and had a great news. He was in the Australians. He'd competed in the heavy events – putting and hammer throwing with my brother round the north games circuit before the War. He told me to tell Peter that he won the Western Australian Championship at hammer throwing. Charlie was a big powerful fellow. A coincidence here – the present day champion, Colin Matheson's father was in the Scouts with me and belonged to Dunphail of Forres.

A cousin of mine – John MacGregor won the VC at Ypres with the Princess Patricia's own Regiment of Canada. John was out in Canada before the War and had joined up there. I remember he got the freedom of Nairn when he came home on a visit from Vancouver once.

William MacGregor, Lovat Scouts

I remember when a Canadian lot landed up beside us, seeing Ben Stewart and Willie Horsack from round here. We had a grand news and after that they came prowling about looking for the Cromarty lads all the time they were there.

Then some of the Australians from round here came looking for us as well and man! it was surprising who you met in with for a blether. Some were relations and some of the lads even had brothers among them.

We had a lot of big strong heavy men. Peter MacAlister from Dingwall was one. When we came out of the trenches he would help the little fellows by taking their pack on top of his own. He was always in beautiful order.

Robert More MM, 4th Seaforth Highlanders

Jock Begg fae Dufftown wis a nephew o Dr Bodie.

Jimmy Reid, 6th Gordon Highlanders

We were on the march beside Lille when Sergeant Major George Hay came up to me and told me I had got promotion to officer and would be leaving next day. He told me not to go without seeing him.

After breakfast next morning I said goodbye to my platoon whom I had came through a lot of hard times with. Then I went round to see my friend George. He accompanied me on foot for two miles just as we would back home. There we parted company not knowing whether we'd meet again.

…

Sergeant Major Hay's father had a croft at Haddo House.

…

A Johnnie Rennie I knew was sent home with bad feet but was taken back when the Army got hard up for men.

Corporal Collie from Newmachar was a shoemaker to trade and Essolment from Cairnorrie was a blacksmith.

I knew an Ogston – a sergeant major from New Deer. We were both very friendly when we were both sergeants together.

I knew a slater – Sergeant Major Eadie – a well set up fellow, he was an older man than me. He was from Fyvie.

Duggie Clark was a slater with Eadie I think – he too was with me.

Jimmy Garland of the Farm of Letham was a private at the start but was picked to be an officer. He came out to France first with a John Watt who had a cycle business in Ellon. This man Watt became regimental quartermaster sergeant.

We also had regimental sergeant major Mort from Tarves.

Alec Robertson, 5th Gordon Highlanders

There wis ae sergeant, fin he fell us in on the march eense to say in pure Buchan, 'Are ye aa in ower yet?' as we formed up in fours.

J. Fowlie, 7th Gordon Highlanders

A cockney was in my company. He hid been a pickpocket in London an gid us great fun wi his slight o han tricks.

Alec Pratt MM, Royal Horse Artillery

I was in the line at Point Dieppe and saa the 5th Gordon Highlanders comin alang the road and I jist steed there and saa a lot o lads I kent fae Strichen – Broch wy. I wis jist wishin I could hae geen wi them, I couldna help it.

Bit we hid a feoy Strichen lads wi us; I mind a lad Gow – a Piper. Then there wis a lad Thamson.

Then I mind meetin wi Dod Leel fae Strichen eence.

Jimmy Milne, 2nd Gordon Highlanders

Oor sergeant major wis Slater Eadie o Fyvie, for a filie in France only.

Albert Connon, 5th Gordon Highlanders

50. Members of the cavalry resting their horses by the side of the road, in France. The men are milling around in front of their horses. They all look fairly glad to be having a rest.

Reproduced by permission of the National Library of Scotland

When we came out of the line at Mont-St-Éloi, the Black Watch were lying at Roclincourt. We were away on high ground and when I looked across at Roclincourt, I thought it looked to be only three miles or so away. This was a Saturday and as I had the day off I decided to go down and look up some of the lads of the village I knew in the Black Watch. Instead of a mile or two it turned out to be a walk of about 15 miles or so. It was worth it though – I met a lot of the boys I knew and had a grand news.

…

I saw Dodds of Celtic[42] once on horseback but didn't speak to him.

Dave Pitkethly, 4th Seaforth Highlanders

36

Armistice and after the War

Efter the Armistice, a battalion mutinied for hame. Anither een wis sent to disarm them. They jist jined them.

A puckle os fae oor unit got the job o burnin ammunition efter the feenish. We put it in a trench an set fire tult. It gid on exploding bit we jist steed aside it, nae batherin to ging back. The bullets niver deein ony ill at aa. If ye held oot a han, you could feel a ping noo an an.

John Webster, Royal Field Artillery

Fin we relieved Brussels I bade wi a lady in digs, her brither wis er; like a skeleton an fair fite in the face. She had hidden him fae the Germans below the stair for fower year.

Alec Pratt MM, Royal Horse Artillery

I mind I wis hairsrin ae time and a lad stoppe't wi a Land Rover and socht some address in Turra; I says, 'I'll gang in wi ye masel as I am needin something'. He said he cam fae Monymusk and I telt him I only kent ae man fae there – that wis Sir Arthur Grant. On the road to Turra I telt him aa aboot him and I suppose on the wy back cis he wis aye speirin. 'Weel,' he says fin he lat me aff, 'That wis very interesting. Sir Arthur Grant was my grandfather!'

John Rennie, 5th Gordon Highlanders

hairsrin harvesting

My brither got oot o the Army afore me and wis workin at Farquhar's o Skelmanae. My ald boss wrote to my CO – Lt Colonel Gair, Seaforth Highlanders, to get me oot and I got oot in time to bigg corn rucks that hairst.

Robert MacRobbie, 1st Gordon Highlanders

Fin I wis demobbed, I aye drappit to the grun at the least soon like a pail laid doon or onything it gid a clatter.

John Webster, Royal Field Artillery

I got married the first Feberwar efter the War. This wis the time o the afa flu. The second horseman de-ed wi the flu an I got hame for his job at Kennerty.

Sellars made the lang boord ploos for the plooin matches and we jist got their socks waaled fin nought. That wis afore the broken fur wis heard o ye ken.

Jimmy Reid, 6th Gordon Highlanders

I got a suitie like a rag efter the War an £60. £60 wis like a fortune ti me.

I gid back ti the feein and gid hame as foreman ti Earlstone, Cruden Bay, a place o three pair and an orra beast.

John Brown, 5th Gordon Highlanders

After the War I joined the police force at Greenock but packed it in and sailed for a new life in Canada in 1923. I went and visited my Uncle Sandy first and from there I struck out for the prairies of Saskachewan where there was a lot of other North-East lads. I got a job with a trader. Later I came back east and worked there for a while. Then I decided to try my luck in the States. I had the good fortune to find a job helping at a summer camp. A cousin of Sir Douglas Haig had a cottage there. I then went and helped build a boathouse for a family from New York, where I met my future wife.

A. MacEwan, 6th Gordon Highlanders

Fin the War wis feenished, we war sent up ti occupy Germany. There wis an afa racket caused amang oor lads fin the officers decided to smertin us up wi deein drill an mairchin us back an fore in the barrack square fae mornin ti nicht. Then as weel, we hid ti dole up oor kit aa spik an span. Noo iss wis ti keep the lads occupied an awa fae ill tricks. Weel maist o them rebatted cis they hid jined up for the duration of War only an, a gie lot hid been in fae the day one, so a petition wis got up an we aa signed wir name – iss wis objectin to aa at drillin cairry on. That document wis presented ti wir commander an dee ye ken he didna like wir little antics one bit an ordered us ti be aa lined up in the square farr he lectured us at great length aboot the great benefits to the British soldier of real discipline an aa at, bit I think it jist gid in ti ae lug an oot the idder. We didna mind as lang as the War wis on, bit noo it was feenished we war needin hame withoot aa that capers. Aa the same, conditions improved efter at.

William Shearer, Royal Field Artillery

De'y ken I listed on efter the War and spent three year in India wi the 1st Battalion the Black Watch; a lot o ma time on the North West Frontier.

Peter Baigrie, 7th Cameron Highlanders/6th Black Watch

After the War I went to America. I did two years at a fruit farm at Springfield. When I lost my job there, I applied for a job I saw advertised in a match factory.

'Diamond' matches they produced. The pay seemed good, so up I went this wintry morning to the employee manager and told him I wanted the job advertised, as floor sweeper.

'You're not American?' he said.

'Oh no – but will that make any difference?' I asked.

'Oh no, but you don't look like a fellow that would sweep floors!'

I explained that I could sweep floors as good as anybody, and he said he would take my name but there wasn't much hope.

I went down next day to a toy factory and tried there but I was told that there were many more looking for a job also. I said, 'That's all right, but I'm here now and have you anything going?'

'No,' the boss replied, 'but keep coming back – you never know.'

That was the whole story all over.

Alec Robertson, 5th Gordon Highlanders

I recuperated fae ma wounds for eicht months an got ma first leave hame since the War started. Fin I reported for duty they widna lat me back to France as I wis noo medically classed as category C an wis sent ti Woolwich ti yoke an brak in new horses wi a lot o idder ex-wounded category C men.

My CO there took an interest in me an even offered me a job. He said, 'When you are finished with the Army I could use you if you would like to come out to the Argentine!' I telt him that i widna mind and wid keep his offer in mind fin I got ma discharge.

Weel I eventually got discharged although I was still on the reserve – the War wis feenished by iss time and I took him at his word an set sail for Argentine.

The officer's name was Bridget and he hid anither brither an a sister – the three o them owned the place. They lived in England the half the eer an only cam oot in the simmertime so they hid a simmer aa the time in idder words.

I became manager o this place that wis something like 60-mile lang by 40-wide wi 200 thoosan sheep and 26 shepherds, some Scots lads amang them. I is there for 15 eer an enjoyed ivery meenit ot.

...

In the Argentine I didna like the Devon oxen that drew wir wagons; they hid ower lang legs and laired easily in the boggy grun. They war a hellava size for aa that. I hid the idea that I could cross them wi a Heelan bull. I got een sent oot and in time he did his wark an the off spring seen brocht doon the hicht o them, bit still left the big horns that we yokit them wi.

The Indians got a great fleg at the dockside fin we took this Heelan bull off the ship. They hid niver seen a reed shaggy haired beast like it – oh aye it caased a commotion aa richt.

James Smith, Royal Field Artillery

I gid hame fae Kennerty to Anderson, up at Durris. I was twal eer wi him. In aat time I wis twice first at plooin matches and a hantle o idder prizes foreby.

I wis then wi a descendent o the Black Douglas at Tullyfolly. Then I wis a lang time wi the Marquis o Huntly.

Efter aat I wis 15 eer wi Lady Jaffrey – Sir Thomas's widow and I liked her best.
Jimmy Reid, 6th Gordon Highlanders

I got discharged efter bein wounded the hinemist time. This wis a nesty abdominal wound. This wis at Third Ypres.

Still I got better o that and gid doon to Langside market an met in wi a grieve I kent fae Logie and fe-ed hame as hairst man. There we hid three horse yokit in the binder.

The suitie I got discharged in wis jist a rag. It wisnae worth weein.
Wullie Gavin, 5th Gordon Highlanders

Fit ist aa for the day onywy. Fit gweed did it dae? [Demob suit]
Tom Rearie, 5th Gordon Highlanders

Fin I came hame fae the War I didna fancy the feein an jined a boat fishin oot o Macduff. I hid anither think aboot it and didna ging. For that I wis fined but didna care a damn. I gid hame to Camalynes instead. There wis 32 aacre in the shift. We plooed it wi three pair. Fin I moved to Ardley we hid 45 acre to the shift.

We hid some great breed o horse there. Dunlop cam oot and bocht aa wir foals as they kent fit they war buyin. They couldna be deein wi Dunure Footprint stock as they were heelava kittle beasts – ay he left a lot o bad buggers and ill-nettered eens ana.

Still I feenished up as grieve and fair liked it.
George Barclay, Royal Field Artillery

A lot os that hid been in the War for a start an wisna A1, got the chance to gang hame an dee ferm work aboot 1918 an I wis een. Captain Manson fae Old-meldrum hid lost an airm at Beaumont-Hamel on the Somme battle, an he wis in charge o the depot at Aiberdeen. Weel I hid to report to him an he wintit men that could work horse. I hid vrocht horse an he sent me to the ferm toon o Newton o Barra aside Meldrum that belanged to Dr Forbes, an I wis there till the War feenished.

I left there and gid oot to the Argentine to help ma brither it wis manager there. I supervised the shepherds on this 250-square mile estate, an I nought a string o horses to masel, that wis aboot ten. They were aa trained to keep close to their lead meer. This beast had a bell roon its neck and ilkey troop o horses kent the soon o their ain bell. Ye see that made it easy to keep them aa thegither fin they were oot grazin aa nicht and easy for me to get them in aboot an awa in the morning again. They war the best Arab horses an there wis some great horsemen oot there ye ken.

Charles Smith, 7th and 4th Gordon Highlanders

Fin I took this flu – I think I telt ye already, I wis richt determined to get hame. I hid been demobbed an took this killin flu an stuck her oot withoot reportin sick. I cam aff this train at Aiberdeen an conkit oot on the street. Folk fun ma lying there ryput ma pooches to see fa I wis an they hid got ma Army pay book an got ma address oot o it. They got me hurled hame wi somebody and I didna ken a thing aboot it till I wakened up in my midder's hoose in bed hame at Reimshill, a craftie up the brae there atween Auchterless an Inverythan. I lay there eicht wicks afore I got better.

Jimmy Scott, Royal Engineers

I was sent home from Salonica by train through Italy and France with no food laid on and arrived at Cherbourg hardly able to stand with hunger. I went aboard a troopship and there got a cup of soup. We sailed and were later coming into dock at Southampton when the ship was intercepted by a Royal Navy one. Our captain was hailed to stop and wait because we weren't expected. We eventually got ashore next day where all Scots were ordered to one side and sent on our way to Scotland by train.

We Cameron Highlanders went all the way to Inverness to depot and when on arrival there was a hot meal waiting for us which was fantastic. I later ended up at Edinburgh Castle where I was informed that I was sleeping in Queen Margaret's Room.

When I was demobbed I suffered from malaria for years and took doses of quinine for it. I also got a pension of 3/6 the week to which I donated part to my mother.

Jim Burgess, 2nd Cameron Highlanders

A William Low wis in France as an officer in the 5th Gordon Highlanders. Although he wisna in oor company, he wis wounded the same day as masel at Ypres.

Efter the War he emigrated to Canada. Forty-five eer later my wife and I were oot at a weddin there – oor dother is there.

Wir son-in-law introduced us to a friend o his and lo and behold! fin we got spikin we discovered we were in the War thegither. We hid a great news aboot aa the times and the lads we kent.

Albert Connon, 5th Gordon Highlanders

We hid a lot o gran fiddlers in my day – Jimmy Dickie, Charlie Sutherland o Percyhorner, Sandy Begg o Kincardine O'Neil, Tam Gregson o Gartly. Sandy

Milne o Banchory an of coorse Hector MacAndrew fa bade jist up the road and we eence ti play a tunie or twa ivery day thegidder. Bit it wis Charlie Sutherland that hid the Strad fiddle an I hid a tune ot at some o his great fiddle nichts he held at Percyhorner. I wis richt feart ti play it ower hard or drap it.

Harry Nicoll, Royal Engineers

Notes

1   See https://projects.handsupfortrad.scot/hall-of-fame/performers/ [accessed February 2019].

2   Small, Judy (1986).

3   For a detailed discussion of the BEF, and indeed of all aspects of the Scottish experience of the Great War, see Trevor Royle's excellent book *The Flowers of the Forest: Scotland and the First World War* (2007A).

4   For more detail on this in relation to Scottish soldiers see Royle, Trevor (2007A), pp. 261–62.

5   A War Office Instruction issued in June 1916 allowed parents to request that their underage sons be sent home.

6   'It is sweet and fitting to die for one's country.' Wilfred Owen, 'Dulce et Decorum Est'.

7   Royle, Trevor (2007A), p.92.

8   Sir James Taggart KBE was Lord Provost of Aberdeen from 1914–19.

9   The Lourin Fair has been held in August in the village of Old Rayne, Aberdeenshire, for at least five centuries, and continues to this day.

10   This is not the same man as features in David Kerr Cameron's book, *Willie Gavin, Crofter Man: a Portrait of a Vanished Lifestyle* (Victor Gollancz Ltd, 1980), Willie Gavin being a pseudonym for Kerr Cameron's maternal grandfather, Willie Porter.

11   The Derby Scheme was initiated in the autumn of 1915 by the Director General of Recruiting, Edward Stanley, 17th Earl of Derby. It was aimed at assessing to what extent the War could be sustained through volunteering, or whether conscription would be necessary. It failed to convince the government that relying on volunteers would supply enough men, and conscription was therefore introduced in March 1916.

12   *The Hairst o Rettie* is a well-known bothy ballad. Many versions of it have been recorded for the School of Scottish Studies Archives, University of Edinburgh, and can be heard on the Kist o Riches website.

13   Gavin Greig (1856–1914) was one of the most important collectors of folk song Scotland has ever produced. Working with the minister, James Duncan (1848–1917), they collected around 2000 songs, mainly in the North East, between 1902 and the outbreak of the War. These have since been published in 8 volumes: Shuldam Shaw P. and E. B. Lyle (eds) 1981–2002; followed by a single volume selection aimed at singers: Campbell, Karen (2009).

14   Secunderabad is a city in the state of Telangana in India.

15   Lord George Stewart-Murray was a son of the 7th Duke of Atholl. He was killed at the 1st Battle of the Marne on 14th September 1914. In June 2018 the Atholl Highlanders paid tribute to him at his memorial, the Marquis of Tullibardine, eldest son of the present Duke of Atholl, parading with Lord George's sword. Also present was Jock Duncan's son, Pipe Major Ian Duncan.

16 Colonel John Raymond Evelyn Stansfield, died of wounds on 29th September 1915, and is buried at Chocques Military Cemetery, France.

17 Charlie Innes was born in Rothes, enlisted in Keith, and died aged 18. He was the son of Mrs Christina Innes of Moss Street, Keith (*Aberdeen Weekly Journal*, 26th March 1915).

18 If an injury was deemed serious enough to be returned back to England for hospital treatment it was known as 'a Blighty one'.

19 Corporal Charles Young, who died on 5th August 1915. He was the son of William Young, Davah Farm, Inverurie. His brother had been killed a month previously (*Aberdeen Weekly Journal*, 20th October 1916).

20 The town of Albert in Picardy had a cathedral crowned with a basilica on which stood a statue of the Virgin Mary holding her child out to God. Constant shelling badly damaged the building, and caused the statue to hang at a precarious angle. The 'hanging virgin' became a famous landmark for troops of both sides. The cathedral was destroyed in 1918.

21 The Hindenburg Line was a German defensive line built in the winter of 1916/17, and ran from Arras to Laffaux.

22 The 'Cambrai Cross' was made by fellow members of the 4th Battalion of the Seaforth Highlanders in memory of all of their comrades who died at Cambrai in November 1917. It was removed to Dingwall in 1924, and unveiled the following year. See https://dingwallscotland.com/war-memorials [accessed February 2019].

23 When transcribing this passage, Jock Duncan made the following note: 'Mr Mowat's mother lived to 102. Mr Mowat is still alive at 102 in 1996.'

24 This was HMHS *Lanfranc*, built as an ocean liner by Caledon Shipbuilding and Engineering Co. Ltd in Dundee and launched in 1906. Having been requisitioned as a hospital ship, it was actually sunk on 17th April, with the loss of 22 British and 18 German soldiers. See https://wrecksite.eu/wreck.aspx?11280 [accessed February 2019].

25 Mailly Maillet, Somme. There is a War Cemetery at Mailly Wood and among those buried there are several Seaforth Highlanders, including Captain Eric James Anderson, Lance Corporal William Cassells, Lance Corporal Donald MacGregor and Sergeant John Wood. See https://livesofthefirstworldwar.org/community/4097 [accessed February 2019].

26 Major Charles Fowlie, who died on 30th May 1915. He had been an officer in the Territorials before the War, and was the son of John and Elizabeth Lawson Fowlie, Udny. Charles had farmed at Mains of Bogfechil, Whiterashes, on the Udny estate, and also served as schoolmaster at Oldmeldrum (*Aberdeen Weekly Journal*, 4th April 1915).

27 A highly contagious respiratory infection in horses.

28 Private George Imlach McIntosh, VC, 1/6th Battalion, Gordon Highlanders, was born at Buckie, Banffshire, on 24 April 1897. He was the youngest son of John McIntosh, a fisherman, and Margaret McIntosh, of 107a Main Street, Buckie. He was awarded the Victoria Cross in 1917 at the age of 20, and later went on to join the RAF, serving with them during the Second World War. He died in 1968. (Gordon Highlanders Museum).

29 Son of Dr Alexander Bruce and Anna Louisa Bruce, Ainslie Place, Edinburgh. He was educated at George Watson's College, Edinburgh and New College, Oxford.

30 Donald Dinnie (1837–1916) was a renowned athlete and strongman from Birse, Aberdeenshire.

31 The Battle of Flers-Courcelette took place on the Somme in September 1916.

32 A popular concert party specialising in the music and song of the North East.

33 Willie MacLean (1876–1957) was born in Tobermory, but brought up in Dumbartonshire. A pupil of Calum MacPherson of Catlodge in Badenoch (Calum Piobaire), Willie became

one of the leading players and foremost piping authorities of his generation. Interviews with him are held in the School of Scottish Studies, University of Edinburgh, and can be heard on the Kist o Riches website.

34 John MacColl (1860–1943), from Oban, is recognised as having been one of the finest pipers and composers of all time. He served as Pipe Major of the 3rd Battalion Black Watch and in the Scottish Horse.

35 The Center family were noted pipers and bagpipe makers from Kildrummy in Aberdeenshire. John Center moved his family to Edinburgh where he established himself as a photographer in Leith, before opening a bagpipe making business in Grove Street. One of his sons, James, joined him in this business. One of his brothers was indeed called William: in this extract Piper MacLeod may be referring to him, or it may be an error, and he may in fact have been referring to James.

36 John MacDonald of Inverness (1865–1953) was born at Glentruim and became highly influential as a player and teacher. Many of today's top pipers can trace their stylistic influences and 'pedigree' directly back to him.

37 Music was very much in the family for Davie and Robin. Settled travellers, their father, Donald, known as Auld Crichie, was a piper, as was his father, Jimmy. Their niece, Lucy Stewart of Fetterangus, was a very highly regarded traditional singer, as is her niece, Elizabeth, in turn. Elizabeth has written of Robin in very proud terms: 'Fighting was in his blood and he was a professional soldier in the 2nd Battalion Gordon Highlanders. Efter a year in Cairo at the beginning of the First World War, the regiment went tae France. Robin wis decorated wi the Distinguished Conduct Medal and the Russian Order of St George. Sadly he was killed at Loos on 25th of September 1915.' (Stewart, Elizabeth 2012).

38 G. S. Maclennan (1883–1929) was a prolific composer and virtuosic piper. Born in Edinburgh, he joined the Gordon Highlanders as a boy soldier, and rose to become Pipe Major of the 1st Battalion by the age of 21. He served for the whole of First World War, although became ill in the trenches in 1918, collapsing shortly after playing his company 'over the top'. He left the Army in 1922. Many of his tunes have become classics, and several form a standard part of every piper's repertoire.

39 Willie Lawrie (1881–1916), a close friend of G. S. Maclennan, was born in Ballachulish, and enjoyed considerable success as a piping competitor from a young age, becoming Pipe Major of the 8th Argyllshire Battalion of the Argyll and Sutherland Highlanders in 1914. He also composed several tunes which remain highly popular to this day, including the most famous pipe composition to emerge from the War, *The Battle of the Somme*. He did not actually die of the flu epidemic, but rather became ill while serving on the Front, and was evacuated to hospital in Oxford where he died in November 1916.

40 Very lights were gun-fired flares named after Edward W. Very (1847–1910), an American naval officer who invented the form of pistol which fired them.

41 Corporal W. B. Wood, 4th Battalion Gordon Highlanders, was the man killed in this incident. Many hundreds of men marched on Etaples in protest, their anger aimed at the Military Police (the Red Caps). As a result of this 'mutiny', many soldiers were charged with a range of military offences, including Corporal Jesse Robert Short of the Northumberland Fusiliers who was sentenced to death, and shot by firing squad on 4th October 1917.

42 Joe Dodds (1887–1965), who played for Celtic, Cowdenbeath and Queen of the South, and who won three Scotland caps.

Bibliography

Cameron, Ewen (2010): *Impaled Upon a Thistle: Scotland Since 1880* (Edinburgh: Edinburgh University Press).

Campbell, Katherine (2009): *Songs from North East Scotland: A Selection for Performers from the Greig-Duncan Folk Song Collection* (Edinburgh: John Donald).

Carter, Ian (1979): *Farm Life in North East Scotland, 1840–1914* (Edinburgh: John Donald).

Falls, Cyril (2014): *Gordon Highlanders in the First World War* (Uckfield: Naval and Military Press).

Goldie, D. and Watson, R. (2014): *From the Line: Scottish War Poetry 1914–1945* (Glasgow: The Association for Scottish Literary Studies).

Grassic Gibbon, Lewis (2006 edition): *Sunset Song* (Edinburgh: Polygon).

Harrison, Michael (2017): *High Wood* (Barnsley: Pen and Sword).

Hart, Peter (2013): *Gallipoli* (London: Profile Books).

Morpurgo, Michael (1982): *War Horse* (London: Egmont).

Wilfred Owen (1921): 'Dulce et Decorum Est', *Poems* (New York, NY: Viking Press).

Royle, Trevor (2006): *The Black Watch: a Concise History* (Edinburgh: Mainstream Publishing).

Royle, Trevor (2007A): *The Flowers of the Forest: Scotland and the First World War* (Edinburgh: Birlinn).

Royle, Trevor (2007B): *The Gordon Highlanders: a Concise History* (Edinburgh: Mainstream Publishing).

Royle, Trevor (2012): 'The First World War' in Spiers, Crang and Strickland (eds), *A Military History of Scotland* (Edinburgh: Edinburgh University Press).

Schofield, Victoria (2017): *The Black Watch: the 42nd Highlanders at War from the Boer War to Iraq* (London: Head of Zeus Publishing).

Shuldham-Shaw, P. and Lyle, E. B. (eds) (1981–2002): *The Greig-Duncan Folk Song Collection*, vols 1–8 (Aberdeen: Aberdeen University Press).

Small, Judy (1986): *The Judy Small Songbook* (Orlando, FL: Orlando Press).

Stevenson, David (2004): *1914–1918: the History of the First World War* London: Penguin Books.

Stevenson, Randall (2013): *Literature and the Great War, 1914–1918* (Oxford: Oxford University Press).

Stewart, Elizabeth (2012): *Up Yon Wide and Lonely Glen: Travellers' Songs, Stories and Tunes of the Fetterangus Stewarts*, compiled and edited by Alison McMorland (Jackson, MS: University of Mississippi Press).

Van Emden, Richard (2009): *Sapper Martin: the Secret War Diary of Jack Martin* (London: Bloomsbury).

Van Emden, Richard (2016): *The Somme: The Epic Battle in the Soldiers' Own Words and Photographs* (Barnsley: Pen and Sword).

West, Gary (2012): 'Military Music' in *A Military History of Scotland* (Edinburgh: Edinburgh University Press).

West, Gary (2012): *Voicing Scotland: Folk, Culture, Nation* (Edinburgh: Luath Press).

West, Gary (2018): 'Understanding Scotland Musically: reflections on place, war and nation' in McKerrell, S. and West, G. (eds), *Understanding Scotland Musically: Folk, Tradition and Policy* (London and New York: Routledge).

Young, Derek (2008): *Scottish Voices from the Great War* (Stroud: The History Press).

Index of Contributors

Index

Titles in the Regional Flashback series
and the Flashback series co-published by the
European Ethnological Research Centre
and NMS Enterprises Ltd – Publishing

REGIONAL FLASHBACKS

Whithorn: An Economy of People, 1920–1960
edited by Julia Muir Watt

Stranraer and District Lives: Voices in Trust
edited by Caroline Milligan

FLASHBACKS

The Making of *Am Fasgadh*: An Account of the Origins of
The Highland Folk Museum by its Founder
Isabel Frances Grant

From Kelso to Kalamazoo: The Life and Times of
George Taylor, 1803–1891
edited by Margaret Jeary and Mark Mulhern

Scotland's Land Girls: Breeches, Bombers and Backaches
edited by Elaine Edwards

Showfolk: An Oral History of a Fairground Dynasty
Frank Bruce

An Orkney Boyhood
Duncan Cameron Mackenzie

Galoshins Remembered: 'A penny was a lot in these days'
edited by Emily Lyle

From Land to Rail: Life and Times of Andrew Ramage 1854–1917
edited by Caroline Mulligan and Mark Mulhern